Saints, Heretics, and Atheists

Saints, Heretics, and Atheists

A Historical Introduction to the Philosophy of Religion

JEFFREY K. McDONOUGH

OXFORD UNIVERSITY PRESS

OXFORD
UNIVERSITY PRESS

Oxford University Press is a department of the University of Oxford. It furthers the University's objective of excellence in research, scholarship, and education by publishing worldwide. Oxford is a registered trade mark of Oxford University Press in the UK and certain other countries.

Published in the United States of America by Oxford University Press
198 Madison Avenue, New York, NY 10016, United States of America.

CIP data is on file at the Library of Congress

ISBN 978-0-19-756385-4 (pbk.)
ISBN 978-0-19-756384-7 (hbk.)

DOI: 10.1093/oso/9780197563847.001.0001

1 3 5 7 9 8 6 4 2

Paperback printed by Marquis, Canada
Hardback printed by Bridgeport National Bindery, Inc., United States of America

Contents

Preface

Saints, Heretics, and Atheists: A Historical Introduction to the Philosophy of Religion has grown out of a hope, two convictions, and a course.

The hope was to offer an introduction to philosophy that would meet students halfway in their interests. Most students—most people—are, I think, philosophers at heart. The issues that philosophy deals with—the nature of things, what we should believe, what we should value—are issues that all of us wrestle with at various points in our lives. But relatively few students are ever exposed to careful, systematic philosophy. They are left to popular presentations and their own devices. The philosophy of religion is both an exceptionally interesting area of philosophical inquiry and a potential gateway to further philosophical study. The general questions taken up in the philosophy of religion are general questions of philosophy. The philosophy of religion asks questions about the nature of things, what we should believe and what we should value. But the specific questions that the philosophy of religion asks are also specific questions that many students ask themselves. *Does God exist? Why is there evil in the world? Should I accept religion or not?* The hope that gave rise to this book is that by meeting students halfway in their interests, I could share the joys of careful, rigorous philosophy with students, that we could think through their own questions together, and prepare them to ask new questions of which they had not yet dreamed.

The first of the two convictions that gave rise to *Saints, Heretics, and Atheists* was that it is difficult to understand either religion or the philosophy of religion without at least some historical context. The issues, views, and puzzles we confront today in the philosophy of religion have deep historical roots. Many contemporary philosophers explicitly or implicitly understand those roots and see their own work as contributing to a conversation that has been going on for millennia. But students are typically in a very different place. Many have had very little exposure to the history of philosophy and religion. Indeed, many have had essentially no exposure at all. Many introductions to the philosophy of religion largely neglect the historical dimensions of their subject. The first conviction that gave rise to the present book is that—for at least some teachers and students—a historical approach to the philosophy of religion might work better. This conviction has only deepened with experience. *Saints, Heretics, and Atheists* thus aims to offer a historical on-ramp to topics in the philosophy of religion as they have arisen in the context of great writings of the past.

The second conviction behind *Saints, Heretics, and Atheists* is that the philosophy of religion should not be seen as a simple debate between two opposing camps of believers and nonbelievers. Philosophical viewpoints on religion vary more than any straightforward dichotomy might hope to capture. Many viewpoints occupy a nuanced middle ground between what we are inclined to think of as theism and atheism. It is unclear, for example, if Spinoza is best characterized as an ardent theist or a die-hard atheist, if Hume is attacking religion or defending it, or if secular humanism is a rejection of religion or a new kind of religion in its own right. And even with respect to views that are more clearly theistic or atheistic, much of what is most interesting lies in their details and variations—for example, in the difference between Augustine's Platonism and Aquinas's Aristotelianism, in the contrast between Anselm's rationalism and al-Ghazali's mysticism, in the ambiguities of Nietzsche's appraisal of traditional religion. *Saints, Heretics, and Atheists* thus also aims to put on display a wider range of religious views than is currently customary in comparable introductions.

The course behind *Saints, Heretics, and Atheists* is a popular class that I have taught for over a decade at Harvard University. Each of the book's twenty-five chapters corresponds to a specific lecture and reading assignment. Links to those reading assignments as well as to supplemental materials are available through the book's website hosted on my homepage. Readers may also find a copy of my course syllabus there. In keeping with the hope of meeting students halfway in their interests, the course was designed to be accessible to a wide audience and has been offered not only through the Philosophy Department but also in Harvard's General Education Program and its Extension School. I owe a huge debt to the students who have taken those offerings. The course and this book have been shaped, refined, and improved over the years as I have tried to adapt to students' interests, responses, and feedback. Imperfect as the results might be, they would surely be much worse without the generous engagement of many students over many years. With much appreciation and many fond memories, this book is dedicated to those students—the saints, the heretics, the atheists, and all those in between.

Acknowledgments

This book is the work of many years, and I owe a debt of gratitude to more people than I can acknowledge here. Bonnie Kent generously started me thinking about medieval philosophy many years ago. Samuel Newlands and Michael Rea welcomed me to the Center for the Philosophy of Religion for an enlightening and productive year. Lucy Randall at Oxford University Press encouraged the project and generously shepherded it along. David Bzdak prepared the index and caught errors in the manuscript. My colleagues in the Harvard Philosophy Department have been a constant source of philosophical support while the course that gave rise to this book took shape. My greatest debt of gratitude related to this volume goes to the students of that course with my heartfelt thanks for their enthusiasm, feedback, and willingness to engage. My own personal greatest debt of gratitude goes, as always, to my family for their love, support, and patience.

The artwork on the cover is an image of a painting by Eugène Lenepveu (ca. 1888) of Joan of Arc being burned at the stake. Famously, Joan reported experiencing religious visions at the age of thirteen. She then led the French army of Charles of Valois to victory but was later captured by English forces. She was burned at the stake on charges of heresy in 1431. Twenty years later she was cleared of those charges and declared a martyr. In 1920 she was canonized and became the patron saint of France. A saint and a heretic. Two out of three.

1
Plato's *Euthyphro*
What Is Piety?

1.1. The Setting

Plato (ca. 424–348 BCE) lived during a golden age of Greek history and is considered by many to be the most influential philosopher ever in the Western tradition. One of his most famous dialogues, the *Euthyphro*, features two main characters, Socrates and Euthyphro. Although he appears as a fictionalized character in Plato's dialogues, Socrates was an actual historical figure and indeed Plato's teacher. He lived from approximately 470 to 399 BCE in ancient Greece and was brought to trial and executed on charges of introducing strange gods and corrupting the youth. We don't know if Euthyphro was an actual historical figure as well, but he is presented in Plato's dialogue as a professional priest and a talking head on matters of ritual and piety.

At the start of the dialogue, Socrates has left the Lyceum—a large, open space in Athens—in order to present himself at court on a charge of corrupting the youth. On his way to court, he runs into Euthyphro, who is on his way to prosecute his father for murder. Euthyphro explains the case to Socrates as follows:

> The victim was a dependent of mine, and when we were farming in Naxos, he was a servant of ours. He killed one of our household slaves in drunken anger, so my father bound him hand and foot and threw him in a ditch, then sent a man here to inquire from the priest what should be done. During that time, he gave no thought or care to the bound man, as being a killer, and it was no matter if he died, which he did. Hunger and cold and his bonds caused his death before the messenger came back from the seer. (4c–d; this chapter follows Jowett's translation of the *Euthyphro* in Plato [1892])

It is important for understanding the dialogue to recognize that Socrates thinks that this case is complicated for at least two reasons. First, Socrates

Saints, Heretics, and Atheists. Jeffrey K. McDonough, Oxford University Press. © Oxford University Press 2022.
DOI: 10.1093/oso/9780197563847.003.0001

finds the case itself morally unclear. Today, we'd certainly disapprove of such treatment even of a murder. In Socrates's day, however, murderers were thought to have few if any rights, and it really would have been unclear that Euthyphro's father had done anything wrong, even though the murderer died in his custody. Second, there is a question of the appropriateness of Euthyphro prosecuting his own father. Even if the case were morally clear, one might think that something is off about Euthyphro pursuing his own father's execution.

Because Socrates thinks the case is morally complex, he is surprised that Euthyphro is so certain that he is doing the right thing in prosecuting his father. In characteristic fashion, Socrates suggests that if Euthyphro is right to be so certain, he must have a deep and exact understanding of piety. Accordingly, Socrates asks Euthyphro to explain to him what piety and impiety are. With the stage set, the heart of the dialogue then begins as Euthyphro offers a series of different accounts of piety that Socrates critically examines in turn.

1.2. First Attempt: Examples of Piety

Euthyphro first attempts to provide an account of piety by suggesting that pious and impious actions should be identified with the sorts of things that he and the gods do and refrain from doing:

> Euthyphro: I say that the pious is to do what I am doing now, to prosecute the wrongdoer, be it about murder or temple robbery or anything else, whether the wrongdoer is your father or your mother or anyone else; not to prosecute is impious. And observe, Socrates, that I can cite powerful evidence that the law is so. I have already said to others that such actions are right, not to favor the ungodly, whoever they are. These people themselves believe that Zeus is the best and most just of the gods, yet they agree that he bound his father [Chronos] because he unjustly swallowed his sons, and that he in turn had punished his own father [Uranus] for a similar reason, in a nameless manner. But they are angry with me because I am prosecuting my father for wrongdoing. They contradict themselves in what they say about the gods and about me. (5e, translation slightly modified)

Socrates is characteristically unsatisfied with this first attempt to explain what piety and impiety are. He was hoping for an account, definition, or *logos* of piety that would allow him to identify any pious act and distinguish it from any impious act. Instead, Euthyphro has given him a set of (dubious) examples. The dialogue continues:

SOCRATES: Bear in mind then that I did not bid you tell me one or two of the many pious actions, but that idea itself that makes all pious actions pious, for you agreed that all impious actions are impious and all pious actions pious through one idea, or don't you remember?

EUTHYPHRO: I do.

SOCRATES: Tell me then what this idea itself is, so that I may look upon it and, using it as a model, say that any action of yours or another's that is of that kind is pious, and if it is not that it is not. (6d)

Socrates is looking for something like a rule or definition that will allow him to distinguish all pious actions from all impious actions. He finds Euthyphro's first attempt to explain what piety is unsatisfying because it merely offers examples of pious and impious actions. We, of course, might have some reservations about Socrates's demand in general. For it could be the case that piety is a vague concept with various examples of piety bearing only a family resemblance to one another. Just as we might think that there is no precise rule that will allow one to distinguish all chairs from all nonchairs, all games from all nongames, so there may be no precise rule that will allow one to distinguish all pious acts from all nonpious acts. Be that as it may, we can nonetheless feel the force of Socrates's objection here especially because Euthyphro's examples are themselves morally unclear and because it is precisely Euthyphro's ability to distinguish pious and impious actions that is in question. Euthyphro's own extreme confidence that he is doing the right thing in prosecuting his father suggests that he thinks there are clear and unambiguous criteria for distinguishing pious from impious actions.

1.3. Second Attempt: What Is Dear to the Gods

In response to Socrates's questioning, Euthyphro next suggests that what is pious is whatever is dear to the gods, and that what is impious is whatever is not dear to the gods: "Well then, what is dear to the gods is pious, what is not is impious" (7a). Earlier in the dialogue (6c), Socrates confirmed that Euthyphro believes in the Greek gods and all of the stories about them—that, for example, he believes that they fight, and that there is war between them, and that they disagree about many things. Socrates now notes that this presents a prima facie difficulty for Euthyphro's second definition of piety: if what is dear to the gods is pious (and what is not dear to the gods is impious), and the gods nonetheless disagree and fight over what is dear to them, then it seems that one and the same action must be both pious and impious (since it will be both dear to some gods and not dear to others).

There is of course a contemporary corollary to Euthyphro's second attempt to define piety. Just as Euthyphro must admit that the gods disagree among themselves, most theists today grant that members of different religions, and even members of the same religion, often disagree with one another. Such disagreements do not, of course, rule out the possibility that some people are simply right and others wrong, but they do suggest that as long as such disagreements reign, theists need some means to distinguish pious actions from impious actions. For even if it were granted that pious actions are indeed what some gods or religions hold dear, there would still be a need for a means of identifying which god or religion to follow.

As an aside, we might note that the question of religious diversity is itself an important topic in contemporary philosophy of religion. Although we won't dig into that topic deeply here, it might be worth briefly noting three main views—apart from atheism and agnosticism—that philosophers have taken with respect to the issue of religious diversity.

The first view is *exclusivism*. Exclusivists maintain that there is one correct religion, and that only those who believe and act in accordance with that religion can enjoy its benefits and rewards. In a relatively pluralistic society like our own, this can seem like a harsh view, but it can claim strong support from various religious texts and is certainly coherent. People disagree about all sorts of matters, and we don't generally assume that disagreement alone indicates an absence of fact.

A second view is *inclusivism*. Inclusivists maintain that there is one true religion, and generally one set of revealed or sacred texts. Nonetheless, they maintain that even those who do not share belief in the true religion may enjoy its benefits and rewards, typically by pursuing a strictly false religion in a way that resonates with the moral dictates of the true religion. So, for example, an inclusivist Muslim might maintain that Christian doctrine is strictly false or incomplete, but nonetheless maintain that even a Christian may receive salvation as long as she has lived a pious life.

Finally, a third view is *pluralism*. The pluralist maintains that many different religions may be striving after the same truth, but that none have a complete and full grasp of that truth. It is as if we were all to go to the fair and describe different parts of the fair—you see the Ferris wheel, I see the roller coaster, and so on. None of us has it all correct, but none of us is simply wrong. This view can claim some support from a long historical tradition that treats God as being in some sense knowable, but always beyond our full grasp. The pluralist view should not be confused with *relativism*. The relativist claims that all religious views are equally true, or true relative to a set of beliefs. The pluralist, in contrast, may insist on one objective truth, but nonetheless maintain that no one religion has a full account of it.

1.4. Third Attempt: What All the Gods Love

After some prompting by Socrates, Euthyphro next settles on the following definition of piety: "the pious is what all the gods love, and the opposite, what all the gods hate, is the impious" (9e). This of course helps to remove the prima facie objection to Euthyphro's second attempt at defining piety. But it also represents, I think, an intuitive move for contemporary defenders of so-called natural law or divine command theories—that is, theories that hold that what is right aligns with, or is determined by, divine decree. Many religious believers might allow that various idiosyncrasies of particular religions are not really all that important. They might grant that it is not so important whether you, for example, eat fish on Fridays or rest on Shabbat. What really matters, it might be insisted, are those core "religious values" common to many religions. Euthyphro's third definition captures that sentiment quite nicely.

At this juncture, Socrates raises the most famous point of the entire dialogue: "Is the pious being loved by the gods because it is pious, or is it pious because it is being loved by the gods?" (10a). The idea here is that, even granting that the gods love the pious, the order of explanation is important: do the gods recognize pious things and love them *because* they are pious, or are these things pious simply *because* the gods love them (the reasons for loving them being unimportant)?

We seem to face a dilemma: If, on the one hand, we say that things are pious simply because the gods love them, then it looks like what is pious or impious depends on the arbitrary whim of the gods—for what the gods may love or not love seems to be as arbitrary as, say, whether you like or dislike Wisconsin cheese. One might well think that if what makes pious things pious is simply the gods happening to like them, then the fact that they are pious gives us no more reason to hold them in esteem than does the mere fact that I like Wisconsin cheese give you a reason to like Wisconsin cheese.

If, on the other hand, things are pious independent of whether the gods love them or not, then the fact that the gods love pious things seems incidental to defining or understanding piety. What we would like to know, Socrates in effect complains, is what it is about pious things that the gods love. If what is pious is pious independent of the arbitrary decree of the gods, then there should be an explanatory account of pious things that both explains why the gods love them and why we should love them too.

Many philosophers have seen this dilemma as providing a devastating critique of natural law or divine command theories. They suggest that even where what is right aligns with, or is determined by, divine decree, there must either be independent reasons to support that decree, in which case those reasons may be judged independently of religious considerations, or the decree is arbitrary and should have no more hold on us than any other arbitrary decree.

Although I agree that something about the central argument of the *Euthyphro* is profound, I don't think it is as irresitable as many philosophers have suggested. In fact, it seems to me that the theist is in a pretty good position to embrace either horn of Euthyphro's dilemma, although doing so may come at some cost.

She could embrace the first horn, granting that while my arbitrary preference for Wisconsin cheese does not provide any reason for others to esteem it, the case is entirely different when it comes to the divine. She might maintain that if God—the best, most perfect being and creator—prefers us to do x, then that is a very good reason indeed for doing x. (One might analogously suppose that the fact that your parents want you to do x is a good, albeit defeasible, reason for doing x. We certainly tell our children that!)

She might also embrace the second horn, maintaining that God has independent reasons for judging what is right, but that from her own limited position she is not able to discern those reasons herself. That is to say, the theist might maintain that God has good reasons for his decrees, and maintain still that we should simply follow God's lead because we are not in as good a position as God is to appreciate those reasons. Such a response would be unsatisfying to Socrates because it fails to provide what he is really looking for, namely, an illuminating account or definition of the pious itself, but the contemporary theist might insist that to ask for such an account is simply asking for too much.

1.5. Fourth Attempt: Piety Is the Part of Justice That Concerns the Gods

Prompted anew by Socrates, Euthyphro next tries to say how just actions and pious actions are related. He claims that "the godly and pious is the part of the just that is concerned with the care of the gods, while that concerned with the care of men is the remaining part of justice" (12e). The idea is something like this: justice covers a lot of things—things having to do with both gods and humans. Piety, on the other hand, is concerned only with justice as it relates to the gods, and not as it relates to people. So, while all pious things are just, not all just things are pious.

In responding to this suggestion, Socrates first concentrates on what exactly Euthyphro means when he says that "the pious is the part of the just that is concerned with the care of the gods." For he thinks that "care of" indicates bettering something, as it does when someone cares for dogs or horses or cattle. But surely, Socrates argues, the gods aren't bettered by our pious actions; nothing we might do could improve the gods. Under pressure, Euthyphro clarifies that the sort of care he had in mind is the kind of care "that slaves take of their masters" (13d). He goes on to endorse the view that piety (as Socrates puts it) is "a sort of trading skill between gods and men" (14e). We give benefits to the gods, and the gods in turn give benefits to us.

Socrates finds none of this very convincing. In effect, he pushes on a point that has understandably puzzled many philosophers of religion. While it is easy to see how we might benefit from God, it is harder to see how God might benefit from us. Ironically, the issue is perhaps less pressing with respect to ancient Greek gods, who were notoriously vain and resentful, and might well be expected to enjoy human adoration and compliance. Given a conception of God as being omnipotent, omnibenevolent, and indeed, immutable, it seems to be even more challenging to say why our actions should matter to God, or how they could influence him in any way. (Those with an interest in Western church history might see seeds of the Christian Reformation already present here.) We can easily appreciate why Socrates is not impressed by Euthyphro's fourth definition of piety.

1.6. Fifth Attempt: The Pious Is What Is Dear to the Gods

Pressed by Socrates, Euthyphro finally suggests that the pious is "of all things most dear" to the gods (15a). Socrates, however, points out that Euthyphro has now come full circle. He is back to the claim that what is pious is that which is pleasing or dear to the gods. Socrates then starts all over again, saying that they "must investigate again from the beginning what piety is" (15d). At this point, however, Euthyphro is frustrated and takes his leave. The dialogue concludes with the question of the positive nature of the pious and the impious unresolved. Plato's *Euthyphro* ends having shown why we may be unsatisfied with various answers to the question "What is piety?" It does not, however, establish a clear, positive account of its own.

Many of Plato's dialogues end on a similar note. Plato seems to imply that philosophy is not necessarily about finding clear, concrete answers. It is more about asking hard questions and thinking through the implications of various possible answers. It is about exploring a field of study to better understand it, even when a better understanding leaves one with more questions than answers. In this respect Plato's dialogues provide a model for the chapters that follow. Those chapters explore three great themes in the history of philosophical thought about religion:

What is the nature of God or the divine?

What is the nature of the world, including human beings?

How are those two things—the divine and the mundane—related to one another?

Each chapter explores these questions in the company of great thinkers of the past and present in the hopes of gaining better insight into the various answers that might be given to them. The approach is one of inquisitive exploration and eagerness to understand. But be forewarned: no one should be surprised if, at the end, we wind up just where Socrates winds up at the end of the *Euthyphro*—namely, back where we started, hopefully a little wiser, but no more certain, and perhaps even less certain, than when we began.

Further Study

Edith Hamilton, *The Greek Way*. New York: W. W. Norton and Company (reissued), 1993. Popular, accessible summary of Greek history for a general reader.

Richard Kraut, "Plato." *Stanford Encyclopedia of Philosophy* (Spring 2015 edition), ed. Edward N. Zalta, http://plato.stanford.edu/archives/spr2015/entries/plato/. Helpful, more advanced overview of Plato and his philosophical views. Includes an extended bibliography of primary and secondary sources.

Plato, *The Dialogues of Plato*, Volume 2. Trans. Benjamin Jowett. Oxford: Oxford University Press, 1892. Jowett's translation is in the public domain and widely available on the Web, including at http://classics.mit.edu/Plato/euthyfro.html.

Paul Woodruff, "Plato's Shorter Ethical Works." *Stanford Encyclopedia of Philosophy* (Winter 2014 edition), ed. Edward N. Zalta (ed.), http://plato.stanford.edu/archives/win2014/entries/plato-ethics-shorter/. Helpful, more advanced overview of Plato's shorter ethical works, including the *Euthyphro*.

2

Augustine's *On Free Choice of the Will*

Where Does Evil Come From?

2.1. The Setting

With this chapter, we jump forward in history from the golden age of ancient Greece to the beginning of the end of the Western Roman Empire. The Roman Empire traced its own roots back to the fall of Troy, taking 753 BCE as its founding date. In spite of its modest—indeed scandalous—beginnings, Rome soon expanded, first as a kingdom, then as a republic, and finally as an empire.

For roughly its first thousand years, Rome was a pagan state. It was known for its willingness to tolerate, and even embrace, the deities of the lands it had conquered. Rome's religious identity changed dramatically, however, around the time of the fourth century CE. In the previous century, Diocletian had outlawed Christianity and carried out what has been called the Great Persecution. In 310, however, Constantine became the first Christian emperor, setting a precedent that all subsequent Roman emperors save one would follow. With the rise of Constantine, Christianity went from being a persecuted enemy of the state to, in effect, the state religion. It was a dramatic reversal of fortune with incalculable consequences for Western religion.

Augustine grew up and lived in these turbulent times, simultaneously dealing with fallout from the Great Persecution, shaping what would become accepted doctrine, and responding to concerns that Rome's Christian turn would lead to its downfall.

The future saint was born in a small provincial town in North Africa in 354 CE to a pagan father and a famously devout Christian mother, Monica. At roughly the age of fifteen, he moved to Carthage to continue his schooling. There he studied rhetoric, lived a self-described life of sin, and took a mistress who bore him a son, Adeodatus (literally "given by God").

In Carthage, Augustine became a novice of a sect known as the Manicheans. Manicheans believed in a metaphysical dualism of two

Saints, Heretics, and Atheists. Jeffrey K. McDonough, Oxford University Press. © Oxford University Press 2022.
DOI: 10.1093/oso/9780197563847.003.0002

fundamental principles, one good and one evil. They held that good and evil are engaged in an eternal struggle for supremacy. Augustine reports that he was attracted to Manicheanism as a youth in part because of its straightforward account of the presence of evil in the world.

After roughly ten years of teaching rhetoric in Carthage and one year in Rome, Augustine took up a teaching position in Milan. There, under the influence of Saint Ambrose, he renewed his interest in Christianity and broke permanently with the Manicheans. After suffering a spiritual crisis during which he struggled to accept the full implications of his new faith, Augustine converted to Christianity in 386. He would later be elected bishop of Hippo and write over 100 books and treatises, 500 sermons, and 250 letters. His works include *The Confessions* (published in 400) and *The City of God* (completed in 426).

Augustine died during a Vandal siege of Hippo in 430. He was later canonized by popular acclaim and recognized as a Doctor of the Church in 1303. One of Augustine's earliest philosophical works—his *On Free Choice of the Will*—presents a dialogue between himself and his close friend Evodius. It asks, most centrally, what is the cause of evil?

2.2. What Is the Cause of Evil?

Augustine's *On Free Choice of the Will* opens unceremoniously with Evodius asking bluntly, "Isn't God the cause of evil?" Augustine maintains that Christians must believe that God isn't the original cause of evil, although they may grant that God allows people to suffer evil. But why would God allow people to suffer evil? Augustine responds: Because people freely choose to act in evil ways. Evil in the world, according to Augustine, is due not to God but to our evil actions.

What, then, makes an action evil? In taking up this question, Augustine starts by quickly raising and dismissing three possible views. First: evil is violating civil law. Augustine thinks this gets the order of dependence the wrong way around. A law is good if it promotes good behavior, and bad if it promotes bad behavior. Evil is not to be defined in terms of civil laws, but rather civil laws are to be judged good or bad to the extent that they promote pious actions and discourage evil actions. Second: evil is doing to another what you would not want done to yourself. Not so, says Augustine. Some people *want* immoral things done to them! That doesn't make those things right. Third: evil is what is condemned by many. Wrong again, says Augustine. Even a persecuted minority—like the early Christians—might, Augustine thinks, be in the right. Augustine's process of raising and responding to a series of definitions echoes, and is intended to echo, the Socratic method we saw in chapter 1.

Having dispatched some tempting accounts of what makes actions evil, Augustine offers his own view: evil is inordinate desire. But what, exactly, does that mean? Most basically, inordinate desires occur when one values lower goods over higher goods. (Inordinate desires are desires that are literally out of order.) Augustine's account of inordinate desire takes for granted a background understanding of goods not uncommon in earlier eras. Eternal things that are associated with God are assigned a high value, while changeable things associated with earthly matters are assigned a low value. Augustine adds to this background a further thought—namely, that higher goods are also goods that one cannot lose against one's will, while lower goods are always subject to the whims of fate and fortune. You might lose your money to a thief or a flood, but no one can take away the heavenly goods that are due to you. We sin when we value lower goods like money over higher goods like virtue.

It is worth noting that something radical is built into the very structure of Augustine's hierarchy of goods. For Augustine, an unbridgeable gap exists between worldly goods and heavenly goods. Worldly goods are simply incomparable to heavenly goods. Consequently, for Augustine, there is never any reason to sacrifice a heavenly good for a worldly good—no matter how apparently trivial the heavenly good or how grand the worldly good. According to Augustine, committing even a small lie for the sake of a great fortune would be a mistake. It would be wrong to, say, fudge a job application even if one were certain to get away with it and to become rich and famous as a result. Fudging the job application would be to value the lower goods of wealth and fame over the higher good of obeying divine law. It would be evil.

Augustine himself gives us a nice example of just how demanding his view can be. In *On Free Choice of the Will*, Augustine considers a case of self-defense. Distinguishing between civil laws and divine laws, he argues that civil laws are right to allow killing in self-defense because civil laws should favor lesser evils (such as the killing of an attacker) to greater evils (such as the killing of an attacker's victim). Nonetheless, Augustine maintains that anyone who kills in self-defense sins because he acts out of an inordinate desire for worldly goods. The person who kills in self-defense, according to

Augustine, inordinately values his own life over God's commandment not to kill. And so, according to Augustine, even killing in self-defense is *always* forbidden by divine law. Augustine's understanding of evil places great demands on anyone who accepts it.

2.3. The Well-Ordered Person

Augustine has argued that evil is due to our sinful actions, and that our sinful actions are to be understood in terms of inordinate desires. But what would it be for our actions, our desires, to be not disordered but well ordered? In answering this question, Augustine proceeds through three main steps. First, he argues that the crowning virtue of human beings is their reason. He does this, in part, by arguing that we surpass beasts in virtue of our reason, and that this is witnessed by the fact that we are able to tame and subdue animals, while they are not able to tame and subdue humans. (Augustine clearly never met my dog!) While we might balk at Augustine's argument, his first conclusion is nonetheless plausible enough. What sets humans apart from other creatures is our ability to reason—to write poems, build bridges, govern wisely.

Second, Augustine suggests that in a well-ordered person, reason rules one's baser instincts and passions. Conversely, he suggests that a person not ruled by reason is a fool. In these characterizations, Augustine echoes another common theme from Plato's writings. In his *Republic*, Plato had argued that a well-ordered city (ruled by philosophers, of course!) mirrors a well-ordered person ruled by his faculty of reason. For both Augustine and Plato, reason is in charge in both a well-ordered society and in a well-ordered person. Again, we might have some hesitations about Augustine's argument. We might wonder, for example, how similar a well-ordered person and a well-ordered state really are. Nonetheless, Augustine's second conclusion is plausible enough. Being ruled by reason rather than flights of passion and fancy does seem like a mark of a disciplined, well-ordered, virtuous person.

Third, Augustine maintains that what is lower can never, of its own accord, control what is higher, and in particular that no desire or material object is more powerful than reason. He suggests that if a lower object could control a higher object, the lower object by dint of that very fact would not be a lower object after all. If beasts could tame humans, rather than the other way around, then by dint of that very fact beasts would be above humans. Augustine reasons analogously that a righteous mind could never force another righteous mind to inordinately desire something, since the first mind would, by dint of that very fact, not be a righteous mind, and thus would be inferior to the mind it seeks to corrupt. Augustine draws the conclusion that nothing can make a righteous—that is, a well-ordered—mind subject to vice or sin.

Augustine's understanding of what it is to be a well-ordered person fits into his broader understanding of the good life. A good person is a person who lives in accordance with reason and who orders her desires rationally. The good life, for Augustine, is a moderate life dominated by rational reflection. Such a picture of the good life is largely in tune with the picture of the good life favored by Plato and many other early philosophers. Indeed, this picture of the good life has resonated with philosophers throughout history and continues to do so with many people today.

But not with everyone. Augustine's picture of the good life, with its emphasis on moderation and reason, may be opposed by those who afford a greater place in the good life to soaring emotions and profound love. It may also be opposed by those who think that the good life is most firmly rooted in compassion and good deeds. In such different conceptions of the good life, one can see foreshadows of religious disputes that would rage in later centuries. Is the deepest root of religious belief rational reflection, passion and emotion, or good deeds? Is the monk who spends his days secluded in a monastery a model of piety? Is it the mystic lost in ecstatic feelings of love and devotion? Or is it the dedicated nurse who spends her time among the suffering, addressing their needs and providing them with comfort as best she can? Augustine's understanding of what it takes to be a good person is not just the converse of his understanding of what it takes to be a bad person. It is an opening move in his account of what is most central to living well.

2.4. Sin and Ignorance

Having drawn a tight connection between reason and virtue, Augustine faces a potential objection: No one wants to be irrational, so if we are irrational, it seems, we must be irrational against our will. But if we are irrational against our will, then it seems that we are not responsible for our irrational actions—that is, for our sins. Here's the way Augustine puts the problem:

> The question that troubles me most is this: We are certainly fools and have never been wise. And yet we are said to suffer such bitter penalties deservedly because we abandoned the stronghold of virtue and chose to be slaves to inordinate desire. How can this be? (18; this chapter follows Williams's translation of *On Free Choice of the Will* in Augustine [1993])

Augustine's language here is a bit poetic by contemporary standards, but the problem he is raising is intuitive. Augustine is committed to the view that sin is always a mistake. If you think that a lower good is more valuable than a higher good, you are simply wrong. But, of course, no one wants to make mistakes. No one wants to be wrong. So, if we make a mistake—if we sin—it seems we must sin against our will. But from the very beginning of his dialogue, Augustine has granted that we are only responsible for what we will. So, to ask the question again: if there is a tight connection between reason and virtue, how can we be responsible for sinning, if whenever we sin, we make a mistake?

Augustine offers a three-part response to this difficult question. First, he argues that anyone—even a fool—can recognize that a good will is far more valuable than any earthly good, and that all that is required to have a good will is to value it above any earthly good. Augustine's thought is that everyone will recognize that it is more important to be a good person than to have, say, a new iPhone. And furthermore, while that new iPhone might not be available now and will cost you a bundle anyway, you don't need anything external to be honest, sincere, and pious. Augustine concludes that even a fool is responsible for not having a good will, since even a fool must know that a good will is the best thing to obtain, and even a fool is capable of obtaining it (20).

Second, Augustine argues that the person who has a good will also has all other virtues. In order to do this, he draws upon an ancient doctrine known as the "unity of the virtues." According to that doctrine, a person is not able to truly possess one virtue without possessing all other virtues. So, for example, it was held that a thief couldn't really be generous if he isn't also honest and fair. On this view, the thief who gives away stolen items isn't really being generous since one can only be generous if one is also honest and fair. With the unity of the virtues in the background, Augustine argues that if one has a good will, then one must also have the virtues of prudence, fortitude, temperance, and justice. Augustine concludes that since anyone can have a good will, it must also be the case that anyone can have all the virtues. This thought ties back into Augustine's earlier thought that while our possession of earthly goods is subject to fate, our possession of heavenly goods is completely within our power.

Finally, Augustine links having a good will and virtue with leading a good life, arguing that "it is established that people are happy when they love their own good will, in comparison with which they scorn everything that is called good but can be lost even though one wills to retain it" (22). In a dramatic passage, Augustine pulls together his views on sin and ignorance:

AUGUSTINE: So if by our good will we love and embrace that will, and prefer it to everything that we cannot retain simply by willing to retain it, then . . . we will possess those very virtues that constitute an upright and honorable life. From this it follows that all who will to live upright and honorable lives, if they will this more than they will transitory goods, attain such a great good so easily that they have it by the very act of willing to have it.

EVODIUS: I can hardly keep myself from shouting for joy that such a great and easily attainable good has suddenly sprung up within me.

AUGUSTINE: And when that very joy, born of the attainment of this good, calmly, quietly, and steadily bears up the soul, this is called the happy life. For doesn't a happy life consist precisely in the enjoyment of true and unshakable goods?

EVODIUS: Indeed it does. (22)

2.5. An Objection and Two Conclusions

Augustine has argued that we all have it in our power to recognize the importance of having a good will, to thereby have all the virtues necessary in order to lead a good life, and to thereby be happy. Having come this far, however, one might worry that Augustine's argument—if right—would prove too much. Augustine himself recognizes the objection:

> How can anyone suffer an unhappy life by the will, when absolutely no one wills to be unhappy? Or to put it another way, how can we claim that it is by the will that human beings achieve a happy life, when so many are unhappy despite the fact that everyone wills to be happy? (23)

Augustine responds by drawing a distinction: he suggests that while everyone wills to be happy, not everyone wills to be happy in virtue of living a good life. The scoundrel and the saint are similar in both wanting to be happy. They differ in that the scoundrel wants to be happy by leading a sinful life while the saint wants to be happy by leading a pious life. To lead the good life, one must not only will to be happy. One must will to be happy in the right way (24).

With his distinction between willing to be happy in the right way and willing to be happy in wrong ways, we finally arrive at Augustine's full answer to his second question, namely, "What is evildoing?":

> We set out to discover what evildoing is. The whole discussion was aimed at answering that question. So, we are now in a position to ask whether evildoing is anything other than neglecting eternal things, which the mind perceives and enjoys by means of itself and which it cannot lose if it loves them; and instead pursuing temporal things—which are perceived by means of the body, the least valuable part of a human being, and which can never be certain—as if they were great and marvelous things. It seems to be that all evil deeds—that is, all sins—fall into this one category. (27)

Here we get an interesting characterization of evildoing, namely, evildoing is neglecting immutable, eternal things in favor of mutable, transient things. To Augustine's way of thinking, eternal things can be known with certainty and through the intellect, whereas worldly things can never be known with certainty and must be perceived through bodily senses. Relatedly, for Augustine, our acquaintance with eternal things is wholly under our control, and thus the benefits we enjoy from them are wholly under our control, while our possession of earthly goods is always subject to fate and fortune. Our enjoyment of earthly goods is never fully under our control.

And finally, we also get Augustine's answer to the first question he posed, namely, "What is the source of our evildoing?" In summarizing Augustine's answer, however, Evodius raises a further question that will serve as the starting point for the second book of *On Free Choice of the Will*:

> And I think that we have answered another question. After we asked what evildoing is, we set out to discover the source of our evildoing. Now unless I am mistaken, our argument showed that we do evil by the free choice of the will. But I have a further question. Since, as we have found, free choice gives us the ability to sin, should it have been given to us by the one who created us? It would seem that we would not have sinned if we had lacked

free choice, so there is still the danger that God might turn out to be the cause of our evil deeds. (28)

In the next chapter, we follow Augustine's lead and turn our attention from the question "Where does evil come from?" to the question "Why might God give us free will knowing that it will lead to sin?" As we'll see, Augustine's answer to his second question is no less interesting and subtle than his answer to his first question.

2.6. Freedom and Determinism

In this chapter, we have examined Augustine's account of the sources of evil. As we've seen, Augustine thinks that evil comes from the free choices of creatures such as us. In the next chapter, we take up a question that naturally arises from Augustine's account of where evil comes from—namely, why would God give us free wills knowing that we will use them to do evil? In preparation for understanding Augustine's subtle answer to that question, however, it will be helpful to distinguish three theses concerning the nature of freedom itself, namely, the theses of *determinism*, *compatibilism*, and *incompatibilism*, as well as some different positions concerning compatibilism and incompatibilism that we may call *optimistic compatibilists*, *pessimistic compatibilists*, *optimistic incompatibilists*, and *pessimistic compatibilists.*

To begin with, *determinism* is the thesis that future events are causally determined by past events and the laws of nature. So, for example, if I walk into an ice cream store and I am about to order an ice cream cone, determinism entails that it is causally determined that I will select (say) two scoops of chocolate in a sugar cone. A central question that philosophers discuss in connection with free will is whether freedom is consistent with determinism. If I am causally determined to choose chocolate, can I *freely* choose chocolate?

Incompatibilism is the thesis that freedom is not compatible with determinism. Put conversely, it maintains that if, for example, humans are to have free will, it must be the case that some events are not causally determined by prior events and the laws of nature. Most incompatibilists are optimistic incompatibilists (also known as *libertarians*). *Optimistic incompatibilists* maintain that our choices are undetermined, that our wills cause our actions without being causally determined themselves, and that we are free. Freedom as understood by optimistic incompatibilists is often called *libertarian freedom*. Proponents of libertarian freedom insist that if we could rewind the tape of history so that I could relive my experience of being in the ice cream store, I could—with everything else being the same—still choose vanilla rather than chocolate.

Not all incompatibilists, however, are optimistic. *Pessimistic incompatibilists* (also known as *hard incompatibilists*) also maintain that free will is inconsistent with determinism, but—in contrast to optimistic incompatibilists—they also insist that free will is incompatible with indeterminism. Their thought is that libertarian freedom is impossible or incoherent. Why might one be a pessimistic incompatibilist? And, in particular, why might one think that free will is incompatible with indeterminism? Well, one might think that the only way for the world to be indeterminate is for some events to be random or irreducibly probabilistic. If uranium atoms, for example, decay spontaneously—without a determining cause—then determinism is false. But would the occurrence of such an event help to secure free will? The pessimist thinks not. She may argue that random or irreducibly probabilistic events aren't good candidates for free choices either. If my hand shoots up in class randomly or, say, with a 63.8 percent probability, it doesn't seem like I freely raise my hand. The pessimist concludes, whether determinism is true or false, we can't have free will.

Compatibilism, in contrast, is the thesis that free will is compatible with determinism. Compatibilists hold that even if my choice of chocolate ice cream is causally determined, it might nonetheless be free. Compatibilists typically suggest that what is relevant to freedom is not the absence of causal determinism, but rather the way in which our actions are determined. If, for example, the immediate cause of my jumping off a curb is bound up with my desires and beliefs, my action is free. If, on the contrary, the immediate cause of my jumping off a curb is that someone else is pushing me, my action is not free. The difference between free actions and unfree actions on this view is not the difference between actions that are determined or undetermined, but rather between some ways of being causally determined and other ways of being causally determined.

Most compatibilists are *optimistic compatibilists* (also known as *soft compatibilists*). Optimistic compatibilists maintain that our actions are typically causally determined, but also typically free. *Pessimistic compatibilists* are less common but hold a logically consistent view. As you'll have guessed, pessimistic compatibilists (also known as *hard compatibilists*) maintain that although freedom and determinism are in principle compatible, we are nonetheless not free. Insofar as they insist that we can't even clear the lowered bar of compatibilism, the pessimistic compatibilist might be reckoned the most pessimistic of pessimists. In the next chapter we see Augustine raise a series of pessimistic objections to our being free and counter with his own optimistic responses.

Further Study

Augustine, *On Free Choice of the Will*. Trans. Thomas Williams. Indianapolis, IN: Hackett, 1993.

Peter Brown, *Augustine of Hippo: A Biography*. Berkeley: University of California Press, 2000. (Authoritative biography of Augustine.)

Diarmaid MacCulloch, *Christianity: The First Three Thousand Years*. New York: Penguin, 2009. Sweeping, popular history of Christianity from its historical inception to the present day.

Mike Duncan, *The History of Rome*. Audio Podcast, 2007–2013; available online and through iTunes and on the web. (Entertaining, accessible introduction to Roman history.)

Michael McKenna and Justin D. Coates, "Compatibilism." *Stanford Encyclopedia of Philosophy* (Summer 2015 edition), ed. Edward N. Zalta, http://plato.stanford.edu/archives/sum2015/entries/compatibilism/. Helpful, advanced overview of the relationship between freedom and determinism.

Michael Mendelson, "Saint Augustine." *Stanford Encyclopedia of Philosophy* (Winter 2012 edition), ed. Edward N. Zalta, http://plato.stanford.edu/archives/win2012/entries/augustine/. Helpful, advanced overview of Augustine and his philosophical views. Includes an extended bibliography of primary and secondary sources.

3

Augustine's *On Free Choice of the Will*

Why Do We Have Free Will?

3.1. Setup and Structure

In the last chapter, we saw that in the first book of *On Free Choice of the Will*, Augustine argued that free will is a source of evil. The second book of *On Free of the Choice* begins with Evodius asking "why God gave human beings free choice of the will, since if we had not received it, we would not have been able to sin" (29; this chapter follows Williams's translation of *On Free Choice of the Will* in Augustine [1993]).

Augustine initially replies by sketching what he thinks must be accepted on the basis of faith: The gift of free will comes from God and therefore it must be good. Furthermore, since we are punished when we use our wills to sin, and rewarded when we use them to do right, it is clear that God gave us free wills in order to do right and not in order to sin.

Evodius agrees that all of that must be accepted on the basis of faith. Nonetheless, he characteristically presses for a philosophical account as well, invoking the recurring Augustinian theme of not only wanting to believe, but also to understand. Evodius's plea serves as the prompt for Augustine's philosophical response to Evodius's initial question. That response is the central topic of the second book of *On Free Choice of the Will*.

Early in his response, Augustine gives us an important clue into the structure of his account, writing,

> But if you don't mind, let's pose our questions in the following order. First, how is it manifest that God exists? Second, do all things, insofar as they are good, come from God? And finally, should free will be counted as one of those good things? Once we have answered those questions it will, I think, be clear whether free will ought to have been given to human beings. (33)

Saints, Heretics, and Atheists. Jeffrey K. McDonough, Oxford University Press. © Oxford University Press 2022.
DOI: 10.1093/oso/9780197563847.003.0003

This, in fact, captures quite well the contour of Augustine's answer to the question "Why do we have free will?" In the rest of this chapter, we follow Augustine by allowing his questions to structure our own investigation of his views. Taking up those questions up one at a time, let's start by asking, "How is it manifest that God exists?"

3.2. How Is It Manifest That God Exists?

Immediately after posing his structuring questions, Augustine offers several arguments for the conclusion that reason or understanding is the highest faculty in humans. The first argument appears to take for granted a principle to the effect that where A presupposes B, but not vice versa, then A is superior to B. Thus, Augustine has Evodius argue,

> There are these three things: existence, life, and understanding. A stone exists, and an animal is alive, but I do not think that a stone is alive or an animal understands. But whatever understands must certainly also exist and be alive. So I do not hesitate to conclude that something in which all three are present is superior to something that lacks any of them. For whatever is alive also exists, but it does not follow that it also understands; such, I think, is the life of an animal. But from the fact that something exists it does not follow that it is alive and understands; for I can admit that corpses exist, but no one would say that they are alive. And whatever is not alive can certainly not understand. (33)

The argument is supposed to establish that since understanding presupposes life, and life presupposes existence, they are ranked as understanding, life, and existence. Humans are above animals because they have understanding. Animals are above inanimate beings because they have life. It follows for Augustine that understanding is the highest faculty, or crowning virtue, of humans. Augustine's other arguments focus on the capacities of perceiving and judging but are similar in nature.

Having secured to his own satisfaction the conclusion that reason is the highest faculty among creatures, Augustine argues next that God exists. The general structure of his argument goes as follows:

> Premise 1: God is that which is eternal, unchangeable, and superior to reason, and to which nothing is superior.

Premise 2: If there is something eternal, unchangeable, and superior to reason, then either that is God, or there is something else superior even to that, and that is God.

Premise 3: So, if there is something eternal, unchangeable, and superior to reason, then God exists.

Premise 4: There is something eternal, unchangeable, and superior to reason.

Conclusion: God exists.

We might, of course, wish to quibble about the definition implicit in Augustine's first premise or the suggestion of his second premise. Must God be unchangeable? Could there be something eternal, unchangeable, and superior to reason that is neither God nor a rung below God? Augustine, however, sees the fourth premise as the lynchpin of the argument and as the point in most need of defense.

Augustine's argument for his fourth premise may be thought of as having four main steps. First, he argues that just as we each have our own sensory faculties, we each have our own rational faculties. Second, he makes a distinction between subjective and objective objects of sensory experience. The taste of a small piece of cake might be held to be subjective since we can't both taste the very same morsel. The sight of the sun, in contrast, might be thought to be objective since my seeing the sun doesn't preclude you seeing the very same sun. Third, Augustine argues that mathematical truths and the "unchangeable rules of wisdom" must be objective objects of rational perception. They must be *objects* of rational perception because we grasp not only that they are truths, but that they are metaphysically simple, necessarily true, and immutable. They must be *objective* objects because my perceiving an eternal truth doesn't preclude your perceiving the same eternal truth. Fourth, Augustine argues that since reason cannot be superior to the eternal truths (since reason does not make judgments about them, but rather in accordance with them) nor equal to them (since reason is changeable while the truths are unchangeable), the eternal truths must be higher than reason itself. Augustine has put himself in a position to assert the claim of the fourth premise, namely, that there is something eternal, unchangeable, and superior to reason (55).

With the fourth premise defended, however, Augustine is also in a position to answer his first main question: how is it manifest that God exists?

> Now you had conceded that if I proved the existence of something higher than our minds, you would admit that it was God, as long as there was nothing higher still. I accepted this concession, and said that it would be enough if I proved that there is something higher than our minds. For if there is something more excellent than truth, then that is God; if not, the truth itself is God. So, in either case you cannot deny that God exists, and that was the very question that we had agreed to discuss. (58)

3.3. Do All Things, Insofar as They Are Good, Come from God?

Having shown how it is manifest that God exists, Augustine raises his next question: do all things, insofar as they are good, come from God? Augustine's response is easier to understand in light of an important Platonic theme that lies in the background of his discussion. Plato had distinguished between an eternal, immutable realm of forms and the transitory, ever-changing realm of material objects. He held that the eternal forms (including numbers, shapes, and certain "eternal truths") are related to mundane objects through the relation of "participation." Very roughly, the idea is that things in the world are, for example, (imperfectly) square or (imperfectly) wise insofar as they participate in the eternal forms of (perfect) squareness and (perfect) wisdom. Although the stop sign is not a perfect octagon, nonetheless it imperfectly participates in the perfect octagonal form, and in virtue of that participation it is roughly octagonal. Likewise, although no mortal is completely wise, Socrates, for example, might be held to approximate wisdom by imperfectly participating in the form of wisdom.

With the Platonic doctrine of participation in the background, Augustine argues that everything, to the extent that it is good or perfect, participates in form or number. The stop sign participates in form in virtue of its shape. A horse participates in form in virtue of its motion, a dancer in virtue of her rhythm, and so on. Given his Platonic outlook and his broad understanding of form, we can see why Augustine thinks that everything must, to some degree, participate in number or form and thereby participate in eternal truths.

Augustine is now in a position to respond to his second question. If everything insofar as it is good participates in form, and form is either God or from God (if God is even higher than form), then everything insofar as it is good comes from God.

> Therefore, there can be no good thing, however great or small, that is not from God. For what created things could be greater than a life that understands or less than matter? However much they may lack form, and however great may be their propensity not to exist, nonetheless some form remains in them so that they do exist in some way. And whatever form remains in a deficient thing comes from the form that knows no deficiency and does not allow the motions of growing or decaying things to transgress the laws of their own numbers. Therefore, whatever is found to be praiseworthy in nature, whether it is judged worthy of small or great praise, should be referred to the ineffable and most excellent praise of their maker. (64)

3.4. Should Free Will Be Counted as a Good Thing That Comes from God?

Having argued that God exists, and that every good thing is from him, Augustine finally turns to his third question: should free will be counted as a good thing that comes from God? The question isn't answered yet because, for all that has been said, it could still be the case that free will is not a good thing, and consequently does not come from God. Augustine still needs to show that free will is in fact a good thing.

He prepares the ground for his arguments to follow by pointing out that even tremendously good things can be used wrongly:

> Consider what a great good a body is missing if it has no hands. And yet people use their hands wrongly in committing violent or shameful acts. . . . By our eyes we see light and we distinguish the forms of material objects. They are the most beautiful things in our bodies, so they were put into the place of greatest dignity; and we use them to preserve our safety and to secure many other good things in life. Nonetheless, many people use their eyes to do many evil things and press them into the service of inordinate desire; and yet you realize what a great good is missing in a face that has no eyes. (65)

The overarching point is simply that many things, like hammers, eyes, and dogs, are good things, even though they can be used to do bad things. The implication, of course, is that freedom of the will might be a good thing even if it can be used to do evil.

Having readied his readers, Augustine turns to his main argument for the goodness of freedom of the will. It turns on the thought that anything that is necessary for living rightly must be superior to anything that is merely consistent with living rightly. Taking that principle for granted, Augustine argues roughly as follows:

Premise 1: Eyes are good even though they are not necessary for living rightly.

Premise 2: One cannot live rightly without a free will.

Premise 3: Whatever is necessary for living rightly is superior to whatever is not necessary for living rightly.

Conclusion 1: Free will is a good thing (since it is better than eyes, for example, and eyes are good).

Conclusion 2: Since all good things, insofar as they are good, come from God, free will comes from God.

With this argument, Augustine has answered the last of the three questions he raised at the beginning of the second book of *On Free Choice of the Will*. He has shown—to his own satisfaction at least—how it is manifest that God exists. There must be something higher than human reason, and that something is either God or God is superior to even it. He has shown that all things, insofar as they come from God, are good. Everything, insofar as it exists, partakes of eternal, immutable forms, and those forms are either God or from God. Finally, he has shown why free will should be counted as a good thing that comes from God. Although we can use it badly, free will is a good thing because it is necessary for living rightly. Chaining the results of the previous chapter and this chapter together, Augustine has argued that evil comes from the misuse of our free wills, but that free will itself is a good thing because it affords us the possibility of living rightly. It is a good thing that comes from God even though—like a hand or a hammer—it can be misused to do evil.

3.5. Happiness and Immortality

In the third book of *On Free Choice of the Will*, Augustine turns to his last main question: why, if God gave us a will to do good, do we use it to sin? Near the end of the second book of *On Free Choice of the Will*, however (and more thoroughly in other works), Augustine considers the question of whether we can be happy in this life. He concludes that belief in an afterlife is essential to whatever happiness we can enjoy now, and that full and secure happiness is only possible in a life to come. He thus rejects, for example, the Epicurean view according to which we may strive to be happy in this life while holding that death may be "nothing to us" since after we die, we'll be dead. Augustine responds, If you want to be happy, you'll want to be happy forever, and the very prospect of not being happy someday is bound to spoil even your present joy. By Augustine's lights, a belief in immortality is essential to happiness. We can only be happy if we believe that we are immortal.

But would immortality really be a good thing? The contemporary philosopher Bernard Williams (1929–2003) has argued that immortality is not something we should hope for (1973). More specifically, Williams argues (very roughly) that the prospect of an immortal life raises a dilemma with no good options. He thinks that if we were immortal either our interests and passions would stay much the same over time and we would eventually get terribly bored, or our interests and passions would change dramatically over time, and there would be no good reason to suppose that we would be the same people continuously enjoying an eternal life. We might call these two horns, respectively, the *boredom problem* and the *identity problem*.

Is the boredom problem really a problem? In reply to Williams, John Martin Fischer (1952–) has argued that we should distinguish two kinds of pleasures (1994). *Self-exhausting pleasures* are pleasures we can only enjoy for a limited time. You liked a recent pop song when it first came out, but pretty soon, or already, it's going to drive you crazy if you hear it one more time. But other pleasures, call them *nonexhausting pleasures*, Fischer argues, are not like that. Perhaps you are a sports fan and you could enjoy watching your favorite soccer team play every weekend, literally forever. Or perhaps to offer a more serious example, you take deep pleasure in meditation and prayer in such a way that you derive no less—and maybe even more—satisfaction from their regular repetition. Examples such as these are, I think, difficult to assess. Do we really experience any nonexhausting pleasures? (Soccer games are fun to watch, but would you really still be interested after a million years?)

Furthermore, the theist might concede that in this life we don't experience any nonexhausting pleasures, but nevertheless maintain that the continuum of our experiences gives us reason to hope that there could be pleasures that we might enjoy forever.

Is the identity problem a problem? Anticipating a response along the lines of Fischer's nonexhausting pleasures, Williams effectively warns us to be careful what we wish for. He maintains that the only plausible kinds of pleasures that are not self-exhausting are pleasures we commonly describe as ones in which we "lose ourselves." If you love jazz so much that you could listen to *Kind of Blue* forever, then, Williams implies, you must lose yourself in the music, cease to notice what is going on around you, and forget about your own individual identity altogether. In the extreme case, perhaps you could lose yourself for eternity, but then it's not clear that it is *you* who is enjoying anything for eternity.

In reply, Fischer argues that we can resist the second horn of Williams's dilemma as well. Fischer contends that Williams's second horn takes too literally the idea of losing yourself in a pleasure. He maintains that we can distinguish between losing oneself in the sense of not being self-absorbed and losing oneself in the sense of those experiences not being identifiable as one's own experiences. Listing to jazz, I might lose myself in the sense that I'm mostly paying attention to the music, and so not to myself or to my immediate surroundings. Nonetheless, it is obviously *me* that's listening to the music, and indeed it is obviously me that's enjoying the music.

Perhaps, however, there is something to Williams's second horn that even theists might be reluctant to deny. A common theme of many religious traditions is that much of what is so good about the afterlife is that you become absorbed into a larger whole or higher being, that your false and artificial sense of being an independent person dissolves. This suggestion, however, gives another route into Williams's identity concern: if *I* am to dissolve into a greater and more inclusive being after my bodily death, then in what sense do *I* survive my bodily death, and why should *I* be comforted by such a conception of the afterlife? (We see Spinoza taking up this issue in a very different context in chapter 16.) The debate between Williams and Fischer by itself, however, should be sufficient to indicate that the connections between immortality and happiness are at the least more complicated—and more interesting—than at first might appear.

Further Study

Peter Adamson, *The History of Philosophy without Any Gaps: Philosophy in Later Antiquity*. Podcast, 2011–13; available online and through iTunes. An excellent, entertaining introduction to philosophical currents before and during Augustine's time.

Augustine, *City of God*. Trans. Thomas Merton. New York: Random House, 1993. Augustine's defense of Christianity in the wake of the sack of Rome by the Visigoths in 410 CE.

Augustine, *On Free Choice of the Will*. Trans. Thomas Williams. Indianapolis, IN: Hackett, 1993.

Sissela Bok, *Exploring Happiness from Aristotle to Brain Science*. New Haven, CT: Yale University Press, 2010. A highly readable study of happiness that takes up the views of philosophers including Plato, Aristotle, and Augustine.

John Martin Fischer, "Why Immortality Is Not So Bad." *International Journal of Philosophical Studies* 2, no. 2 (1994): 257–70.

Bernard Williams, "The Makropulos Case: Reflections on the Tedium of Immortality." In *Problems of the Self*. Cambridge: Cambridge University Press, 1973.

4

Augustine's *On Free Choice of the Will*

Why Do We Sin?

4.1. Why Do We Sin, and Who Is to Blame?

The last two chapters showed Augustine arguing that our free wills are the source of evil in the world, and that God gave us free will in order to live rightly. In Book III of *On Free Choice of the Will*, Augustine pursues two further, related questions. First, why do we sin, or as Evodius puts it, what "is the source of the movement by which the will turns away from the common and unchangeable good toward its own good, or the good of others, or lower goods, all of which are changeable" (70; this chapter follows Williams's translation of *On Free Choice of the Will* in Augustine [1993])? Second, who or what is responsible for our sinning? In particular, are we to blame, or is our maker?

Augustine begins by arguing that the will is not moved to sin by its very nature: he insists that it is evident that the will's sinning is blameworthy, and that if it were moved to sin by its nature, its sinning would not be blameworthy. Evodius makes the point by drawing a comparison with the natural and blameless movement of a stone:

> I don't deny that this movement, by which the stone seeks the lowest place, is a movement of the stone. But it is a natural movement. If that's the sort of movement the soul has, then the soul's movement is also natural. And if it is moved naturally, it cannot justly be blamed; even if it is moved toward something evil, it is compelled by its own nature. But since we don't doubt that this movement is blameworthy, we must absolutely deny that it is natural, and so it is not similar to the natural movement of a stone. (71)

Augustine's suggestion here is that the will must not be determined by its very nature to will one way or another. Rather, it must be free in the sense that it could, consistent with its nature, choose either what is blameworthy

Saints, Heretics, and Atheists. Jeffrey K. McDonough, Oxford University Press. © Oxford University Press 2022.
DOI: 10.1093/oso/9780197563847.003.0004

or praiseworthy. In this passage at least, Augustine thus appears to hold that freedom and responsibility presuppose a libertarian conception of freedom. Such a conception suggests that if we could rewind history, keeping everything else the same, we could make choices differently the second time around. Augustine—rightly, I think—recognizes that given such a conception of the will's freedom, the question "Why do we sin?" cannot be given a deeply explanatory answer. It's just something we do.

Having suggested that the question "Why do we sin?" must bottom out in an appeal to our free choices, Augustine next suggests that it is nonetheless utterly clear that *we* are to blame for our sinful actions. Evodius is made to say,

> There is nothing I feel so firmly and so intimately as that I have a will by which I am moved to enjoy something. If the will by which I choose or refuse things is not mine, then I don't know what I can call mine. So if I use my will to do something evil, whom can I hold responsible but myself? . . . If the movement of the will by which it turns this way or that were not voluntary and under its own control, a person would not deserve praise for turning to higher things or blame for turning to lower things, as if swinging on the hinge of the will. Furthermore, there would be no point in admonishing people to forget about lower things and strive for what is eternal, so that they might refuse to live badly but instead will to live rightly. And anyone who does not think that we ought to admonish people in this way deserves to be banished from the human race. (72–73)

This paragraph gives voice to a number of important themes that we won't dwell on here but that reappear in later chapters—for example, the thought that praise and blame presuppose libertarian freedom, and that there could be no point in rewarding or admonishing people if they were determined by their natures to act in a certain way. Most important for our present purposes is that with his declaration of our responsibility for our sinful actions, Augustine has essentially completed his answer to the overarching question of Book III. We sin because we choose to sin—and because we choose to sin, we are responsible for sinning. In the rest of the dialogue, Augustine defends this line of thought against a number of natural objections.

4.2. Is Libertarian Freedom Consistent with Divine Foreknowledge?

The first worry Augustine raises concerns the compatibility of his libertarian view of freedom with his doctrinal commitment to God's omniscience. Augustine pinpoints the tension himself:

> How is it that these two propositions are not contradictory and inconsistent: (1) God has foreknowledge of everything in the future; and (2) We sin by the will, not by necessity? For, you say, if God foreknows that someone is going to sin, then it is necessary that he sin. But if it is necessary, the will has no choice about whether to sin; there is an inescapable and fixed necessity. And so you fear that this argument forces us into one of two positions: either we draw the heretical conclusion that God does not foreknow everything in the future; or, if we cannot accept this conclusion, we must admit that sin happens by necessity and not by will. (74)

In a nutshell, Augustine's worry is that God must know what we are going to do even before we do it. But if God knows that, say, I'm going to steal the car even before I steal it, then it seems that there's no way that I'm not going to steal the car, so it seems that not stealing the car is not really an option, and this might seem to conflict with Augustine's libertarian conception of free will.

Augustine's narrowest response to this first worry essentially skirts the explanatory problem by clarifying the content of what God foreknows. According to Augustine, God foreknows not only that you will do x and that the stone will do y, but that you will freely do x and that the stone will necessarily do y. Since what God foreknows is that you will freely do x, it follows that you will freely do x, and so it follows that you are responsible for doing x! This might seem to skirt the explanatory problem insofar as it tells us that libertarian freedom and God's foreknowledge are consistent, but it doesn't really explain *how* they are consistent. It seems unlikely that anyone who earnestly raised Augustine's first worry would be fully satisfied with Augustine's narrow response.

Perhaps anticipating that not everyone would be satisfied with his narrow response, Augustine also offers an analogy that might be thought to make his position more palatable. He suggests that just as our being pretty sure that someone is going to sin doesn't undermine the sinner's responsibility, we shouldn't suppose that God's knowing with absolute certainty that someone is going to sin undermines the sinner's responsibility either. Augustine writes,

> Unless I am mistaken, you do not force someone to sin just because you foreknow that he is going to sin. Nor does your foreknowledge force him to sin, even if he is undoubtedly going to sin—since otherwise you would not have genuine foreknowledge. So if your foreknowledge is consistent with his freedom in sinning, so that you foreknow what someone else is going to do by his own will, then God forces no one to sin, even though he foresees those who are going to sin by their own will. (78)

The thought here perhaps makes Augustine's narrowest response more satisfying. Augustine seems right that I can be pretty certain that someone is going to sin without thereby causing him to sin. So why can't God be completely certain that someone is going to sin without causing her to sin? Nonetheless, we might still crave a fuller explanation of how responsibility and foreknowledge could be compatible. We'll return to such concerns in section 4.5 after considering two more questions that Augustine raised.

4.3. Can't God Be Blamed for Creating Beings That He Knows Will Sin?

Having suggested that God knows that some beings will sin, and are responsible for their sinning, Augustine has Evodius raise another natural concern: even if all this is granted, isn't God nonetheless responsible for creating a being that he knows will sin? We have already seen a version of this worry, when Evodius asked why God would give us free will if he knew we were going to sin. This version is slightly different insofar as it asks not why God would give us free will, but if God has not in fact erred in making creatures that sin, that is, in making creatures that are in an important sense imperfect.

The foundation of Augustine's response can be found in two principles of his theodicy—that is, his explanation of why a good god would allow evil. The first principle is that since existence itself is good, each individual thing, insofar as it exists, is good. Although a bad turtle might be worse than a good turtle, even a bad turtle, insofar as it is an existing thing, is good, and indeed is even better than a stone or a stick. (Augustine makes this point by insisting that a drunk person is still better than the good wine that he drinks.) A turtle is thus rightly called "bad" only in the sense that it is not as good as other turtles (or not as good as a turtle should be). The second principle is that while there are different degrees of goodness, God's justice demands that he create every level of goodness. Although zebras might be better than turtles, which in turn might be better than stones, the world would not be better if God had created only zebras and not turtles or stones. No one should thus complain that the world contains lesser beings—for example, turtles and stones—as well as greater beings—for example, zebras and humans.

With his two principles in hand, Augustine is in a position to respond to Evodius's question: There is nothing blameworthy in God creating not only angels and nonsinning humans but also sinning humans, turtles, and stones, since all of these things are good insofar as they exist, and the world is better for having all levels of being. In short, it is better for God to have created even inveterate sinners than to have not created them at all:

> Why, then, should we not praise God with unspeakable praise, simply because when he made those souls who would persevere in the laws of justice, he made others who he foresaw would sin, even some who would persevere in sin? For even such souls are better than souls that cannot sin because they lack reason and the free choice of the will. And these souls in turn are better than the brilliance of any material object, however splendid, which some people mistakenly worship instead of the Most High God. In the order of material creation, from the heavenly choirs to the number of the hairs on our heads, the beauty of good things at every level is so perfectly harmonious that only the most ignorant could say, "What is this? Why is this?"—for all things were created in their proper order. How much more ignorant, then, to say this of a soul whose glory, however dimmed and tarnished it might become, far exceeds the dignity of any material object! (82)

Augustine's answer to the question "Can God be blamed for creating beings that he knows will sin?" is thus, in a way, remarkably straightforward. His answer is "no." On the contrary, God, according to Augustine, should be praised for creating sinners just as he should be praised for creating sunsets and rainbows, and indeed, he should be praised even more for creating sinners—who are superior by their very nature—than for creating sunsets and rainbows. Even if sinners are not as good as they should be, they are still—by their very natures—very good indeed.

4.4. Is It the Case That Some of Us Must Sin?

Augustine now takes up another natural line of objection: Why didn't God simply order creation in such a way that no one was unhappy? After all, it seems that if God is good he would want everyone to be happy, and if he were omnipotent he could have brought it about that everyone is happy. Augustine initially responds by claiming that, first, the order of the world is just (since nothing has a right to a higher place on the great chain of being than it actually enjoys) and, second, that since existence itself is good, the world could not be better by lacking the existence of anything that actually does exist. Augustine even gives us a nice little analogy: just as the world is better for having the moon and the sun, even though the moon is not as bright as the sun, so the world is better for having people destined to suffer even though they are not as good as those destined to be happy.

But Augustine's discussion of happiness is really intended to set up a deeper objection: The sinning and suffering of at least some people now seem necessary for the perfection of the universe, and thus it seems to be the case that at least some of us must sin. And if that's right, then it might seem unfair that God punishes sinners, since their sinning is after all necessary for the perfection of the world. Here's Augustine:

> Someone . . . might raise this objection: "If our unhappiness completes the perfection of the whole, then this perfection would be missing something if we were always happy. Therefore, if no soul becomes unhappy except by sinning, it follows that even our sins are necessary to the perfection of the universe that God created. How then can God justly punish our sins when they are necessary to ensure that his creation is complete and perfect?" (89)

The objection is a good one and it arises naturally from Augustine's own theodicy. If God creates turtles because they are good and an essential part of a good world, it doesn't seem right to blame turtles for existing or having hard shells. But, analogously, if God creates sinners because they are good (in themselves) and an essential part of a good world, what sense does it make to blame them for existing as sinners, that is, for their sinning?

Augustine responds to this challenge by essentially arguing that it is not sinners that are required for the perfection of the universe but rather freedom and justice. That is to say, the universe's perfection requires the creation of creatures capable of sinning as well as the punishment of those creatures *if* they sin. It does not, however, require sin and unhappiness themselves:

> What is necessary to the perfection of the universe is not our sins or our unhappiness, but the existence of souls that, simply because they are souls, sin if they so will and become unhappy if they sin. . . . When those who do not sin are happy, the universe is perfect; but when those who sin are unhappy, the universe is no less perfect. The fact that there are souls that will be unhappy if they sin and happy if they do not sin means that the universe is complete and perfect with respect to every nature that it contains. Sin and the punishment for sin are not natures, but characteristics of natures, the former voluntary and the latter punitive. The voluntary characteristic that comes about when one sins is disgraceful, so the punitive characteristic is used to place the soul in an order where it is not disgraceful for such a soul to be, forcing it to conform to the beauty of the universe as a whole, so that the ugliness of sin is remedied by the punishment of sin. (89)

Augustine's profound suggestion here runs as follows: (i) The harmony of the whole requires the existence of creatures that can freely choose to sin or not to sin. (ii) Those that freely sin introduce a kind of disorder into the world by making themselves unworthy of the position they hold in the hierarchy of being. (iii) God restores that order by punishing those sinners, and in doing so effectively moves them down the chain of being, restoring harmony to the whole. Perhaps, in Augustine's view, it doesn't really matter so much whether you sin or not, what really matters is that those who don't sin are rewarded, and that those who do sin are punished: that order and justice prevail.

4.5. Three Views on Divine Foreknowledge

As we've seen, in Book III of *On Free Choice of the Will*, Augustine raises a concern that has long exercised theists: how can human freedom be consistent with divine foreknowledge? Compatibilism provides one relatively straightforward solution to this apparent tension. In chapter 2, section 7, we noted that optimistic compatibilists hold that humans can be free and responsible for their actions even if their actions are causally determined by past events and the laws of nature. Under such a view, it seems that God can know what I will do tomorrow in much the same way that I can know what a billiard ball will do when I strike it with my cue stick. Since optimistic compatibilists deny that we must have libertarian freedom in order to be responsible for our actions, they see no difficulty in supposing both that God knows that we will sin and that we are nonetheless responsible for sinning. Although it provides a relatively clear-cut response to the tension engendered by divine foreknowledge, many theists in particular reject optimistic compatibilism because they think that libertarian freedom is necessary for our being responsible for our actions.

Other approaches attempt to reconcile libertarian freedom and divine foreknowledge—indeed, far too many to consider here. Nonetheless, we might highlight two especially interesting, and I think interestingly opposed, views. The central difference between these two views can be seen in the following scenario: Suppose you decided to go to class today. Do you know what you would have done for the rest of the day, the rest of the year, the rest of your life, if you hadn't decided to go to class today? Your decision to cut class might have led you to encounter different options, and to make still other decisions. Since each decision you make quickly ramifies and intersects with new decisions (and the decisions of others), it seems that it would be very difficult—practically impossible—for you to know exactly what you would have done had you not gone to class today. But what about God? Does God know how the rest of your life would have turned out if you had decided not to go to class? In terminology that philosophers commonly use, we can ask, does God know not just all factual truths, but also all *counterfactual* truths about you?

Molinism, named after Luis de Molina, a sixteenth-century Jesuit, maintains that while we enjoy libertarian freedom, God knows all the factual and counterfactual truths about how we would choose in any given circumstance. So, with this view, although I am free to choose whatever flavor I want when I walk into the ice cream store, God knows with absolute certainty what flavor I will choose in those circumstances. Furthermore, he knows what flavor I would have chosen under different circumstances, indeed under all possible circumstances. If I had decided to go to a different ice cream store, God knows what flavor I would have freely chosen in those circumstances as well.

Molinism can claim several advantages as a view of God's foreknowledge. First, it promises a way of reconciling libertarian freedom and divine foreknowledge, since it allows God to know exactly what we will do while still allowing that we choose freely and that we could have done otherwise.

Second, under this view, God is able to exercise full providential control over creation. In other words, God knows exactly what he is getting into when he creates the world and each creature in it. He is never surprised by what unfolds. Third, Molinism is consistent with a common response to the problem of evil. Since counterfactual truths are independent of God's will (because they are dependent upon what we choose), God may be credited with having created the best possible world (or at least a sufficiently good world), even though our world contains free creatures that introduce sin and suffering into it.

In spite of its apparent virtues, many theists have found Molinism unacceptable as an account of divine foreknowledge. Let's considered two objections. First, one might wonder if the Molinist view is at root coherent. In particular, one might wonder how it can be both that I enjoy libertarian freedom and that there are all these counterfactual truths about what I would exactly do in various circumstances. In short, how could it be that I could have chosen otherwise, and yet it also be the case that God could know with certainty what I would choose? Second, some theists have worried that Molinism makes God too involved in our sinful choices. If God knows ahead of time that if I'm placed in the ice cream store, I'll eat too much ice cream, and he puts me in the ice cream store anyway, isn't he implicated in my eating too much ice cream? Perhaps I should be blamed for eating too much ice cream, but—if the Molinist is right—isn't God also responsible? If the Molinist is right, isn't God an accomplice to our sins?

Another school of thought, known as *open theism*, offers a very different response to the problem of divine foreknowledge. Open theists maintain that there are no counterfactual truths, or even merely future truths, about what a free agent will do before she chooses. The future is truly open on this account, and so no one, not even God, can know with absolute certainty that I will, say, choose chocolate ice cream until I actually choose chocolate ice cream. After all, given a libertarian conception of the will, I could always, at the last moment, decide to get vanilla.

Like the Molinists, open theists can claim many virtues for their account of divine foreknowledge. First, many religious philosophers have thought that open theism puts the relationship between God and creatures in a better light. As we saw earlier, there's a way of viewing Augustine's God as being indifferent to our sinning and punishment: what is really important is the perfection of the world as a whole, which requires the existence of creatures with free will, but isn't really affected by whether those creatures sin or not. Open theism maintains that this approach is all wrong. Open theism suggests that once we are created, what we choose next is literally up to us, and that the world will be a better place if we choose well. In this sense, we have an active role to play in perfecting the world. We might even imagine God as rooting for us to do the right thing. Second, some philosophers have also maintained that open theism offers an especially good basis for responding to the problem of evil. With the open theist view, that creatures will sin is not foreordained, and so it need not be any part of God's plan for there to be sin in the world in addition to free creatures.

Not surprisingly, there are also strong objections to open theism. Again, let's consider two. First, just as one might worry that Molinism doesn't really allow us to have libertarian freedom, so one might worry conversely that open theism doesn't really satisfy the demands of divine foreknowledge because God doesn't know what we'll do next. The open theist will resist this suggestion by insisting that this is not a genuine problem. She'll insist that the fact that God doesn't know what we'll do next is no slight against divine omniscience because there is literally nothing to know about what we will do next until we do it. But the open theist's opponent might understandably worry that the open theist paints God as being omniscient in a rather anemic sense. Second, and relatedly, some have worried that open theism doesn't afford God sufficient providential control over the created world. Having created beings with free will, God literally doesn't know what they will do next, and so can't be sure how his own creation will unfold. Some have thought that such a picture cannot be squared with their own views on providential control and accepted religious doctrine. No surprise then that the question of how to reconcile freedom and divine foreknowledge continues to be much debated among philosophers and theologians.

Further Study

Augustine, *On Free Choice of the Will*. Trans. Thomas Williams, Indianapolis, IN: Hackett, 1993.

Thomas Nadelhoffer, Flickers of Freedom (Blog), http://philosophycommons.typepad.com/flickers_of_freedom/ . Advanced group blog focused on philosophical issues concerning freedom and responsibility. Unfortunately, no longer active.

James Rissler, "Open Theism." *Internet Encyclopedia of Philosophy*, http://www.iep.utm.edu/o-theism/. Helpful overview of open theism with an extensive bibliography.

5
Anselm's *Proslogion*
Does Reason Prove That God Exists?

5.1. The Setting

With this chapter we are once again jumping ahead in time. Augustine's *On Free Choice of Will* was written during the waning days of the Western Roman Empire. In 476 CE, the "barbarian" Odoacer displaced Romulus, the last Roman emperor in the West. Wisely refusing the title of emperor, Odoacer had himself crowned king of Italy. The West did not completely change overnight, but the fall of Rome can nonetheless be seen as an omen of the diverging fates of the eastern and western halves of the Roman Empire.

The center of the empire had already begun to shift to the east during the rule of Constantine, who not only converted the empire to Christianity but also moved its capital to modern-day Istanbul in 330 CE. The Eastern Empire was generally wealthier, more cultured, and more oriented to Greek culture than the Western Empire. It also developed its own version of Christianity, now generally known as Orthodox Christianity. The Eastern Empire would outlast the Western Empire by almost a thousand years, enjoying a rapid expansion under Emperor Justinian I (450–527) before falling much later, in 1453, to the Turks. Although commonly referred to today as Byzantium, citizens of the Eastern Roman Empire thought of themselves as Romans—that is, as citizens of the enduring Roman Empire that traced its roots all the way back to the fall of Troy.

The remains of the Western Empire were soon divided among the Visigoths, Franks, and Ostrogoths. While many of thc "barbarian" invaders were eager to emulate Roman culture, the fifth century marks the beginning, in the West, of what Petrarch would famously call the Dark Ages. For many in Europe, life became more difficult, less cultured, less civilized. The rise of the Carolingian dynasty in the eighth and ninth centuries provided a brief reprieve, as did the rise of monasteries as centers of intellectual sanctuary and learning.

Saints, Heretics, and Atheists. Jeffrey K. McDonough, Oxford University Press. © Oxford University Press 2022.
DOI: 10.1093/oso/9780197563847.003.0005

Born in modern-day France in 1033 CE, Anselm joined one of those monasteries in the village of Bec. His brilliance and piety led to his rapid advancement, and he was elected abbot in 1078. Under his leadership the already impressive reputation of the Bec monastery continued to grow. In addition to his many duties as abbot, Anselm published a number of works, including the *Monologion* (1076), the *Proslogion* (1077–78), and four dialogues. In 1093, reportedly over his strenuous objections, Anslem was enthroned as archbishop of Canterbury and became involved in the English power struggle between royal authority and the Roman Catholic Church that is now known as the Investiture Controversy. Although those struggles led to his being exiled twice, Anselm nonetheless managed to write several important works, including *Cur Deus Homo* (1094–98) and *De Concordia* (1107–8). He died on 21 April 1109 and was canonized in 1494.

5.2. Anselm's Ontological Argument

Among philosophers today, Anselm is most famous for a short argument for the existence of God that he provides in his *Proslogion*. A key first step of the argument suggests that God just is the greatest thing we can possibly imagine:

> Therefore, Lord, who grants understanding to faith, grant me that, in so far as you know it beneficial, I understand that you are as we believe and you are that which we believe. Now we believe that you are something than which nothing greater can be imagined. [This section follows Jasper Hopkins's translation of Anselm's *Proslogion*.]

This seems a plausible definition of God, and indeed Augustine offers a similar definition of God in *On Free Choice of Will*. Anselm's definition merely suggests that God is not simply the greatest thing that exists, but the greatest thing that *could* exist.

At a first pass, it seems that we should be able to accept Anselm's definition of God, grant that we have such an idea of God, and yet still deny that God exists. Here's Anselm:

> Then is there no such nature, since the fool has said in his heart: God is not? But certainly this same fool, when he hears this very thing that

> I am saying—something than which nothing greater can be imagined—understands what he hears; and what he understands is in his understanding, even if he does not understand that it is. For it is one thing for a thing to be in the understanding and another to understand that a thing is.

So it seems the atheist may agree with Anselm's definition of God, maintain that he has an idea of God in mind, and yet deny that there is anything that fits that idea. The situation seems analogous to the case of, say, the labradoodle denier, who agrees that a labradoodle would be the offspring of a Labrador retriever and a poodle, who insists that she has a perfectly good idea of a labradoodle in mind, yet who denies that there are any labradoodles in the world.

Anselm, however, maintains that the atheist who accepts his definition is really forced to admit that God exists, since even the atheist should allow that existence in reality is a good thing, and that whatever she is imagining could only be the best imaginable thing if it is indeed imagined as existing:

> And certainly that than which a greater cannot be imagined cannot be in the understanding alone. For if it is at least in the understanding alone, it can be imagined to be in reality too, which is greater. Therefore if that than which a greater cannot be imagined is in the understanding alone, that very thing than which a greater cannot be imagined is something than which a greater can be imagined. But certainly this cannot be. There exists, therefore, beyond doubt something than which a greater cannot be imagined, both in the understanding and in reality.

The thought here is that if what the atheist is really imagining is God, she should admit that what she is imagining must be thought to exist. For if what she is imagining is not thought to exist, then she could imagine something even better than what she is imagining (perhaps whatever she was imagining before, but now with existence thrown in), and this thing has a better claim to being identified with God than the thing she was previously imagining (since what she is now imagining is better, and God is the best of all possible things). It is here, of course, that the analogy with the labradoodle case is supposed to break down. The atheist, according to Anselm, is guilty of a conceptual mistake—she has not fully appreciated the implications of the concept of the greatest possible being—while the labradoodle denier is guilty of merely a factual mistake (since nothing about the concept of a labradoodle requires that labradoodles exist). Anselm concludes that we can know by reason alone that God exists.

5.3. A Perfect Island?

Not surprisingly, there is a long history of responses to Anselm's argument. One of the earliest critical replies was made by Gaunilo, a Benedictine monk and contemporary of Anselm. In a work to which Anselm himself responded, Gaunilo considered how "someone, on behalf of the fool," might respond to Anselm's argument. In the elegant piece, Gaunilo offers three specific objections as well as the most famous one ever made to the ontological argument.

Gaunilo saw Anselm's argument as resting on two principal claims. The first is that "the very one who doubts or denies the existence of this nature already has this nature in his understanding when, upon hearing it spoken of, he understands what is said." That is to say, the atheist understands what he is talking about when he says that God does not exist. He understands the concept of God being used. The second is that the concept of God and the nature of existence are related in that "it is necessary that the greater than all others, having already been proved to exist in the understanding, exist not only in the understanding but also in reality." That is to say, the concept of God together with the nature of existence entails that God exists not only in the understanding but in reality as well.

Having pinned down what he sees as Anselm's two main points, Gaunilo is ready to present his three specific objections. First, he objects that there is a crucial difference between "having the thing in the understanding and subsequently understanding the thing to exist." His thought is quite intuitive. It is one thing to have something in the understanding in the sense of comprehending something and quite another thing for that very thing to exist. It is one thing to understand the concept of Santa Claus. It is something else altogether for Santa Claus to exist. Gaunilo's own example makes the same point. It is one thing for the painter to have a certain subject or scene in mind; it is another thing for that subject or scene to be depicted in oil on a canvas. The implication, of course, is that Anselm has improperly run roughshod over this basic distinction in moving from the "fool" having the concept of God in mind to God existing in reality.

Second, Gaunilo objects, "it could scarcely at all be plausible that when this thing is spoken of and heard of, it could not be thought not to exist in the way that even God can [be thought] not to exist." This objection is perhaps a little less clear at first. Nonetheless, I think we can see Gaunilo's idea. It seems to be the case that I can doubt the existence of anything that I can understand. If I understand the concept of Santa Claus, I can doubt that Santa Claus exists. If I understand the concept of the mayor of Cambridge, I can doubt that the mayor of Cambridge exists. Perhaps a couple of cases are more puzzling. As Gaunilo notes, and as Descartes would later make famous, it is at least more difficult—if not impossible—to doubt that oneself exists. I think, therefore I am! I doubt, therefore I am! But even in this special case Gaunilo notes that I can at least doubt that I existed earlier and that I will exist later. Even if I can't doubt my existence while I'm thinking, I needn't suppose that I exist necessarily.

Third, Gaunilo objects that Anselm's claim that God exists "would have to be proved to me by means of an indubitable consideration, not by means of the [consideration] that this thing is already in my understanding when I understand what I have heard." Again, we can feel the force of Gaunilo's objection. His thought is that the truth of existence claims in general are to be determined not by rational reflection on the concepts involved but rather on the basis of evidence. If I'm trying to convince you that duckbill platypuses exist, I should not try to get you to simply reflect harder on the concept of a duckbill platypus but rather show you pictures or take you to the zoo. Perhaps the existence of theoretical objects will be thought to be an exception to this general rule. If I'm trying to convince you that atoms exist, I can't very well just show you an atom. But I think Gaunilo's point is safe here as well. Although I might not be able to show you an atom directly, if I want to convince you that atoms exist, I should give you some evidence—perhaps quite indirect evidence—that they exist. I'll get nowhere by just asking you to reflect on the concept of an atom.

All three of Gaunilo's points are, I think, intuitive and reasonable. He's right that generally there's a crucial difference between having something in mind and that thing actually existing, that generally we can doubt whatever we can understand, that existence claims should generally be settled not by reflection but by evidence. Nonetheless, it is not clear that Gaunilo has put his finger on a non-question-begging argument against the very particular case that Anselm has in mind. Anselm grants that a crucial difference exists between having something in mind and that thing actually existing, but he thinks that the latter follows logically from the former in the very special case of God. Likewise, Anselm can grant that, in the typical case, we can doubt the existence of anything that we understand, while still denying that we can do just that in the very special case of God. Likewise with respect to evidence for existence claims: Anselm can grant that if I want to convince you that a duckbill platypus exists, I had better give you some empirical evidence, even while still insisting that the existence of God can be established on the basis of rational reflection alone. In short, with his three objections, Gaunilo raises a series of intuitive and reasonable points, but it is not clear that they undermine Anselm's specific ontological argument.

Gaunilo's most famous objection to Anselm's argument, however, is to be found not in any of the specific principles just highlighted but in an analogy that attempts to show the absurdity of Anselm's line of thought. Gaunilo suggests that if Anselm's ontological argument worked, the same line of reasoning could be used to show that innumerable absurd things exist. To drive his point home, he imagines someone presenting the following argument to Anselm:

> You can no more doubt that this island which is more excellent than all [other] lands truly exists somewhere in reality than you [can] doubt that [it] is in your understanding. And since [for it] to exist not only in the understanding but also in reality is more excellent [than for it to exist in understanding alone], then, necessarily, it exists in reality. For if it did not exist [in reality], then whatever other land did exist in reality would be more excellent than it, and thus this [island], which has already been understood by you to be more excellent [than all other lands], would not be more excellent [than all others]. [Translation by Jasper Hopkins, paragraph 6 of Gaunilo's "On Behalf of the Fool"]

It is easy to appreciate the point of Gaunilo's analogy and to feel its force. If the perfect being must exist because it must have any relevant perfection and existence is a perfection, then why shouldn't it be the case that the perfect island must exist because it must have any relevant perfection and existence is a perfection? The analogy is powerful insofar as it suggests that something, somewhere, has gone wrong with Anselm's argument. Gaunilo's perfect-island argument seems to mirror the reasoning in Anslem's ontological argument, but we find the notion that we might prove the existence of a perfect island from reasoning alone to be absurd. The implication is that we should find Anselm's argument equally absurd. Nonetheless, Gaunilo's analogy has an obvious weakness: it implies that something has gone wrong with Anselm's reasoning but doesn't tell us what; it encourages us to think that there's a difficulty but doesn't tell us what exactly that difficulty is. Let's close, therefore, by looking at two attempts pioneered by later figures to say what exactly (if anything) is wrong with Anselm's argument.

5.4. Two Objections

The second-most-famous objection to Anselm's argument was made hundreds of years after Gaunilo's, by Immanuel Kant in the eighteenth century. Anselm's argument, of course, takes for granted that many predicates should be applied to God. The concept of God involves, for example, the predicates *is good, is wise, is simple, is eternal.* Put differently, it suggests that we should suppose that God has the properties of being good, wise, simple, and eternal. Anselm's argument implies that one additional predicate should also be ascribed to God, namely, *exists.* That is, we should think that God not only has the properties of being good, wise, and simple but also has the property of existing.

Kant objected to the thought that *exists* is a predicate denoting a particular property. Kant's thought is that it is a mistake to think of existing as just another property that a subject has, to think that *exists* is a predicate on par with *is good, is wise,* or *is eternal.* Existence is better understood, according to Kant, as something like a precondition for having properties at all. The existence of my dog isn't just another property like her curly hair or friendly disposition. It is not the case that my dog has curly hair, is friendly, *and* exists. Rather, my dog's existence is a precondition for her having any of the other properties. If she didn't exist, she couldn't have curly hair, be friendly, or have or be anything else.

Kant's objection is often held to be decisive against Anselm's argument, but I think the issues here are actually quite difficult. Kant seems right to insist that there is an important difference between existence and other properties, and even to suggest that it is natural to think that other properties presuppose existence for their existence. But we might also be inclined to think that Santa Claus has the property of having a big beard and that Sherlock Holmes has the property of living in London. But of course, Santa Claus and Sherlock Holmes don't exist, and so their existing doesn't seem to be a precondition for their having properties (if indeed they do have properties). In short, Kant's objection seems to relate to something deep and important about Anselm's ontological argument, but we might still long for more clarity than the doctrine "Existence is not a predicate" offers us by itself.

A third, well-known, but less famous objection was made decades before Kant by Gottfried Wilhelm Leibniz. Leibniz, in fact, accepted a version of Anselm's ontological argument, but he thought that it crucially required a preliminary step. Leibniz held that Anselm's ontological argument works, but only if it can be shown that the concept of God is in fact consistent. It is perhaps easiest to bring out Leibniz's point via a mathematical analogy. Suppose we assert that the biggest possible number is bigger than any even number. Have we asserted something true? We might be tempted to think that we have. Take any even number. Since it is even, we can add one to that number. But when we add one to a number, we get a bigger number. So the biggest possible number must be bigger than any even number!

This all sounds convincing and even has the air of a logical demonstration, but it is all nonsense, right? The problem comes straight at the start. The very idea of the biggest possible number is incoherent, since for any number we could add one and get a bigger number. If the concept of the biggest possible number is coherent, it is bigger than any even number, but the concept of the biggest possible number is not coherent, and so it is not true to assert that the biggest possible number is bigger than any even number. Leibniz's thought is that if the concept of a greatest possible being is coherent, it follows that it exists. But the argument isn't valid until it has been shown that the concept of a greatest possible being is coherent. For all Anselm has argued, the concept of a greatest possible being could be like the concept of the biggest possible number. For all Anselm has argued, according to Leibniz, God—understood as the greatest possible being—might not exist. Indeed, for all Anselm has argued, God—understood as the greatest possible being—might be impossible, just like the greatest possible number.

Further Study

Anselm, *Proslogion*. Trans. Jasper Hopkins. Minneapolis: Arthur J. Banning Press, 2000. Available online via Hopkins's homepage.

Graham Oppy, "Ontological Arguments." *Stanford Encyclopedia of Philosophy* (Spring 2015 edition), ed. Edward N. Zalta, http://plato.stanford.edu/archives/spr2015/entries/ontological-arguments/. A detailed, advanced discussion of ontological arguments with an extensive bibliography.

Robin Pierson, *The History of Byzantium*. Podcast, 2012–; available online and through iTunes. An engaging survey of the Byzantine Empire.

R. W. Southern, *Saint Anselm: A Portrait in Landscape*. Cambridge: Cambridge University Press, 1990. Definitive biography of Anselm in English.

Thomas Williams, "Saint Anselm." *Stanford Encyclopedia of Philosophy* (Spring 2011 edition), ed. Edward N. Zalta, http://plato.stanford.edu/archives/spr2011/entries/anselm. A helpful overview of Anselm's philosophical thought, together with a useful bibliography.

6

Ibn Sina's *The Book of Salvation*

What Is the Nature of the Soul?

6.1. The Setting

The founding of Islam as a tradition distinct from Judaism and Christianity dates to the seventh century CE. Muhammad reported revelations from God beginning in 610, and a community grew around him first at Mecca and later at Medina. Muhammad, however, was not only the founding prophet of Islam but also an adroit civil and military leader. Islam expanded rapidly under his leadership. Muhammad died in 632, but expansion of the Islamic Empire continued. By the early eighth century, the Islamic Empire reached from parts of central Asia, through Egypt, across the Mediterranean, and included much of modern-day Spain. During its peak, the Islamic Empire far outstripped any other society in the West in terms of learning, science, and culture.

In the eighth century a massive translation project was undertaken to render Greek philosophical and scientific works into Arabic. Through those efforts an enormous body of intellectual work was transmitted into Arabic-speaking lands, including works by Plato, Neoplatonists, early Greek commentators, and Aristotle. Indeed, many ancient Greek writings have survived today only because they were once translated into Arabic. Philosophers and theologians in Arabic-speaking lands, however, did not simply translate and preserve ancient Greek thought. Mixing it with their own reflections, experiences, and beliefs, they gave birth to a distinct tradition known as *falsafa*. When Greek philosophy was later reintroduced into the Latin West around the thirteenth century, it was accompanied by extensive commentaries and elaborations by Muslim, Jewish, and Christian thinkers who lived within the Islamic Empire.

Ibn Sina, also known as Avicenna, was born in the east of the Islamic Empire in 980 near Bukhara in Central Asia. He began studying medicine at the age of thirteen and reports that it came very easily to him. It certainly

Saints, Heretics, and Atheists. Jeffrey K. McDonough, Oxford University Press. © Oxford University Press 2022.
DOI: 10.1093/oso/9780197563847.003.0006

served him well. He was consulted as a physician by the sultan of Bukhara and treated him successfully. In return, the sultan granted Ibn Sina access to his extensive library, which burned down shortly thereafter. Luckily, Ibn Sina had an extraordinary memory and was able to work in later years largely from his recollection of the texts he had once read in the sultan's library. With the death of his patron and the decline of the Samanid Dynasty, Ibn Sina's fortunes took a turn for the worse. He was forced to seek support and positions from a series of beneficiaries and spent much of his adult life in modern-day Iran. Suffering from a severe case of colic while on a military march, he died in 1037 and was buried in Hamadan.

Ibn Sina wrote many works. His most important is *The Book of Ḥealing* (*Kitab al-shifa'*) in which he offers a comprehensive treatment of subjects ranging from logic and mathematics to metaphysics and the afterlife. Ibn Sina also wrote a number of logical treatises, including his *Remarks and Admonitions* (*al-Isharat wa-'l-tanbihat*) as well as a commentary on Aristotle's *Prior Analytics*. In addition, Ibn Sina penned an autobiography as well as an autobiographical, allegorical work *The Living Son of the Vigilant* (*Hayy ibn Yaqzan*). From these writings we know that he was precocious, brilliant, and not terribly humble about it. We also know that he was no ascetic and notoriously enjoyed sensual pleasures and wine, a point that his opponents would later seize upon in criticizing him and his works. In this chapter we focus on the nature of the soul as discussed in Ibn Sina's *The Book of Salvation* (*Kitāb al-najāt*), a work that is a self-abridgement of Ibn Sina's *The Book of Healing* (*Kitab al-shifa'*).

6.2. What Does the Intellect Do?

In earlier chapters, we saw Augustine argue that the intellect is the crowning feature of human beings. But what exactly does the intellect do? Ibn Sina's answer takes for granted a bit of Aristotelian philosophy. In the Aristotelian tradition, particular things like my dog Martha were thought to be composites of matter and form. Very roughly, form is what makes a thing the kind of thing that it is, while matter is what the form inheres in and what differentiates that thing from other things of the same kind. So, for example, suppose that Martha and George are both Labradoodles. What they have in common is the form of being a Labradoodle. Their respective matter is what makes them different. Martha is Labradoodle-ness in this parcel of matter and George is

Labradoodle-ness in that parcel of matter. The same story would apply, for example, to two students. Since forms were often held to be common to more than one thing, they were also called "universals."

For Aristotelians, knowledge and science concern immaterial forms or universals, that is, forms or universals free from any individuating matter. This is all rough and ready, but you can get a feel for the driving idea. Suppose we ask, "Why is Martha a mammal?" You might say, "Well, Martha is a Labradoodle, and all Labradoodles are mammals, so Martha must be a mammal." Likewise, we might ask, "Why can James laugh?" You might reply, "James is a human, all humans can laugh, so James must be able to laugh." Our ability to have scientific knowledge, according to the Aristotelian tradition, ultimately rests on our ability to receive—to literally have in mind—immaterial forms or universals that can be applied to many different particulars.

We are now in a position to say more specifically what sort of thing the intellect is according to the Aristotelian tradition. The intellect is the capacity (of the soul) that allows us to receive immaterial universals and thus to know things scientifically. Aristotelians typically hold that only humans (and higher species) have this sort of capacity. Animals, like my dog Martha, can be acquainted with particular things. They have a faculty of memory and instincts that help them navigate and respond to the world. But they can't grasp immaterial forms or natures. They can see and chase particular cats, but they can't have scientific knowledge of the universal nature of cats.

6.3. Is the Soul Immaterial?

Following Aristotle, Ibn Sina thinks that for the intellect to receive immaterial universals—that is, universals without individuating matter—the intellect must itself be immaterial. In his *Book of Salvation*, Ibn Sina makes two arguments for the conclusion that the (theoretical) intellect is immaterial. Let's focus on the first one here. It has the logical form of a reductio ad absurdum. That is to say, Ibn Sina's argument begins with an assumption, attempts to show that that assumption leads to an absurdity, and then concludes that that assumption must therefore be false. Perhaps an analogy would be helpful. Suppose I assume for *reductio* that triangles have an even number of sides. I know triangles have three sides. So, triangles have an odd number of sides. In my example, triangles have an even and an odd number of sides. But that is absurd. I conclude that my initial assumption was false. It is not true that triangles have an even number of sides.

Ibn Sina's opening assumption—the one he wants to show is absurd—is that the intellect is material. He begins by arguing that if the intellect were material then it would either be (i) indivisible or (ii) divisible. That seems reasonable. All material things do seem to be either indivisible or divisible. Ibn Sina's next step is to argue that both options (or "horns") of his dilemma lead to absurdities. His overarching aim is to conclude that the assumption that the intellect—a part of the soul—is material must be rejected. Let's look briefly at the arguments he uses to develop each horn of his dilemma.

(i) Let's suppose first that the intellect is material and indivisible. If so, says Ibn Sina, then the intellect would either have to (a) inhere in a point and have no magnitude or (b) inhere in an atom, that is, something that is extended but indivisible. (ia) So let's suppose first that the intellect inheres in a point. Ibn Sina maintains that a point is just a limit of a divisible magnitude and so has no existence independent of that magnitude. It's like the shape of a vase—the shape is a limit of the vase but doesn't have an independent existence. Ibn Sina infers that if anything inheres in a point, it must therefore do so in virtue of inhering in the thing of which the point is a limit. So, for example, if the shape of the vase is purple, it must be purple in virtue of the vase's being purple. Ibn Sina concludes that if the intellect were to inhere in a point, it would have to do so in virtue of inhering in a divisible magnitude after all. The thought that the intellect inheres in a point thus collapses into horn (ii).

(ib) Could a material intellect inhere instead in an extended but indivisible magnitude, that is, an atom? Ibn Sina understands the relevant sense of indivisibility here to be conceptual indivisibility and argues that the very notion of a conceptually indivisible atom is incoherent. Ibn Sina's own argument can be a bit difficult for contemporary readers to follow, but the gist of it should be easy enough to appreciate. Suppose you have an extended atom. Does it have a left half and a right half? If, on the one hand, it does have halves, then it is conceptually divisible. If, on the other hand, it doesn't have halves, then it isn't extended. Either way, Ibn Sina concludes, universals can't inhere in indivisible extended matter because indivisible extended matter is itself impossible. The first horn of Ibn Sina's initial dilemma leads to absurdity (or collapses into the second horn) and therefore must be rejected.

(ii) If Ibn Sina's arguments are on track so far, it must be the case that *if* the intellect is going to inhere in something material, it has to inhere in something *divisible*. But, Ibn Sina maintains, the universals grasped by the intellect can't inhere in something divisible. Why not? Whatever inheres in something divisible, Ibn Sina maintains, is at least potentially divisible itself. For example, if sourness inheres in something divisible, then sourness itself must be at least potentially divisible. If I cut a lemon in half, I get sourness here and sourness there. So, if the immaterial universals grasped by the intellect were to inhere in divisible matter, those universals would be potentially divisible too. And that, Ibn Sina thinks, would be a problem.

To show why universals can't be divisible, Ibn Sina employs yet another dilemma. He argues that if a universal were divisible, its parts would have to be either (iia) similar or (iib) dissimilar, and that either option leads to absurdity. The parts of a universal, Ibn Sina argues, couldn't be similar to one another because if you were to recombine them you'd get the same thing as each one of them alone. But Ibn Sina insists that a whole is *never* the same as its parts. A six-pack of soda can't be identical to any one of its cans. So, Ibn Sina concludes, embracing (iia) would lead to an absurdity and therefore must be rejected. Ibn Sina also gives a bunch of reasons why he thinks that the parts of a universal couldn't be dissimilar from one another either. For example, he argues that if a universal could be divided into dissimilar parts, then it would have an infinite definition, which Aristotelians commonly held to be absurd. So, Ibn Sina thinks embracing (iib) would also lead to an absurdity and therefore must also be rejected. The upshot of his overarching argument is that the intellect, and therefore the human soul, must not be material—that is, the human soul must be immaterial.

6.4. Is the Soul Immortal?

For Ibn Sina, the immateriality of the soul has important further consequences. In *The Book of Salvation*, Ibn Sina argues that human souls come into existence with their bodies. How does he argue for this? Well, at root, he offers another dilemma. If the soul predated the body, then either there would have to be (i) a bunch of not-yet-embodied souls (waiting to be embodied, as it were) or (ii) just one not-yet-embodied soul (that gets paired with many different bodies in the creation of many embodied human beings). Ibn Sina argues that the first option is not possible since it is precisely matter that is needed to individuate souls (at least initially, and this is related to the thought that matter is what makes you distinct from me). But the second option is no better, according to Ibn Sina. For if there were originally one not-yet-embodied soul, then you and I would either (a) have the very same soul or (b) we'd each have parts of the same soul. Ibn Sina finds both options to be absurd.

Ibn Sina has thus argued that it must be the case that our souls come into existence with our bodies. But all this raises a pressing question: If our souls come into existence with our bodies, do they also go out of existence with our bodies? That is to say, are our souls mortal? Ibn Sina's response to this question might be thought of as having two main parts. The first part argues negatively that the corruption of the body does not entail the corruption of the human intellect-or-soul. The second part argues positively that the human intellect—unlike the body—is not the sort of thing that is susceptible to corruption. Let's focus here only on the first part, which might itself be thought of as coming in two big steps.

In the first step, Ibn Sina considers the possibility that the intellect and body might be *codependent*. If they are codependent, he suggests, then they must be codependent in one of two distinguishable ways: (aa) They could be *essentially* codependent, like a concave and a convex curve. If the body and the intellect were essentially codependent, then the intellect would have to perish with the body. (If you destroy the concave curve of a vase, you thereby also destroy the convex curve of the vase.) Ibn Sina, however, argues that the body and the intellect can't be essentially codependent in this way. Why not? The core of his thought seems to be that since the intellect is immaterial and the body material, they can't be essentially the same thing, and if they can't be essentially the same thing, then they can't be essentially dependent on one another like concave and convex curves. I think the argument here is a bit stronger than it might at first appear. *If* you accept the immateriality theses, then the suggestion that the intellect and the body can't be *essentially* codependent probably shouldn't seem unreasonable to you.

(bb) Alternatively, the body and intellect could be accidentally codependent, like the existence of my teacup and its saucer. Ibn Sina allows that the body as a material substance and the intellect as an immaterial substance could be related in this way, but argues that if they are only accidentally codependent, then the extinction of one should not entail the extinction of the other. Just as my saucer may survive the destruction of my teacup, so my soul may survive the destruction of my body. Again, I think, this should seem pretty plausible. *If* you accept that the body and intellect are only accidentally related, then the suggestion that one could survive the other seems plausible. One thing we might take away from all this is that the immateriality of the intellect really does seem to lend support to the possibility of the immortality of the intellect.

In the second step, Ibn Sina considers the possibility that either (i) the intellect is causally dependent upon the body or (ii) the body is causally dependent upon the intellect. In essence, he argues that in no way can the intellect be causally dependent upon the body (as in (i)). Working through Aristotle's four causes, Ibn Sina argues that the body just isn't the right sort of thing to be the cause of the intellect: since the intellect is immaterial, the body can't be its *material cause*; since the intellect is active and matter passive, the body can't be its *efficient cause*; since the intellect accounts for our living activities, the body can't be its *formal cause*; since the body is designed for the intellect rather than the other way around, the body can't be the intellect's *final cause*. It might be worth noting that contemporary materialists essentially deny this branch of Ibn Sina's argument. One way of being a materialist—that is, one way of denying the existence of immaterial things—is to maintain that the body is the cause of the mind, and that the mind is thus in fact dependent upon the body after all.

Might the body be causally dependent upon the mind (as in (ii))? If the body were causally dependent upon the intellect, that wouldn't entail that the intellect perishes with the body. A painting, for example, might be causally dependent upon an artist. But the destruction of the painting won't entail the destruction of the artist. Nonetheless, as Ibn Sina notes, if the intellect were causally prior to the body, the destruction of the body might indicate the destruction of the intellect. If a fire causes heat, we might reasonably infer from the heat's ceasing that the fire has gone out. Ibn Sina argues in response that the destruction of the body would only be a sign of the destruction of the mind if there were nothing about the body itself that could explain its own destruction. (If the only thing that could explain the destruction of the body were the destruction of the mind, then the destruction of the body would indeed be a strong indication of the destruction of the mind.) But, Ibn Sina argues, facts about the body itself can explain its own destruction—we don't need to suppose that the intellect ceases in order to understand how our bodies can perish. He concludes that we needn't infer that the intellect perishes from the fact that the body perishes.

We've now seen Ibn Sina's two-step argument for the conclusion that the intellect needn't perish with the body. The first step established that the body and the mind are not essentially codependent. The second step established that the intellect is neither causally dependent upon the body (so the mind needn't perish when the body does), nor is the body causally dependent upon the mind in such a way that the perishing of the body is a strong indication of the perishing of the mind. That's a lot! But it's still not all we wanted, right? After all, we wanted assurance that the intellect doesn't actually perish. The second stage of Ibn Sina's argument takes up that challenge.

Ibn Sina's positive argument for the immateriality of the soul is reminiscent of arguments found in Plato's *Phaedo* and Plotinus's *Enneads*. Without getting into the details, we can at least get a feel for how it goes. Here's the basic idea. In the Aristotelian framework, form is what makes something actually this or that, while matter is what makes something potentially this or that. So, for example, in the case of a statue, the form is the shape and the matter the clay. The clay is what makes the thing potentially a statue (and not potentially, say, an automobile). The form/shape is what makes the statue what it actually is, say, a statue of Socrates. Ibn Sina has argued, however, that the intellect is an immaterial substance. It therefore can't be potentially anything (because it is not material in any way). It can't, Ibn Sina argues, even potentially cease to exist. But if it can't even potentially cease to exist, then it must be incorruptible, that is, indestructible. Here again, we see Ibn Sina drawing heavily on his earlier result that the soul is immaterial in order to establish (in this case) the conclusion that the intellect is immortal.

6.5. What Am I?

When we worry about immortality we usually worry about whether *we* will survive the deaths of our bodies. Put differently, we typically worry about *personal* immortality. The question of whether *I* will survive the death of my body might be thought to raise an important prior question, however—namely, what am *I* anyway? That's the question of what it takes to be a person—to be me, for example—both at a particular time and through time. This isn't the place to go into all the fascinating issues that arise in connection with issues of personal identity, but it might be helpful to at least sketch three broad views on personal identity.

(1) One traditional view of personal identity is that I am a mind or a soul, and that I persist through time as long as my mind or soul persists through time. This may well be the view of personal identity that most nonphilosophers have if they give the topic of personal identity any

thought at all. To the extent that we take this view for granted, Ibn Sina's argument for the immortality of the mind-or-soul is also an argument for personal immortality. If this is the right view of personal identity, and Ibn Sina is right that our minds-or-souls are immortal, then it follows that we are immortal.

(2) Some philosophers, including some Aristotelians, however, have thought that—at least for now—I am not just a soul. When I eat a spicy meal, I experience a certain kind of pleasure that might be attributed to my mind. But I also feel satiated, I might even perspire a bit, and my eyes might tear up. It might seem more plausible to attribute such visceral reactions to my body. If, however, they are also my reactions—as of course they seem to be—we might conclude that I am not just a soul, but a union of a soul and a body. As a rational animal, I'm both rational *and* an animal. I am both a soul *and* a body. If that's right, however, we might ask again, what happens to me when my body perishes? Three possibilities seem especially salient.

(2a) Although I'm currently a soul-body union, when I go down in the plane crash, I lose an inessential part of me, and I become just a soul. (The case is analogous to my losing a hand, also an inessential part of me.) Perhaps someday I'll get my body back and be a union again, but in any case, the immortality of my soul is sufficient in this view to guarantee my personal immortality.

(2b) Although I'm currently a soul-body union, when I go down in the plane crash, I lose an *essential* part of me (my body), and *I* perish. Even if my soul lives on, I don't live on. And indeed, Ibn Russd (Averroes, 1126–98) would later seem to suggest that something like this scenario is exactly what happens—my intellect may be immortal, but I myself am not.

(2c) Although I'm currently a soul-body union, when I go down in the plane crash, I lose an essential part of me (my body), and I go out of existence. But this doesn't mean that I'm not immortal in an important sense. For it could be the case that there is a stretch of time during which I—a particular union—exist, followed by a stretch of time during which I don't exist because my body is gone, followed by an infinite stretch of time that begins after I get my body back and during which I exist again. Some passages in the works of Thomas Aquinas (1225–74) suggest that this is his considered view, a view related to the religious doctrine of bodily resurrection.

(3) Some philosophers, including many contemporary philosophers, maintain that what is really important for personal identity is not so much the continuation of a particular body, or even a particular soul, but rather psychological continuity. Very roughly, I persist if and only if there is a continuous chain of my beliefs, memories, and desires. Thus, *I* could survive if my ideas were transplanted into another body. *I* could even survive if my ideas were transplanted into another soul. But if I woke up on Wednesday with entirely new beliefs, memories, and desires, I would not be the same person I was on Monday. According to this view—commonly associated with John Locke (1632–1704)—I am immortal if and only if my psychological continuity goes on forever. I could be mortal even if my soul is not, and immortal even if my soul perishes when the plane goes down.

Further Study

Peter Adamson, *The History of Philosophy without Any Gaps: Philosophy in Later Antiquity*. Podcast, 2011–13; available online and through iTunes. An excellent, entertaining introduction to philosophical currents in the Islamic World; includes podcasts devoted to Ibn Sina.

Peter Adamson, *Philosophy in the Islamic World: A Very Short Introduction.* New York: Oxford University Press, 2015. A brief introduction to philosophy in the Islamic world by a leading scholar.

Muhamad Ali Khalidi, *Medieval Islamic Philosophy*. Cambridge: Cambridge University Press, 2005. An excellent collection of English translations of works in medieval Islamic philosophy. Includes a selection from Ibn Sina's *The Book of Salvation* discussed in this chapter.

Reza Aslan, *No god, but God: The Origins, Evolution and Future of Islam*. New York: Random House, 2011. A popular, engaging introduction to Islam.

Christina D'Ancona, "Greek Sources in Arabic and Islamic Philosophy." *Stanford Encyclopedia of Philosophy* (Winter 2013 edition), ed. Edward N. Zalta, http://plato.stanford.edu/archives/win2013/entries/arabic-islamic-greek/. Overview of the so-called Greco-Arabic translation movement with an extensive bibliography.

Jon McGinnis, *Avicenna.* Great Medieval Thinkers. New York: Oxford University Press, 2010. An excellent introduction to Avicenna and his philosophy by a leading scholar.

Eric T. Olson, "Personal Identity." *Stanford Encyclopedia of Philosophy* (Fall 2015 edition), ed. Edward N. Zalta, http://plato.stanford.edu/archives/fall2015/entries/identity-personal/. An overview of philosophical issues concerning personal identity with an extensive bibliography.

Sajjad H. Rizvi, "Avicenna (Ibn Sina) (c. 980–1037)." *Internet Encyclopedia of Philosophy*, ed. James Fieser and Bradley Dowden. Helpful overview of Ibn Sina's philosophy with extensive references for further reading.

7

Al-Ghazali's *The Rescuer from Error*

Is Religious Belief Founded in Reason?

7.1. The Setting

Al-Ghazali was born in 1058 CE in the city of Tus in northeastern Persia (modern-day Khurasan). In his youth he received a traditional Islamic education and later studied Kalam—speculative Islamic theology—from a distinguish theologian in Nishapur. In 1091 al-Ghazali moved to Baghdad to head an influential school that had evolved to defend Sunni orthodoxy against its Shiite rival. During this period he began to intensively study philosophy, and his most important philosophical work, *The Incoherence of the Philosophers* (*Tahafut al-Falasifah*), dates from his time in Baghdad. Although he met with great success as a teacher, al-Ghazali soon suffered a deep spiritual crisis. Disillusioned with his work and worldly success, al-Ghazali sought a more profound spirituality in Sufi mysticism. In 1095 he dramatically renounced his prestigious teaching position, adopted Sufi practices, and traveled broadly. Eleven years later he briefly returned to teaching in the city of Nishapur but resigned once again two years afterward. He died in 1111 CE but has continued to exert a tremendous influence over philosophy in Islamic lands up to the present day.

Al-Ghazali's mature views are best understood against the backdrop of the views of his predecessors, including those of Ibn Sina—whom we met in the last chapter. Ibn Sina agreed with many traditional views. He held, for example, that only God is the cause of his own existence and that all other things must be created by God. Nonetheless, drawing on his understanding of ancient Greek philosophy, Ibn Sina also argued for more radical views. He maintained, for example, that God cannot know about the world as we experience it, that God could not have made the world different than he did, and that even now God cannot change the world in any way. In boldly drawing out many themes arguably implicit in ancient Greek philosophy, Ibn Sina

Saints, Heretics, and Atheists. Jeffrey K. McDonough, Oxford University Press. © Oxford University Press 2022.
DOI: 10.1093/oso/9780197563847.003.0007

came to defend a conception of God that is far removed from the personal deity that many believers in the Judeo-Christian-Islamic tradition accept.

In works such as *The Rescuer from Error* (*al-Munqidh min al-Dalal*) and *The Incoherence of the Philosophers*, al-Ghazali attempted to push back against the views of Ibn Sina and other philosophers. His most accessible work, *The Rescuer from Error* is presented as an autobiographical tale of al-Ghazali's learning, his spiritual and philosophical anxiety, and his eventual embrace of mysticism. This book has often been compared to Descartes's *Meditations* as well as to Augustine's *Confessions*. Like the former, *The Rescuer from Error* has two sides. On the one side, al-Ghazali argues that many philosophical arguments fail by the standards of philosophy itself. Ibn Sina's bold claims concerning God should be deemed unjustified even by Ibn Sina's own standards. On the other side, al-Ghazali argues that his own mature view—mysticism—provides a better route to understanding God, a route that leads to views that are consistent with more traditional theological convictions.

7.2. Three Views on Faith and Reason

A central theme of al-Ghazali's *The Rescuer from Error* is the relationship between faith and reason. It might be helpful to begin by sketching three broad views concerning the relationship between faith and reason. A first view, known as *strong rationalism*, suggests that in order for religious beliefs to be properly and rationally accepted, giving compelling independent evidence in support of them must be possible, evidence that could in principle anyone could accept.

The core idea of strong rationalism was dramatically expressed by the English mathematician W. K. Clifford (1845–79) in his widely read *The Ethics of Belief*:

> It is wrong always, everywhere, and for anyone, to believe anything upon insufficient evidence. . . . If a man, holding a belief which he was taught in childhood or persuaded of afterwards, keeps down and pushes away any doubts which arise about it in his mind . . . and regards as impious those questions which cannot easily be asked without disturbing it—the life of that man is one long sin against mankind. . . . Inquiry into the evidence of a doctrine is not to be made once for all and then taken as finally settled. It is never lawful to stifle a doubt; for either it can be honestly answered by

> means of the inquiry already made, or else it proves that the inquiry was not complete.

The main idea here is that religious beliefs are acceptable only if compelling arguments can be raised in their defense, arguments that might be convincing to anyone. According to Clifford, the following are not good reasons for accepting religious beliefs: you grew up accepting those beliefs, it is a comfort to you to believe as you do, you have never really given the matter much thought.

Although strong rationalism has had its followers, many people today are perhaps more attracted to a second, less demanding view often referred to as weak rationalism. According to *weak rationalism*, the subject matter of religion is a topic that is amenable to debate. Arguments for and against religious beliefs can be offered and evaluated. Furthermore, those arguments should be used to shape our religious beliefs. So far this is all very much in keeping with strong rationalism. The two approaches part ways, however, in their expectations concerning the strength of those arguments. The weak rationalist insists that arguments in favor of religious belief needn't be convincing to everyone. We might think of the weak rationalist as being more skeptical about the strength of human reasoning in general. Reason has a role to play in the formation of our religious beliefs, but not necessarily a decisive role. After all—she might argue—we don't have absolutely compelling reasons for most of our beliefs. Why should we suppose that the situation is any different with respect to our religious beliefs?

A third view, often referred to as *fideism*, maintains that even weak rationalism assigns too strong a role to reason in the formation of religious belief. Fideists hold that religious beliefs must rest on faith rather than reason. According to fideism, religious beliefs are justified—to the extent that it makes sense to speak of them as being "justified"—not on the basis of arguments that can be marshaled for or against them, but rather on the basis of one's commitment to them. In its strongest form, fideism goes so far as to suggest that the search for rational grounds for religious beliefs is inimical to faith. One way of developing this thought is to suggest that the search for rational arguments reveals that one doesn't really have faith. If one has faith, one doesn't need arguments. And if one has compelling arguments, one can't really have faith. If I trust that you have my best interests at heart, I don't need evidence that you do. And if I have proof that you have my best interests at heart, my trust in you isn't based on faith alone.

7.3. The Quest for Certainty

Al-Ghazali begins *The Rescuer from Error* by relating that he was curious about the foundations of religious belief even as a child. He was struck in particular by differences among religious beliefs and by the fact that children often adopt the religious beliefs of their parents. His curiosity inspired him to seek certain knowledge "in which what is known is laid bare in such a way as to leave no room for doubt and is unaccompanied by the possibility of error or illusion, to the point that the mind cannot even conceive it" (61; this chapter follows the translation of Al-Ghazali's *The Rescuer from Error* in Khalidi [2005]). In short, al-Ghazali's initial curiosity led him to seek absolutely certain foundations for religious belief.

In examining his beliefs according to this high standard, al-Ghazali initially supposed that his immediate sensory beliefs and his beliefs about necessary truths might serve as epistemic foundations. Further reflection, however, led him to question whether sensory beliefs could be held with absolute certainty:

> Where does this confidence in sensory beliefs come from? The strongest sense is vision, which looks at a shadow and sees that it is stationary, and judges that there is no motion. But then as a result of experience and observation, after an hour, it is cognizant that the shadow is indeed moving. Moreover, it finds that it did not move suddenly, all at once, but rather incrementally atom by atom, in such a way that it was never actually stationary. Likewise, vision looks at a celestial body and sees that it is small, around the size of a dinar, but then geometrical proofs indicate that it is in fact larger than the earth in size. In this and other such sensory matters, the judge of sensation makes its judgments, but the judge of reason then judges it to be false and disproves it irrefutably. (62)

Al-Ghazali's argument is clear enough. We see a shadow. Our vision suggests that it is stationary. But an hour later it is clear that the shadow has moved substantially. We reason that the shadow must have been moving very gradually after all, initial appearances to the contrary. Likewise, looking at the sun, we might think that it is small, or at least not very big. But by reasoning, we know that the sun is extremely large. Once again initial appearances are misleading. Through such considerations, al-Ghazali calls into question the certainty of sensory beliefs. If his senses could deceive him in some cases, he suggests, then they could deceive him in other cases as well. He draws the conclusion that the senses do not provide absolute certainty.

Arguments from sensory illusion may seem to leave nonsensory beliefs untouched. And, indeed, having cast doubt on the absolute reliability of his sensory beliefs, al-Ghazali immediately suggests that "Perhaps one can only trust the rational beliefs, which are among the first principles, such as the statements 'Ten is greater than three,' 'Negation and affirmation cannot coexist in the same thing,' and 'The same thing cannot be both originated and eternal, or existent and nonexistent, or necessary and impossible' " (62). Soon, however, al-Ghazali offers reasons for doubting even nonsensory beliefs, beliefs that seem to be founded wholly on reason alone:

> The sensory beliefs replied, "How can you be sure that your confidence in rational beliefs is not like that in the sensory beliefs? You trusted in me, but the judge of reason disproved me. Were it not for the judge of reason, you would have continued to believe me. Perhaps behind rational apprehension there is another judge who, if he were to manifest himself, would disprove the judgment of reason, just as the judge of reason manifested himself to disprove the judgments of sense perception. The fact that such an apprehension has not manifested itself does not indicate that it is impossible. (62)

Al-Ghazali's skeptical suggestion here is that even if we cannot bring ourselves to directly doubt that, say, 2 + 2 = 4, we can imagine that there is a higher authority to whom it is manifest that 2 + 2 = 5, and who recognizes that we are mistaken in much the way that our reason recognizes that our sensory faculties are mistaken in judging that the sun is the size of a small coin.

Al-Ghazali reports that he was deeply troubled by his skeptical doubts for a couple of months. He recognized that there is no way to directly rebut the reasoning that led him into skepticism. As he puts it, "For they could be rebutted with a proof, and a proof can only be constructed by combining the first [principles of] knowledge. If these are not given, then it is impossible to arrange a proof" (63). Only God's intervention, al-Ghazali tells us, was capable of curing his skeptical predicament:

> Eventually, God cured me of this disease and my mind was restored to health and balance. The rational necessary beliefs were once again accepted and trusted, both securely and certainly. This did not come about by composing a proof or by an arrangement of words, but rather by a light that God

> Almighty cast into my breast, which is the key to the greater part of cognizance. Whoever supposes that enlightenment depends upon explicit proofs has narrowed the expanse of God's mercy. (63)

To al-Ghazali it is important that God cured him of his skepticism not by reminding him of certain arguments or even revealing new proofs. Rather God cured him through a direct revelation that could not be doubted or called into question. The deep lesson al-Ghazali wishes to impart is that our most basic beliefs do not rest on argument or human foundations but rather must ultimately be grounded in God's revelation.

7.4. Three False Foundations

Having found a resolution to his skepticism, al-Ghazali goes on to consider alternative paths that one might follow in searching for religious foundations. Setting aside for now the way of the mystics, he identifies three classes of seekers: "(i) Theologians, who claim that they are the party of opinion and theoretical speculation; (ii) Esotericists, who claim that they are the party of instruction and are privileged to receive instruction from the infallible imam; (iii) Philosophers, who claim that they are the party of logic and demonstration" (64). Having identified these three routes, he goes on to argue that none of them are able to offer a path to true certainty.

Theologians: Interestingly, al-Ghazali implies that while theology is fine at what it does, its task is simply not the task he has in mind. Theology, according to al-Ghazali, aims to preserve religious dogma and beat back heresy by arguing from accepted principles. Al-Ghazali does not deny the importance of this task, but merely insists that it is not the task of establishing first principles or certainty. Theology simply takes religious dogma as a given starting point. Insofar as it does not seek to establish certain belief, but instead takes certain belief for granted, it is of no assistance to him in establishing firm foundations for his own religious beliefs. Note, this all amounts to the suggestion that if religious belief is to be deeply justified, or certain, it cannot rest merely on religious tradition—for religious tradition stands in need of the same sort of justification as religious belief itself.

Esotericists: The central doctrine of esotericists, according to al-Ghazali, is that knowledge of truth is not possible without a teacher, and the only teacher whose teaching cannot be doubted is an infallible teacher or imam.

The most pressing difficulty that al-Ghazali sees with this view is that it offers no good means of identifying infallible teachers. He is willing to grant that the prophet is an infallible teacher, but the esotericists provide no special means of accessing his teachings, and no way of identifying or accessing other infallible imams. There is, of course, a very general and intuitive worry here. If the foundation of religious belief is to rest on spiritual authority, how we are to identify that authority? Note, this amounts to the suggestion that if religious belief is to be deeply justified, or certain, it cannot rest merely on religious authority—for the identification of a true religious authority stands in the same need of justification as religious belief itself.

Philosophers: Many of al-Ghazali's criticisms in *The Rescuer* are directed at philosophers, and in particular at what he sees as the rationalist tradition reaching back to Socrates, Plato, and Aristotle and continuing through the likes of al-Farabi and Ibn Sina. Simplifying a bit, al-Ghazali divides their teachings into three main topics: mathematics and logic, physics and metaphysics, and morality and politics. He then argues that the threat posed by the teachings of the philosophers varies considerably with respect to each of these topics. An overriding theme, however, is that religious certainty cannot be founded on rational argument alone.

Taking up his first topic, al-Ghazali insists, "The mathematical sciences pertain to the sciences of arithmetic, geometry, and astronomy, and none of them is relevant to religious matters, either by way of negation or affirmation. Rather, these are demonstrative matters that one cannot deny once one has understood them and become cognizant of them" (68). Considered narrowly, mathematics and logic are neither a boon nor a threat to religion. Al-Ghazali maintains that in the hands of the philosophers, however, even mathematics and logic become potentially dangerous—for people may be so impressed by philosophers' use of logic and mathematics that they may blindly follow philosophers in their irreligious beliefs as well. Or—going to the other extreme—people may be so eager to reject the impiety of the philosophers that they may foolishly deny their discoveries in logic and mathematics and in doing so undermine their own credibility. It is not hard to see plausible examples of both phenomena even today. On the one side, scientists, for example, may be afforded undue authority in religious matters about which they have no special knowledge. On the other side, religious authorities may overreach themselves in denying well-confirmed scientific results in a way that may undermine their own credibility in spiritual matters.

Turning to the second topic, al-Ghazali maintains that the greatest threat to piety from philosophers stems from their views on physics and metaphysics. In these domains, he suggests, the philosophers "are not able to fulfill the conditions on demonstrations that are set down in logic, and they therefore disagree considerably among themselves about metaphysical questions" (72). In short, in forming their views in physics, and especially in metaphysics, philosophers overreach themselves and arrive at heretical (bad) or blasphemous (worse) views. Those who follow philosophers in these areas are led to false foundations for religious beliefs. In particular, they may come to believe on the basis of philosophers' arguments that (i) God has knowledge only of universals and not particulars; (ii) God cannot act to change the world in any way—that, for example, miracles are impossible and prayers ineffective; and (iii) the world follows necessarily from God in such a way that he could not have created the world in any way other than he did. In short, al-Ghazali thinks that if you follow the philosophers, you might end up with views as heretical as those of Ibn Sina!

With respect to the third topic, al-Ghazali maintains that in the case of ethics and politics, the philosophers have jumbled together a variety of views, including those derived from the mystics and the prophets. This again gives rise to the threat of two dangers, "one pertaining to its acceptance, and the other to its rejection." The danger pertaining to acceptance is that by adopting the views of the philosophers, one will come to hold not only proper views, but also improper ones mixed in with them. The danger pertaining to rejection is just the converse: in rejecting the views of the philosophers, one might inadvertently reject not only improper beliefs but also proper ones mixed in with them. An overriding theme of al-Ghazali's critique of the philosophers is that human reason is not sufficient to secure foundations for religious knowledge. Human reason—while impressive in some domains—is inadequate to the deeper mysteries of metaphysics and religion.

7.5. Is God Hidden?

Al-Ghazali's exploration of the relationship between philosophy and belief provides an opportunity to consider a topic that has recently attracted a great deal of attention. The problem of divine hiddenness suggests a tension between traditional monotheistic conceptions of God and the apparent fact that there are many people who—through no fault of their own—do not stand in a personal relationship to God. Traditional monotheistic religions often suggest that God is like a loving father and that humans are like his children. But what kind of father would let his children earnestly seek his help, support, and comfort in vain? How, if God cares about us, can he let so many of us be uncertain of that very fact? A wide range of replies has been offered to this apparent problem. Let's briefly consider three of them.

A first line of response would simply deny that God exists. There's no problem, for adults at least, about the hiddenness of Santa Claus, the Easter bunny, or the tooth fairy. Those figures are silent to us because they don't exist. Perhaps God is likewise silent to us because he doesn't exist. Or perhaps God is silent to us because God is not like a loving parent at all. Perhaps God is simply too abstract to care about us in the manner of a father or a mother. It was a commonplace view in the ancient world that the gods exist but that they are simply not concerned with human affairs. What gods care about most is not humans but gods! Or perhaps God is too all-encompassing and concrete to enter into a personal relationship with humans. In later chapters, we see both Spinoza and Hume entertain versions of deism according to which God is not like a person at all. If their views are right, there is no mystery as to why God does not make himself manifest even to earnest seekers.

A second line of response denies the alleged fact that many people—through no fault of their own—do not stand in a personal relationship to God. This response may be developed in two rather different ways. The first way would, in effect, deny that there is anyone who does not, or will not, stand in a personal relationship to God. With this approach, one might maintain that in fact we all experience moments in which we are in personal contact with God. The atheist is either in denial concerning her own experiences or misinterprets them. Another possibility in the same line is that while some people may have not *yet* entered into a personal relationship with God, it is just a matter of time. The atheist is like a prodigal son who will eventually be welcomed by his divine father. The second way of going would maintain that while there are people who do not stand in a personal relationship with God, they are nonetheless responsible for their own failure to "hear" God's presence. From this perspective, one might maintain that only the willfully stubborn fail to perceive God's presence, or that God's silence is punishment for our individual or collective guilt.

Finally, a third line of response argues that God's hiddenness serves some greater good. That good might be our own. Perhaps God's making his own presence more obvious would undermine our agency. As things stand, we can seek God out. We can reason and reflect and come to our own conclusions about God's existence. Perhaps that is all for the best—that is, all for the best for *us*. Alternatively, perhaps the greater good that God's hiddenness serves is, first and foremost, his own. The contemporary philosopher Michael Rea, for example, has suggested that perhaps what we take to be divine silence is simply the most apt way for God to express his own nature. God could speak to us from the clouds or appear on public television. But to do so, God would have to express himself in a way that would be both inappropriate and disingenuous. God's silence, in Rea's view, serves a greater good—not necessarily our greater good, but rather the good of God expressing himself in a way befitting his own being. It serves God's greater good.

Further Study

Peter Adamson, *The History of Philosophy without Any Gaps: Philosophy in Later Antiquity*. Podcast, 2011–13; available online and through iTunes. An excellent, entertaining introduction to philosophical currents in the Islamic World; includes podcasts devoted to al-Ghazali.

Frank Griffel, "Al-Ghazali." *Stanford Encyclopedia of Philosophy* (Winter 2014 Edition), ed. Edward N. Zalta, http://plato.stanford.edu/archives/win2014/entries/al-ghazali/. Overview of al-Ghazali's life and works with an extensive bibliography.

Muhammad Hozien, ghazali.org, updated 2021. A comprehensive website devoted to al-Ghazali, including links to texts, timelines, and maps.

Muhammad Ali Khalidi, *Medieval Islamic Philosophy*. Cambridge: Cambridge University Press, 2005. An excellent collection of English translations of works in medieval Islamic philosophy. Includes selection from al-Ghazali's *The Rescuer from Error*.

Michael Rea, "Divine Hiddenness, Divine Silence." In *Philosophy of Religion: An Anthology*, 6th ed., ed. Louis Pojman and Michael Rea, 266–75. Boston: Wadsworth/Cengage, 2012. A helpful, engaging introduction to the problem of divine hiddenness written for an undergraduate audience.

J. L. Schellenberg, *Divine Hiddenness and Human Reason*. Ithaca, NY: Cornell University Press, 1993. Seminal contemporary presentation of the problem of divine hiddenness; written for an advanced audience.

8

Al-Ghazali's *The Rescuer from Error*

Is Religious Belief Founded in Experience?

In the last chapter we saw al-Ghazali reject what he considered to be three insufficient or false foundations for religious belief: tradition, authority, and reason. In this chapter we turn to his positive attempt to ground religious belief in mystical experience. Toward that end, we start by briefly recalling al-Ghazali's report of his journey into mysticism. We then explore some different ways of thinking about the nature of mystical experience. Finally we consider a contemporary attempt to defend mystical experience as a foundation for religious belief.

8.1. Al-Ghazali's Turn to Mysticism

Al-Ghazali reports that the way of mysticism is brought about "by a combination of knowledge and practice." It is clear, however, that al-Ghazali found the knowledge part of the mystic's way far easier than the practice part. Emphasizing the difference between the theory and practice of mysticism, al-Ghazali writes,

> There is a world of difference between knowing the definitions of health and satiety, their causes, and their preconditions, and actually being healthy and satiated. Likewise, there is a world of difference between being cognizant of the definition of inebriation . . . and actually being inebriated. . . . There is a similar difference between knowing the reality of asceticism, its preconditions, and its causes, and the soul's actually being in a state of asceticism and renunciation of the world. (77; this chapter follows the translation of Al-Ghazali's *The Rescuer from Error* in Khalidi [2005])

Al-Ghazali's distinction between the intellectual and practical sides of mysticism foreshadows an important feature of mysticism as a foundation of

Saints, Heretics, and Atheists. Jeffrey K. McDonough, Oxford University Press. © Oxford University Press 2022.
DOI: 10.1093/oso/9780197563847.003.0008

religious belief. Mysticism is commonly accompanied by doctrine and background belief. Clearly, however, the heart of mysticism, and its claim to being a foundation for religious belief lies elsewhere. The heart of mysticism, and its claim to being a foundation for religious belief, must ultimately be located in mystical experience itself.

Like Augustine before him, al-Ghazali appears to have been hesitant to follow his religious beliefs even after having been intellectually convinced of them. In a passage reminiscent of Augustine's plea for "chastity and continence but not yet," al-Ghazali writes,

> One day, I would be determined to leave Baghdad and walk out on my whole situation, and the next I would lose my determination entirely. I put one step forward then took another back. My desire to pursue the afterlife would take hold one morning, only to be dispersed by the forces of appetite by evening. The temptations of the temporal world enchained me and tugged at me to remain, while the voice of faith cried out: "Depart! Depart! You have only a short time left to live, you have a long journey ahead, and your knowledge and practice are all hypocrisy and illusion. If not now, when will you prepare for the afterlife? If you do not sever these attachments now, when will you do so?" (78)

Like many mystics, al-Ghazali presents the mystic's path as simultaneously a turn away from worldly goods and toward an ascetic life, that is, toward a life in which bodily needs are neglected or at least minimally fulfilled. Given the intense physical demands of the mystic's way, it is perhaps not surprising that al-Ghazali should have hesitated in following the mystic's path. In a later chapter, we see Nietzsche trying to tease out the appeal of practices such as those common among Jewish, Muslim, and Christian ascetics.

Al-Ghazali reports that after six months of vacillating, the decision to abandon his former way of life was made for him as he found himself no longer physically able to teach. He left behind his fame and wealth, and even his "family, children, and friends," and traveled to Syria:

> Then I entered Syria and resided there for almost two years, occupying myself exclusively with isolation, solitude, spiritual exercises, and mystical devotion. I was engaged in purifying my soul, moral education, and cleansing my heart for the recollection of God Almighty, in accordance with what I had read in the books of the mystics. Each day, I would withdraw to the

> Mosque of Damascus, ascend the minaret, and lock myself up there for the duration of the day. (80)

From Syria, al-Ghazali traveled to Jerusalem while following the same ascetic routine. He then made a pilgrimage to Mecca and Medina, eventually returning home to Baghdad.

Like many mystics, al-Ghazali maintains that mystical experience itself cannot be fully articulated. Of the mystical path and experience, he writes,

> On the whole, what can one say about their way? Purity, which is its first precondition, is the complete purification of the heart from everything but God Almighty. The key to their way, which follows from this first step, just as prayer follows from sanctity, is the complete absorption of the heart in the recollection of God. The final step is complete obliteration in God. . . . The mystical state progresses from the level of visions of images and similitudes to levels about which it is difficult to give utterance. Any interpreter who has tried to articulate such a state has inevitably committed a clear error of expression, which cannot be guarded against. . . . Whoever has managed to attain that state must not say more than the following: "I do not remember what happened, so assume the best, and do not ask for a report!" (81)

There are hints here of a kind of ascent familiar from Platonic and Neoplatonic philosophy. Plato himself had suggested that we cannot immediately grasp the eternal, immutable form of beauty, but that we must approach it step by step. We must first contemplate beautiful physical objects, then beautiful abstract objects, and then finally beauty itself. But al-Ghazali's ascent really describes just the on-ramp to mystical experience. About the experience itself, al-Ghazali is largely silent. The mystical experience itself—the very heart of the mystical way—cannot be fully articulated. It can only be experienced.

Insofar as mystics insist that religious experience is ineffable and that it must be lived to be understood, mysticism may not seem amenable to philosophical investigation. How are we supposed to analyze what cannot even be articulated? Even if religious experience is ineffable, however, we might nonetheless pursue two related questions. First, what is the nature, or "structure," of religious experience? This question asks how we are to understand in general terms the phenomenon of religious experience, even if it is granted that the intrinsic or specific nature of the experience can only be fully understood by the person who has experienced it. Second, how might religious experience relate to, or even support, religious belief? Many mystics take their religious experiences as confirmation of, or even foundational grounds for, religious belief. We might want to know if, or how, that might be so. Although our two questions are intimately related, we focus on the first question first, and then explore the second by considering some recent views on religious experience as a foundation for religious belief.

8.2. Three Accounts of Religious Experience

What, then, is the basic structure of religious experience? How can we understand the core nature of religious experience, even if we don't share in it directly ourselves? We can begin to get a feel for the range of responses that have been given to these questions by considering three broad views on the nature of religious experience.

A first view suggests that, at its core, religious experience is not an intellectual or cognitive experience, but an intuitive, unmediated feeling often involving a sense of oneness or dependence. We can get some sense of this view of religious belief from one of its most famous proponents, Rudolf Otto (1869–1937). Describing his own mystical experience, Otto writes,

> The feeling of terrifying mystery (*mysterium tremendum*) may at times come sweeping like a gentle tide, pervading the mind with a tranquil mood of deepest worship. It may pass over into a more set and lasting attitude of the soul, continuing, as it were, thrillingly vibrant and resonant. . . . It may burst in sudden eruption up from the depths of the soul with spasms and convulsions, or lead to the strangest excitements, to intoxicated frenzy, to transport, and to ecstasy. (1923, 12–13)

What is most important for our purposes about Otto's understanding of religious experience is his suggestion that religious experience is, in his words, a "non-rational, non-sensory experience or feeling." In Otto's view, religious experience is like a passion that overtakes one, a passion that is not a reasoned response, nor an experience of the physical senses, nor even something that admits of conceptual analysis. In Otto's view, the mystic's religious experience is first and foremost a kind of emotional experience.

Views like Otto's have received criticism that, under such accounts, religious experience would not be sufficiently cognitive to serve as a foundation for religious belief. It has been suggested that to the extent that religious experience is ineffable, nonconceptual, and impossible to characterize, it is not the sort of thing that could ground our beliefs, dogmas, or traditions. This objection grants that the mystic might have ineffable experiences, but questions how ineffable experiences could lend justification to conceptually loaded beliefs. Perhaps the most obvious reply to this sort of objection suggests that perceptual experience itself needn't be conceptual in order to lend support to conceptual beliefs. We might think, for example, that the way something strikes us or the conviction it produces are nonconceptual elements that lend support to conceptual beliefs without themselves being conceptual.

Views like Otto's have also been accused of mischaracterizing emotions. Some philosophers, for example, have argued that emotions themselves essentially involve a robust conceptual component. This line of thought directly challenges the mystic's claim to have truly ineffable experiences. If those experiences are genuine feelings or emotions, then they must, according to this line of objection, have some conceptual content that can be cogently expressed. Perhaps the most obvious response to this kind of objection would be to argue that while some feelings and emotions are conceptually laden, not all experiences need be, and that religious experiences in particular might serve as examples of ineffable experiences.

A second view of religious experience suggests that, at its core, religious experience is a kind of perception. The contemporary philosopher William Alston, for example, has argued that we can distinguish three crucial elements common to both ordinary perceptual experience and religious experience. To begin with a mundane case, suppose I see my dog, Martha. In this case, we may distinguish between the perceiver (me), the object of the experience (Martha), and the mode of the experience (e.g., Martha's clear appearance when my glasses are on, or Martha's hazy appearance when my glasses are off). Likewise, Alston argues, with respect to religious experience, we can distinguish the religious perceiver, God as the object of that perception, and the mode of God to the perceiver. The mystic's experience may be unusual in its mode of appearance and in its being related to a supernatural object of experience. Nonetheless, Alston claims, the basic structure of religious experience is the same as the basic structure of ordinary experience.

One might object to this proposal by pointing out a rather obvious disanalogy between ordinary perceptual experience and religious experience, namely, that the former appears to be much more common than the latter. Most of us can see, hear, and touch ordinary objects every day, and most of us are able to do this essentially whenever we want. Although there are many reports of religious experience throughout history, it seems undeniable that most people do not claim to have perceived God directly, and even those who do are likely to admit that they do not perceive God as readily as they see tables and chairs. In response, it might be noted that, although such considerations might speak to our willingness to accept the existence of veridical religious experience, they need not undermine the view that religious experience has the same structure as perceptual experience. Even if there were only one person in the world who could perceive normally, and even if she could only do so for thirty minutes a week, that would be no objection to describing her experience as having the structure of perceiver, object, and mode of presentation.

It is worth noting that the perceptual account of religious experience leaves open the possibility that purportedly religious experiences are in fact misperceptions. For if it turns out that a purported religious experience is not caused by something divine, then one might plausibly hold that it is not really a religious experience after all. The point can perhaps be made more clearly with the help of an analogy. I might report seeing Martha running down the hall toward my colleague's office, but if it turns out that my experience is caused by something else—say, a stray cat—then I will not have had a Martha perception after all, but rather a misleading cat perception. So, similarly, if I report having a perception of God, but it turns out that my experience is caused by low blood sugar levels, or a misfiring in my brain, then I should allow that I didn't really have a perception of God after all, but instead a misperception or hallucination.

A third view of religious experience might be motivated by the intuition that what is essential to a religious experience is not its causal origin, but the fact that it is taken to be a religious experience. The central idea of such a view is that an experience is a religious experience if and only if it is understood to be a religious experience by the person who has the experience. We might think that religious experience so understood is more akin to a scary experience than, say, an experience of a dog running down the hallway. An experience is a scary experience if the person who has the experience thinks it's scary, while an experience is an experience of a dog running down the hallway only if it is caused by a dog running down the hallway.

It has been argued that if religious experience is irreducibly subjective in this way, the only interesting question we can ask in connection with religious experience is why the person takes that experience to be an experience of the divine. The contemporary philosopher Wayne Proudfoot, for example, argues that consideration of external causes is irrelevant with respect to an investigation of religious experience:

> [Since] the concepts and beliefs under which the subject identifies his or her experience determine whether or not it is a religious experience, we need to explain why the subject employs those particular concepts and beliefs. We must explain why the subject was confronted with this particular set of alternative ways of understanding his experience and why he employed the one he did. What we want is a historical or cultural explanation. (1985, 223)

The thought here is that the external cause of the mystic's experience is irrelevant as far as her having a mystical experience is concerned—just as the cause of my scary experience is irrelevant as far as my having a scary experience is concerned. The only relevant question, Proudfoot suggests, is why the mystic interprets her experience as religious, and for an answer to that question we must investigate the cultural and historical beliefs that shape her interpretation of her experience.

Of course, regarding this account of religious experience one might object that the cause of the religious belief is not as wholly independent of the mystic's interpretation of her belief as Proudfoot implies. She might argue that at least part of the reason she interprets her experience as being of the divine is that it is of the divine! Furthermore, one might argue that we are not *just* interested in why someone interprets his or her belief as a religious belief, but also in whether or not it has a divine object as its cause. Either way, it might thus be objected that Proudfoot's model leaves something significant out of what is interesting and important about religious experience, namely, the purported object of the experience—that is, God.

8.3. Is Religious Experience a Good Reason for Belief?

Having considered three different analyses of the structure of religious experience, we are in a better position to see why someone might think that religious experience *by itself* could never justify one's religious beliefs. One might argue that on any of the above accounts, religious experience can only provide an objective reason for religious belief when supported by other religious beliefs. One would need to have, say, good, independent reasons to suppose that one is actually experiencing or perceiving God. Many philosophers have concluded that mysticism lends little independent support to religious beliefs. They have often thought, in short, that religious experience per se can only be convincing to the already convinced, and thus cannot serve as a legitimate, objective source of religious justification. They have concluded that religious experience, at least by itself, cannot *justify* religious beliefs.

This fairly standard view has recently been challenged by some contemporary philosophers of religion. In order to better understand their position, it will be helpful to recall a very general and pervasive view concerning the foundations of our ordinary, nonreligious beliefs. According to *foundationalism*, all our beliefs are either basic, foundational beliefs, or nonbasic, derived beliefs. One might suppose, for example, that my belief that 2 + 2 = 4, that there is a dog in front of me, or that the sun will rise tomorrow are either foundational beliefs or close to them. As such, they might be taken to be essentially self-evident and the basis for other, less certain, nonfoundational beliefs, beliefs such as that my checkbook is balanced and that I should put on some sunscreen. Relatively nonfoundational beliefs are assumed to derive their evidential support from more foundational beliefs.

But how do foundational beliefs get their evidential support? According to one account, our foundational beliefs are supported by certain epistemically basic practices such as mathematical deduction, sensory perception, and empirical induction. Importantly for our present concerns, while these practices might be thought to provide immediate justification for our foundational beliefs, it is not clear how they might be given wholesale, noncircular justification themselves. It seems that I may check my mathematical proofs, the reliability of my vision, or my inductive generalizations, but only if I assume that my practices of mathematical deduction, sensory perception, and empirical induction are at least generally reliable. Putting the point conversely, if, for example, the use of mathematical deduction is wholly unreliable, it is hard to see what we might use to evaluate a particular mathematical proof or discovery.

When it comes to our nonreligious beliefs, many contemporary philosophers are inclined to allow that our foundational beliefs might be wrong, but that it is not unreasonable to proceed on the assumption that they are correct. I *could* be wrong that Martha is standing in front of me—perhaps I have been drugged, perhaps I am dreaming, or perhaps I am being tricked by an evil demon. I *could* be wrong that the sun will rise tomorrow—perhaps the future will be nothing at all like the past. These skeptical scenarios might be worrisome in the seminar room, but there is no reason to allow them to undermine our day-to-day epistemic practices (or so many philosophers have concluded). In short, when it comes to our nonreligious beliefs, many contemporary philosophers have come to accept that our epistemic foundations are fallible, but that they might nonetheless be perfectly legitimate and provide justification for our derived, nonbasic beliefs.

Some theistic philosophers have argued that once such a picture of justification is accepted, there is no reason why religious experience should not be counted as an epistemically basic practice, or why religious beliefs formed on the basis of religious experience should not count as foundational beliefs. Those who claim to have religious experiences treat the religious beliefs they form on the basis of those experiences as certain and indubitable. Such practices and beliefs have played a long and important role in belief formation. The theist can freely grant that such practices might, in fact, be unreliable and beliefs formed on the basis of them might be false. Nonetheless, she may insist that in this way religious experience differs not at all from our other "ordinary" epistemically basic practices. Parity and fairness, she suggests, require that we recognize that the mystic has just as much basis for her religious beliefs as the nontheist has for her beliefs about mathematics, ordinary objects, and the future. Like our other epistemically basic practices, she will claim that religious experience ought to be assumed reliable until proven otherwise.

Perhaps the most important line of objection to this general attempt to defend religious experience as a foundation for religious belief presses on the thought that religious experience is less universal than other purportedly basic practices. The acceptance of deduction, sensory experience, and induction appears to be common to almost every human being. Someone who went around supposing that 2 + 2 = 5, or that the sun will not rise tomorrow, would probably be deemed crazy (or a philosopher!). In contrast, reports of direct religious experience are relatively uncommon, and perfectly reasonable people may doubt their veracity. Relatedly, most generally accepted epistemic practices are invariant across different cultures and traditions. Reliance on deduction, sensory experience, and induction is essentially the same no matter where you go. Claims of religious experience, however, vary greatly from culture to culture, from religious tradition to religious tradition. Whether such considerations are relevant to the epistemic status of religious experience, or merely differences that don't make a difference, is, of course, a matter for debate.

Further Study

Jerome Gellman, "Mysticism." *Stanford Encyclopedia of Philosophy* (Spring 2014 Edition), ed. Edward N. Zalta, http://plato.stanford.edu/archives/spr2014/entries/mysticism/. Comprehensive overview of mysticism with an extensive bibliography.

Muhammad Ali Khalidi, *Medieval Islamic Philosophy*. Cambridge: Cambridge University Press, 2005. An excellent collection of English translations of works in medieval Islamic philosophy. Includes selection from al-Ghazali's *The Rescuer from Error*.

Daniel O'Brian, "The Epistemology of Perception." *Internet Encyclopedia of Philosophy*, http://www.iep.utm.edu/epis-per/. A concise overview of perception and its relation to epistemology.

Rudolf Otto, *The Idea of the Holy: An Inquiry into the Non-Rational Factor in the Idea of the Divine and Its Relation to the Rational*. New York: Oxford University Press, 1923.

Wayne Proudfoot, *Religious Experience*. Berkeley: University of California Press, 1985. An influential discussion of religious experience for an advanced audience.

9

Aquinas's *Summa Theologica*

Does Experience Prove That God Exists?

9.1. The Setting

With this chapter, we are once again at another important turning point in the history of Western philosophy and religion. Earlier we saw how Greek philosophy was preserved and developed in Islamic lands, having been translated from Greek into Arabic. Around the twelfth century, Greek philosophy began to flow back into Western Europe. Major centers of translation emerged along the seam where predominantly Muslim lands overlapped with predominantly Christian ones. The impact of these translations, and the massive commentaries that accompanied them, was tremendous. For nearly two thousand years, Aristotle had been known in Western Europe—to the extent that he had been known at all—mostly on the basis of a handful of works focused on logic and rhetoric. By the mid-thirteenth century, in contrast, the bulk of Aristotle's extant works had been translated into Latin and were required reading at the University of Paris. There they would be studied by a young Dominican friar from Italy who would make it his life's work to reconcile Christian doctrine and Aristotelian philosophy. That young Dominican friar is, of course, known today as Saint Thomas Aquinas.

Aquinas was born in southern Italy near Naples sometime around 1225. At the age of five, he was placed in the Benedictine Abbey of Monte Cassino and studied there until 1239. When he reached the age of fourteen, his parents shipped him off to the University of Naples. At the university, however, the young Aquinas got into trouble by entering, against his parents' wishes, the recently formed mendicant order of the Dominicans. In response, his parents took the extreme step of having him kidnapped and held at Aquino, the town from which we get the name "Aquinas." After Aquinas had been held against his will for about a year, his parents relented and allowed him to depart for the University of Paris.

Saints, Heretics, and Atheists. Jeffrey K. McDonough, Oxford University Press. © Oxford University Press 2022.
DOI: 10.1093/oso/9780197563847.003.0009

In 1256 Aquinas received his doctorate at the University of Paris and was essentially a professor there for the next three years. In 1259 he was rotated out of his chair at Paris and returned to Italy. There, he wrote his *Summa Contra Gentiles* and started his masterpiece, the *Summa Theologica*. He also began his extensive commentaries on Aristotle's works during this period. In 1268 Aquinas returned to the University of Paris (which was unusual) and completed the bulk of his *Summa Theologica* as well as his Aristotelian commentaries.

Aquinas returned to Italy in 1272 and taught at Naples (and continued to work on his *Summa Theologica*). In 1273, he appears to have had an epiphany or breakdown of some sort. It was at this time he famously declared, "All that I have written seems to me like straw compared with what has now been revealed to me." He died a few months later in 1274 and was canonized in the fourteenth century.

9.2. Is the Existence of God Self-Evident?

Near the beginning of his *Summa Theologica*, Aquinas takes up the topic of God's existence and asks: Is the existence of God self-evident? If not, can God's existence be demonstrated? And if so, how? Taking up the first question first, Aquinas introduces a distinction and effectively turns it into two questions: Is the existence of God self-evident in itself? Is the existence of God self-evident to us?

Aquinas argues that the existence of God is indeed self-evident in itself since God just is his own existence. To say that God exists is like saying that a triangle has three sides or that a bicycle has two wheels. Aquinas is thus willing to grant that it belongs to the very nature of God to exist, and that if we could fully understand the nature of God, then we would see that God must exist—that is, that God's existence is self-evident in itself.

Nonetheless, Aquinas denies that God's existence is self-evident to *us*. Although God's existence follows from God's nature, we—as finite beings—can never fully grasp God's infinite nature. Thus, although there is a necessary connection, as it were, between God's nature and God's existence, we are not in a position to fully understand that connection. Aquinas consequently denies that we can rely on Anselm's ontological argument to prove the existence of God:

> Perhaps someone who hears the name "God" would not understand it to signify "something than which a greater cannot be thought," since some have believed God to be a body. But even if it is granted that everyone understands the name "God" to signify what the objection says—namely "that than which a greater cannot be thought"—nevertheless it does not follow from this that one understands that what is signified by the name exists in the natural order. . . . Nor can it be argued that it exists in reality unless it were granted that there exists in reality something than which a greater cannot be thought, which would not be granted by those who deny that God exists. (Part I, Question 2, article 1, response 2; this chapter follows the translation of Aquinas's *Summa Theologica* in Regan [2002])

Thus, according to Aquinas, while God's existence is self-evident in itself, it is not self-evident to us. If we want to be certain that God exists, we'll have to find a way to prove that God exists.

9.3. Can We Prove That God Exists?

Turning to his second question, Aquinas argues that even though the existence of God is not self-evident to us, God's existence can nonetheless be demonstrated. In making this claim, Aquinas introduces an important distinction between two kinds of possible demonstration: demonstrations *propter quid* and demonstrations *quia*.

A demonstration *propter quid* would involve demonstrating (or explaining) the existence of God from his cause, just as we might demonstrate (or explain) the existence of smoke by appealing to the fire that is its cause. According to Aquinas, God's existence can't be demonstrated in this way because God is not caused to exist by another.

A demonstration *quia*, however, might seem more promising. In such an explanation, a cause is demonstrated by appeal to its effect as when we deduce the existence of a fire from the smoke that it produces. As applied to the divine case, we might hope to deduce the existence of God from God's effects.

All of this is, perhaps, straightforward enough. We might note, however, a perceptible move here from Anselm's a priori demonstration of God's existence to Aquinas's a posteriori demonstration of God's existence that is indicative of a very coarse-grained shift from Platonist rationalism to Aristotelian empiricism. Whereas Anselm had hoped to prove the existence of God from reason alone, Aquinas hopes to prove the existence of God from our experience of the world. (That this shift does not represent a clean break is nicely witnessed by Aquinas's "fourth way" argument for God's existence, which is based on degrees of truth.)

9.4. The Argument from Motion, the First Step

Having suggested that God's existence might be proved from God's effects, Aquinas goes on to offer five main arguments—sometimes called the "five ways"—for the existence of God. He claims that the "first and most evident" of these arguments "is the one from motion," which takes as its starting premise something that Aquinas thinks will be evident to everyone, namely, that there is motion in the world. Note that Aquinas's understanding of motion is not limited to local motion or change of place. Aquinas counts as motion any real change from being potentially something to being actually something—for example, from being potentially in Boston to being actually in Boston, from being potentially warm to being actually warm, from being potentially asleep to being actually asleep.

What we might think of as the first step of Aquinas's argument from motion focuses on things that are moved or changed. Aquinas claims, "Whatever is moved is moved by another." His thought is that the ordinary changes we witness with our senses must be brought about by some distinct agent. In support of this step, he tells us,

> Everything moved is moved by something else, for an object is only moved insofar as it has potentiality for that to which it is moved, while something produces motion only insofar as it is actual. To move something is only to bring it from potentiality to actuality, and only an actual being can do so. But the same object cannot at the same time be actual and potential in the same respect. Therefore, nothing can produce and undergo motion in the same respect and in the same way. Therefore everything moved needs to be moved by something else. (Part I, Question 2, article 3)

Aquinas's premise draws on Aristotle's views on change, but the central idea is intuitive enough. When change occurs, something goes from being potentially F to being actually F—say, from being potentially warm to being actually warm. But if the very nature of the thing in question could make it go from being potentially warm to being actually warm, then it would have been warm already, that is, it couldn't be merely potentially warm to begin with. Real change therefore requires a distinct agent that "reduces" the subject from being potentially something-or-other to being actually something-or-other.

Although the main idea behind the first step of Aquinas's argument is, I think, fairly plausible, it is widely considered today to be one of the argument's weakest links. Two objections are regularly raised against it. The first stems from the apparent possibility of self-moved movers. Ordinary organisms, for example, appear to move themselves without—at least in principle—being moved by another. It is true that all the organisms we encounter have presumably either been created, or brought into being, by something else, and are thus moved movers in Aquinas's broad sense of "moved." Nonetheless, we might still suppose that Aquinas's general principle is not certain, since organisms seem to be able to "reduce" themselves from being potentially something-or-other to being actually something-or-other with respect to at least some properties.

A second objection commonly raised to Aquinas's suggestion that nothing can reduce itself from potentiality to actuality is rooted in the decline of Aristotelian natural philosophy. In the light of Newtonian (and post-Newtonian) physics, it has become natural to suppose that there might be something that is moving—because it has always been moving—and yet is not moved by another. Perhaps some things have always been in motion in the world, and yet were never moved by another. Such things would in a sense be neither moved by another, nor be self-moved, but would rather have motion as their default state. Such things would, of course, violate Aquinas's premise, since they would be things that change without being changed by another.

9.5. The Argument from Motion, the Second Step

The second step of Aquinas's argument from motion turns our attention from things moved to the things doing the moving, from the changed to the changer. Aquinas claims that a changer must either be a derivative source of change or an original source of change. He argues that the changes we witness in the world cannot be the result of an infinite series of derivative changers:

> Therefore, everything moved needs to be moved by something else. And if the cause of motion is moved, the cause itself needs to be moved by another,

> and that other by another. But this regress ought not to be endless, since there would then be no first cause of motion and so no other cause of motion. For example, a stick causes motion only because a hand moves it. (Part I, Question 2, article 3)

At a first pass, Aquinas seems to be arguing that everything that is moved must be moved by another and there cannot be an infinite series of moved movers going backward into the past. It can't be the case, for example, that a chicken causes an egg, an egg causes a chicken, a chicken causes an egg, and so on, all the way back in an infinite temporal regress.

Although it is difficult to imagine an infinite series reaching back in time, many people today think that such a temporal regress is perfectly possible. Why, they ask, couldn't there be an infinite series of moved movers? Indeed, contemporary cosmology might even support such a view: there is a big bang, followed by a big collapse, followed by a big bang, and so forth. Although in such a view there would be no first cause of a first big bang, there would be a cause of every big bang, namely, a big collapse, and a cause of every big collapse, namely, a big bang.

Aquinas himself, however, probably did not have an infinite temporal series in mind in his argument from motion. Indeed, he maintains that philosophically speaking it is an open question whether the world has a beginning in time. What he means to deny is the possibility of an infinite series of dependent per se causes. In a *dependent per se* series of causes, the causal power of each intermediary link is dependent upon the causal power of a prior link. As an example of such a causal series we might think of John Locke's example of the world resting on top of a turtle, resting on top of an elephant, resting on top of . . . , and so on. Such a causal series, it might be thought, cannot be infinite since there must be a first cause from which all the other links ultimately derive their efficacy. (Similarly, you might think that the top floor of a building requires a bottom floor, not just an infinite series of lower floors.)

If Aquinas has in mind a series of dependent per se causes, he would be suggesting that all secondary causes derive their causal powers from higher causes, which perhaps could derive their causal powers from higher causes, and so on, but that such a chain cannot go on indefinitely, since there has to be an original source of all the activity in order for it to trickle down to the lower levels. Such a picture would seem to make the previous step more defensible (although it might raise new worries about its relation to the supposedly empirical premise that we witness change in the world).

9.6. The Argument from Motion, the Conclusion

From the two steps just outlined, Aquinas draws the conclusion that since there are moved movers, and there cannot be an infinite regress of moved movers, there must be an unmoved mover that is the ultimate source of change in the world, namely, God.

There is a natural worry here, however, that Aquinas's conclusion might be inconsistent with the first step of his argument. After all, that step seems to imply that nothing could be a self-mover, and the conclusion seems to suggest that there is a self-mover.

There is a real wrinkle here, but it is far from obvious that it presents a difficulty for Aquinas. What the first step really denies is that beings that undergo change might themselves bring about the change that they undergo. In his conclusion, Aquinas is not claiming that there is something that undergoes change and brings about that change itself. Rather he is claiming that there is an original source of all the change that occurs to things that suffer change. Put in different terms, Aquinas's first step denies that there are any unmoved dependent movers, while his conclusion asserts that there is at least one unmoved independent mover.

It is probably also worth noting that although Aquinas thinks that everyone will grant that the unmoved mover is God, he doesn't really need that concession at this point. It is enough for his purposes at this stage that it be granted that there is an unmoved mover—even an unmoved mover that might possibly be nonintelligent, nonbenevolent, and indeed might not be even unique. As the *Summa* progresses, Aquinas attempts to show that the unmoved mover must have all the canonical attributes of God, in effect arguing that the first cause really is God and not just an unmoved mover.

9.7. The Argument from Providence

Aquinas's "fifth way" takes as its starting point the apparent empirical fact that we find many nonintelligent things that naturally act in such a way as to bring about their own flourishing or their own perfection according to their kind. This is perhaps most evident in the case of plants and animals that act by instinct. Trees grow roots downward where they reach water and leaves upward where they find sunlight. Spiders spin webs that enable them to survive and flourish.

Starting with that premise, Aquinas contends that we must posit the existence of a supreme intelligence that can be identified with God. Here's his argument in total:

> We take the fifth way from the governance of things. Certain things lacking knowledge, namely, natural material substances, act frequently in the same way in order to achieve what is best, and so they evidently achieve their goal by striving for it, not by chance. But things lacking knowledge strive for goals only if a being with knowledge and intelligence directs them, as, for example, an archer aims an arrow. Therefore, there is a being with intelligence that orders all the things of nature to their ends, and we call this being God. (Part I, Question 2, article 3)

Aquinas, selectively following Aristotle, suggests that the fact that unintelligent things regularly act in ways that bring about their own flourishing must be accounted for either by chance or by a providential God. Aquinas further insists that this fortuitous fact cannot be explained by chance. Beneficial things might indeed come about by chance on occasion—as when you run into a friend at the grocery store by accident. So, perhaps, a single tree growing roots downward or a single spider spinning a web might be attributed to chance. But the claim that such beneficial things happen regularly cannot plausibly be attributed to chance, according to Aquinas. The widespread well-directedness of nonintelligent beings thus, according to Aquinas, proves the existence of God.

Darwinian evolution, of course, presents a powerful prima facie counterexample to Aquinas's claim that the well-adapted features of nonintelligent organisms cannot be accounted for by essentially chancy processes. It suggests that the fact that trees grow roots downward and leaves upward, for example, can be explained through a long process of random change and differential selection without any appeal to providential design. Although the theory of evolution is not, as some people imagine, inconsistent with the existence of God, or even with a providential creation, it does present a challenging response to the argument of Aquinas's fifth way. We return to design arguments in more detail when we get to David Hume. For now, it is only important to note that since Aquinas accepts design arguments, he feels entitled to appeal to them when he seeks to establish the impersonal and personal attributes of God later in the *Summa Theologica*.

Further Study

Peter Adamson, *The History of Philosophy without Any Gaps: Philosophy in Later Antiquity*. Podcast, 2011–13; available online and through iTunes. An excellent, entertaining introduction to philosophical currents in the Islamic World; includes an introduction to the Arabic-Latin translation movement.

Thomas Aquinas, *Summa Contra Gentiles*, 5 vols., trans. Anton Pegis, James Anderson, Vernon J. Bourke, and Charles O'Neil. Notre Dame, IN: University of Notre Dame, 1975.

Thomas Aquinas, *The Summa Theologica of St. Thomas Aquinas*, trans. English Dominican Fathers, 3 vols. New York: Benziger, 1947–48; reprinted, Allen, TX: Christian Classics, 1981.

G. K. Chesterton, *Saint Thomas Aquinas*, first printed 1933, widely reprinted. A short, popular biography by the colorful G. K. Chesterton. Copies are widely available on the internet.

Ralph McInerny and John O'Callaghan, "Saint Thomas Aquinas," *Stanford Encyclopedia of Philosophy* (Spring 2015 edition), ed. Edward N. Zalta, http://plato.stanford.edu/archives/spr2015/entries/aquinas/. Advanced overview of Aquinas's philosophical thought from two distinguished scholars.

Richard Regan, trans. and ed., *Thomas Aquinas, A Summary of Philosophy*. Indianapolis, IN: Hackett, 2002. A student-friendly, highly abridged edition of Aquinas's *Summa Theologica*.

10

Aquinas's *Summa Theologica*

What Is the Impersonal Nature of God?

10.1. Is God Simple?

In the previous chapter, we saw Aquinas argue that God is the cause of the world. In this chapter, we see how Aquinas attempts to leverage that conclusion to show that God must have traditional divine attributes, including simplicity, perfection, and infinitude. In short, Aquinas argues that anything that is a first cause must also be simple, perfect, and infinite. There is, however, a small wrinkle that we should note here but that we mostly ignore as we proceed. Aquinas maintains that, strictly speaking, we cannot grasp God's true, positive nature. So, to be precise, in what follows we see Aquinas arguing that the first cause cannot be complex, imperfect, or finite. By bringing out what the first cause cannot be, Aquinas maintains, we may home in, as it were, on the transcendent nature of God. By seeing that God couldn't possibly be complex, imperfect, or finite, we get closer to appreciating the sense in which he must be simple, perfect, and infinite. With that wrinkle noted, however, it generally does no harm to think of Aquinas as arguing for God having certain positive attributes.

In order to understand Aquinas's claim that God is simple, it is essential to have a sense of the ways in which Aquinas thinks other things are complex. Aquinas suggests that an ordinary substance like my dog Martha, for example, is complex in at least two ways. First, as a material object, she can be decomposed into the metaphysical "parts" of matter and form. As a rough first pass, we can take Martha's form to be the nature in virtue of which she is a dog or the nature that she has in common with all other dogs. Furthermore, and again as a rough pass, we can take Martha's matter to be the flesh and bones in which her nature inheres, and that distinguishes her from all other dogs (since they are the same nature in other parcels of matter). Second, as a created object, Martha can be decomposed into her essence and her existence. That these are distinct is suggested by the fact that we could have

Saints, Heretics, and Atheists. Jeffrey K. McDonough, Oxford University Press. © Oxford University Press 2022.
DOI: 10.1093/oso/9780197563847.003.0010

a definition, or conception, of Martha without Martha existing. (In this respect, she could have been analogous to a unicorn.) According to Aquinas, all creatures—material and immaterial alike—can be decomposed along this dimension. So, although an angel is not a composite of form and matter—since it is immaterial—it is nonetheless a composite of essence and existence.

In his *Summa Theologica*, Aquinas argues that God is not complex in the ways that creatures are complex. We might think of his argument for that conclusion as proceeding in two steps. First, Aquinas argues that God cannot be a composite of form and matter. One argument he gives for this step is that form is what reduces matter from potentiality to actuality—that is, form is what causes matter to be this or that specifically. So, for example, form is what causes a lump of copper to be, say, a bowl or a vase. God therefore can't be a composite of form and matter because there would have to be something that is causally prior to God himself, namely, the form of God, but of course there can be no such cause of the first cause. God therefore cannot be a composite of matter and form.

Having argued that God cannot be a complex of matter and form, Aquinas next argues that God cannot be a complex of essence and existence, or as he puts it, that "God's essence and his existing [are] identical in him." Aquinas summarizes his line of thought as follows:

> I answer that God is both his essence and his existing. . . . Were this not so, God's existence would need to be caused by its essential principles or by an external cause. But it is impossible for a thing's existing to be caused by its essential principles, for nothing can be the cause of its own existence if its existence is caused. Therefore, anything whose existing differs from its essence, must be caused to exist by another. But this can't be true of God, since he is the cause of every effect. Therefore, God's essence and existing are identical. (Part I, Question 2, article 4, translation modified; this chapter follows the translation of Aquinas's *Summa Theologica* in Regan [2002] unless noted)

Aquinas's thought is that if God's essence, nature, or form were distinct from his existence, then either God's essence would have to cause its own existence or something distinct would have to cause it to exist. The first option is absurd because nothing is able to cause itself to come into existence. (How could something that doesn't exist cause anything?) The second option, however, can also be ruled out since God is the first cause. (Since God is the first cause, how could something else cause God to exist?) Aquinas concludes that God's essence must be the same thing as his existence. That is to say, he concludes that God must be simple with respect to the essence-existence distinction as well.

10.2. Is God Perfect?

Having argued that God does not have metaphysical "parts," Aquinas goes on to contend that God lacks no perfection—that is, that God is perfect in every way. Aquinas's leading idea is that causation essentially involves the transfer of existence, actuality, or form from a cause to an effect. So, for example, we might think of one billiard ball causing another billiard ball to move as essentially involving the first ball giving motion to the second ball. Likewise, we might think of a hot poker stuck in a bucket of cold water as causing the cold water to become warmer by transferring some of the poker's heat.

With this basic model in mind, Aquinas distinguishes between two kinds of causation, which he calls "univocal" and "equivocal." In the case of *univocal* causation, the cause communicates its form to its effect so that the cause and the effect share the same form in the same way. Aquinas's favorite example of univocal causation involves the begetting of offspring: an oak tree communicates its form to a sapling so that they both come to share the same form in the same way; a parent turtle communicates its form to a baby turtle so that both come to share the same form in the same way.

In the case of *equivocal* causation, the form of the cause does not come to exist in the effect in the same way. So, for example, the artist causes her idea of Caesar to be realized in a lump of clay, but the form does not come to exist in the lump of clay in the same way that it existed in the artist's mind. Aquinas's own preferred example of equivocal causation is heating by the sun. He holds that the sun is the source of all heat in the world, and yet the heat that one finds in the hot sand of a beach is of a lower kind than the heat one finds in the sun itself. According to Aquinas, the sun causes the heating of the sand, but the sun and the sand do not share the same form in the same way.

With the distinction between univocal and equivocal causation in hand, Aquinas argues that God, as the first efficient cause, must be the original source of all the world's perfections. Creating things essentially involves communicating to them all the perfections they have. Now clearly God cannot be the univocal cause of every created perfection, since no creature can enjoy the same form as God in the same way. Aquinas concludes that God must be the equivocal cause of absolutely all things. But to be the equivocal cause of all things, he must have all perfections—either as they are, or in some higher way—within his nature. Thus God, as the first cause of everything, must be perfect in every possible way.

We are now in a position to make sense of Aquinas's main response to the question "Does God possess the perfections of all things?":

> I answer that the perfections of all things exist in God. We can consider this from two perspectives. First, any perfection in an effect needs to be found in its efficient cause either in the same respect if the cause is univocal (e.g., human beings beget human beings) or in a more outstanding way if the cause is nonunivocal (e.g., the likeness of the sun and what the sun produces). Effects preexist in the power of their efficient causes, and efficient causes are perfect. . . . But God is the first efficient cause of things. Therefore, the perfections of all things necessarily preexist in him in a more outstanding way. (Part I, Question 4, article 2)

10.3. Is God Infinite?

Having addressed God's simplicity, perfection, and goodness, Aquinas proceeds to consider God's infinitude. Although Aquinas's discussion of divine infinitude in the *Summa Theologica* covers four articles, its pithy core can be found here:

> I answer that matter does not perfect form. Rather, matter restricts the fullness of form. And so the infinite, as possessed by a form that matter does not limit, has the nature of something perfect. But the most formal of all things is existing itself. Therefore, since God is his subsistent existing, and his existing is not received in something, he is infinite and perfect. (Part I, Question 7, article 1)

In order to get a better grip on what Aquinas is driving at here it may be helpful to set three main ideas out on the table.

First, in suggesting that God is infinite, Aquinas is directly opposing an ancient view of infinity, and indeed he is trying to turn that older notion on its head. According to that older notion, the term "infinity" connotes a lack of distinctness, a privation of exactness, or a mere potentiality for further specification. Thus Aristotle, for example, argues that infinity shouldn't be attributed to the divine, or what is fully actual, but rather to bare matter or what is merely potential. For Aquinas, on the other hand, the term "infinity" (at least in its positive respect) connotes not potentiality, but rather actuality. An infinitude is a superabundance that might become finite by a limitation or privation. Rather than identifying bare matter with the infinite, Aquinas therefore wants to identify the infinite with its opposite, namely, pure form or actuality.

Second, Aquinas suggests that one way in which actuality might be limited is through informing matter. A formal nature in and of itself can be common to many different individuals: it could serve as the nature of this, that, or another thing. By being united with matter, however, it is limited to a particular object and thus it is limited by matter. This is what Aquinas is getting at when he says, "Matter restricts the fullness of form." The upshot of this point is that God, as an immaterial being, may be infinite in a way that no physical object can be.

Third, Aquinas suggests that another way in which actuality might be limited is through realizing some essence. The idea here is, I think, fairly intuitive. If we think of every creature as being made out of existence, or pure being, we can think that the pure being that constitutes a turtle or a grasshopper is extremely limited. (After all, the pure being might have constituted a lion or a tiger.) But what limits pure being in this case is just the essence of the creatures in question. The upshot of this point is that every creature—including immaterial creatures—is a composite of being and essence, and so every creature is limited in some way. God, on the other hand, who is wholly perfect and wholly actual, whose essence is his existence, is not limited even in this way. God is, therefore, according to Aquinas, truly, absolutely infinite.

10.4. Is God One?

Having argued that God is infinite, Aquinas goes on to argue that God is immutable and eternal, but he closes his discussion of "how God is known in himself" with a treatment of God's uniqueness. Recall that the argument from motion insisted that there must be a first mover to get things started, as it were. But Aquinas's argument would seem to be consistent with there being several unmoved movers. So, for all the argument from motion tells us, polytheism is still a live option. In order to block this possibility, Aquinas argues in *Summa Theologica* Part I, Question 11 that we are in a position to see that the unmoved mover must be unique, or, as he puts it, must be "one." In support of this conclusion, he offers three arguments drawing on conclusions he has already established.

A first argument looks back to Aquinas's argument for divine simplicity:

> First, the simplicity of God demonstrates his uniqueness. For the source whereby an individual thing is this particular thing can in no way be communicated to many things. For example, the source whereby Socrates is human can be communicated to many things, but the source whereby Socrates is this particular human being can be communicated to only one thing. Therefore, if Socrates were human by the source whereby he is this human being, there could not be many human beings, just as there could not be many Socrates. But God is his nature and so [he is] God by the source whereby he is *this* God. Therefore, being God and being this God are identical. Therefore, there cannot be several Gods. (*Summa Theologica* Part I, Question 11, article 3)

The main idea here should be clearer when considered in the context of Aquinas's more general metaphysics. As we have seen in passing, Aquinas maintains that two human beings, for example, may have their form (e.g., humanity) in common and yet be different particulars in virtue of informing different parcels of matter (e.g., Socrates is humanity in this parcel of matter, Plato is humanity in that parcel of matter). At a first pass at least, in this case it is matter that makes Socrates and Plato distinct from one another. Aquinas suggests as a general principle that whatever makes something particular or distinct can't be shared by many things—if this parcel of matter is what distinguishes Socrates from Plato, then they can't both share this parcel of matter. Given God's simplicity, however, what makes God something particular or distinct must be his whole being or essence. But if it is granted that what makes anything unique can't be shared, it must follow that no other particular can share in God's being or essence, that is, it must follow that God is unique.

Aquinas's second argument for divine uniqueness looks back to his argument for divine perfection:

> Second, the infinity of God's perfection demonstrates that there is only one God. God includes within himself the whole perfection of existing.

> Therefore, if there were several Gods, they would need to differ. Therefore, something would be proper to one that was not proper to another. But if such a thing were a privation, the one deprived would not be absolutely perfect, and if such a thing were a perfection, the other would lack it. And so there is only one infinite source. (*Summa Theologica* Part I, Question 11, article 3)

The central idea here is that if there were two Gods, then they would have to differ either with respect to some perfection or with respect to some privation (i.e., some absence of perfection). But they couldn't differ with respect to some perfection since God has all the perfections, and they couldn't differ with respect to some privation since no privations are appropriate to God. Aquinas concludes that there can be only one God.

Aquinas's third argument looks back to his fifth way of proving God's existence and aims to make God's uniqueness more intuitive or likely. It reads,

> Third, the uniqueness of the world demonstrates the uniqueness of God. All existing things are related to one another insofar as some are subordinate to others. But different things would not be integrated in one orderly set of relations unless one thing disposed them. For one thing intrinsically causes one thing, and many things cause one thing only accidentally. And so one thing brings many things into an orderly set of relations better than many things would. But what is first is most perfect, and such intrinsically, not accidentally. Therefore, there is necessarily only one first being that brings everything into an orderly set of relations, and this first being is God. (*Summa Theologica* Part I, Question 11, article 3)

The main idea here is that the world displays a certain unity or harmony among its parts. That unity or harmony must have a cause, and that cause must either be one or many. But as anyone who has worked on a committee knows, the likelihood of harmony seems to decrease in direct proportion to the number of individuals involved. That is to say, Aquinas suggests that the extreme harmony of the created world is more likely to be the result of a single author working alone than of many different authors collaborating. The unity of the world gives us reason to suppose that there is only one God.

10.5. Analogical Predication

We have now seen Aquinas argue that God is simple, infinite, perfect, and one. In the next chapter we find him arguing that God is knowledgeable, has a will, and is loving. But does God know things in the same sense in which we know things? Does God love in the same sense in which we love? More generally, how are we to understand the relationship between predicates that are ascribed to God and predicates that are ascribed to creatures? Medieval philosophers struggled to respond to this question and offered many different competing answers. Aquinas's own answer tries to steer a middle course between two more extreme views.

The first extreme position suggests that the relationship between properties ascribed to God and properties ascribed to creatures differs only in degree, not kind. God and creatures are both good in the same sense; it is just that God is much better than any creature. In Aquinas's terminology, in this view, goodness is predicated *univocally* of God and humans.

Much can be said in favor of the univocal account. In particular, a univocal account provides a straightforward explanation of how we can come to understand God's attributes and how we can speak of them. We may come to understand the property of "goodness" by our encounters with everyday people, and we can learn to use the predicate "goodness" in applying it to them.

The univocal account, however, also brings with it a prima facie difficulty. In humans, goodness and intelligence, for example, seem to be distinct properties. I might be good but not intelligent, or my cat might be intelligent but not very good. As we have seen, however, Aquinas is committed to God's goodness being identical to his intelligence as well as to his very being. This might be taken to suggest that goodness as applied to human beings and as applied to God can't really be understood in the same way after all.

Another extreme position suggests that predicates such as "goodness" and "intelligence" are applied in completely different senses to God and humans. According to such a solution, when we say that God is good, we mean something entirely different from what we mean when we say that my neighbor is good. When we speak of God's goodness and my goodness, we are equivocating just as much as when we talk about my credit union being a bank and the town levee being a bank.

There are virtues to the equivocal account. In particular, if we disambiguate the two senses of "goodness" and "intelligence" by calling them "divine goodness" and "human goodness," "divine intelligence" and "human intelligence," there is clearly no problem in supposing that divine goodness is identical to its subject as well as to divine intelligence, while human goodness is distinct from its subject as well as from human intelligence. It can thus solve an important objection to the univocal account. It can also underscore—in a way that might be thought to be pious—the enormous difference in kind between God and his creatures.

The equivocal account, however, also carries with it a rather obvious difficulty, namely, it leaves a complete gap between the predicates that we attribute to humans and those that we attribute to God. If predicates are applied equivocally, we can make absolutely no inferences about God's goodness on the basis of human goodness, or about how to apply the predicate "is good" to God on the basis of how we apply the predicate "is good" to humans. (To do so would be like trying to infer that since financial banks have money, riverbanks must have money too.)

Aquinas's own account attempts to find a middle position between the univocal and equivocal approaches. His proposed solution suggests that predicates like "is good" and "is intelligent" are applied to God and humans neither univocally, nor equivocally, but *analogically*. By this, Aquinas means that predicates like "is good" and "is intelligent" are applied to God and humans in different but importantly related ways. There is a kind of similarity between the way we apply predicates to God and to his creatures that is closer than equivocation, but not as close as univocality.

Aquinas's account may seem to strike a nice balance between the univocal and equivocal accounts. It faces a challenge of its own, however, in explaining what is involved in two terms having an "analogous meaning." This isn't the place to dig too deeply into Aquinas's complex account of analogical meaning, but we might try to get some notion of what he has in mind by way of an example (which I borrow from Robert Pasnau and Christopher Shields [2004, 117]). Consider the way the term "healthy" is used in the three following sentences:

a. To be healthy is to flourish in mind and body.
b. Albert's complexion is healthy.
c. Albert's diet is healthy.

Here it's worth highlighting three points: (1) The meanings of the term "healthy" as used in these three sentences are clearly related to one another (i.e., they are not simply equivocal). (2) Nonetheless, "healthy" does not mean exactly the same thing in each of these sentences (i.e., they are not univocal). In b, for example, "healthy" means something like a sign of health, whereas in c, "healthy" means something like a cause of health. (3) Finally, there's an asymmetry between a, on the one hand, and b & c on the other hand. More specifically, the meaning of b & c seems to depend on the deeper, core meaning provided by a.

Aquinas appears to have something like this picture in mind when he invokes the doctrine of analogical predication in connection with the divine attributes. Consider the three following sentences:

a. God is good.
b. Martha is good.
c. Spring break is good.

Here as well, we can say that (1) the meaning of "good" as used in these three sentences is related (i.e., not simply equivocal); but that (2) the meaning of "good" is not exactly the same in these three cases (i.e., not univocal); and (3) that the meaning of "good" in b & c is asymmetrically dependent upon the meaning of good in a. God, Martha, and spring break are all good, but they are neither all good in exactly the same sense, nor in entirely unrelated senses. Martha and spring break are good in a sense that is analogous, but only analogous, to God's goodness.

Further Study

Thomas Aquinas, *Summa Contra Gentiles*, 5 vols., trans. Anton Pegis, James Anderson, Vernon J. Bourke, and Charles O'Neil. Notre Dame, IN: University of Notre Dame, 1975.

Thomas Aquinas, *The Summa Theologica of St. Thomas Aquinas*, trans. English Dominican Fathers, 3 vols. New York: Benziger, 1947–48; reprinted, Allen, TX: Christian Classics, 1981.

Jennifer E. Ashworth, "Medieval Theories of Analogy." *Stanford Encyclopedia of Philosophy* (Winter 2013 edition), ed. Edward N. Zalta, http://plato.stanford.edu/archives/win2013/entries/analogy-medieval/. A comprehensive overview of medieval theories of analogy, including a section on Aquinas's views and an extensive bibliography.

Robert Pasnau and Christopher Shields, *The Philosophy of Aquinas*. Cambridge, MA: Westview Press, 2004. A helpful introduction to the philosophy of Thomas

Aquinas that does not presuppose prior familiarity with Aquinas or medieval philosophy.

Richard Regan, trans. and ed., *Thomas Aquinas, A Summary of Philosophy*. Indianapolis, IN: Hackett, 2002. A student-friendly, highly abridged edition of Aquinas's *Summa Theologica*.

11
Aquinas's *Summa Theologica*
What Is the Personal Nature of God?

In chapter 9 we saw Aquinas argue that there must be an unmoved mover on which all created things ultimately depend. In chapter 10 we saw him build on that result to argue that the unmoved mover must have impersonal attributes canonically attributed to God. We saw him argue that the unmoved mover must be simple, perfect, infinite, and one. Aquinas's next big step is to argue that the unmoved mover must also have personal attributes canonically attributed to God, attributes including intelligence, will, and love. As we see in this chapter, in arguing that the unmoved mover has personal attributes canonically attributed to God, Aquinas once again attempts to leverage the results he takes himself to have established in earlier questions of the *Summa Theologica*.

11.1. Divine Knowledge

Aquinas's central argument for divine knowledge in the *Summa Theologica* attempts to prove that God has knowledge from the established conclusion that God is immaterial (Part I, Question 14). That argument, however, is both controversial and draws heavily upon aspects of Aquinas's broader framework that we haven't considered. Fortunately for us, he offers another argument that is easier to appreciate in his *Summa Contra Gentiles*. It runs as follows:

> Again, that which tends determinately to some end either has set itself that end or the end has been set for it by another. Otherwise, it would tend no more to this end than to that. Now, natural things tend to determinate ends. They do not fulfill their natural needs by chance, since they would not do so always or for the most part, but rarely, which is the domain of chance.... Since, then, things do not set for themselves an end, because they have no

Saints, Heretics, and Atheists. Jeffrey K. McDonough, Oxford University Press. © Oxford University Press 2022.
DOI: 10.1093/oso/9780197563847.003.0011

> notion of what an end is, the end must be set for them by another, who is the author of nature. . . . We call Him God, as is clear from what we have said. But God could not set an end for nature unless He had understanding. God is, therefore, intelligent. (Book I, Chapter 45; this chapter follows the translation of Aquinas's *Summa Contra Gentiles* in Pegis and Bourke [1975])

The argument here might be thought of as looking back to Aquinas's "fifth way" (touched on briefly in chapter 9, section 7). In that argument, Aquinas maintains that the world is beneficially ordered for its creatures, and that such an ordering is best explained by appeal to a single creator or artificer. Here, Aquinas suggests that such an ordering implies that that artificer—God—must also be intelligent and thus must have knowledge.

Having argued that God is knowledgeable, Aquinas immediately proceeds in the *Summa Theologica* to defend a number of substantial theses about God's knowledge. First, he argues that God has perfect self-knowledge, and indeed that God knows himself simply by being himself. Emphasizing the first point, Aquinas tells us,

> I answer that to comprehend things is to know things as perfectly as they are knowable, and things are knowable insofar as they are actual. But God's power to know is as great as his actuality, since he knows because he is actual and without any matter or potentiality. And so he knows himself as much as he is knowable. And so he perfectly comprehends himself. (Part I, Question 14, article 3; this chapter follows the translation of Aquinas's *Summa Theologica* in Regan [2002])

We might think of Aquinas's suggestion here as having two parts. First, Aquinas thinks of having knowledge as having a perfection or an actuality. When, for example, I learn that a brontosaurus has a long tail, I go from potentially knowing something to actually knowing something. But since God is fully actual—has every perfection—he must actually know everything as fully as it can be known. Second, Aquinas suggests that things can be known only to the extent that they are actual, and indeed the more fully realized something is, the better it can, in principle, be known. As a completely actual, completely realized being, however, God is thus in principle the most fully knowable thing. Putting the two parts together, it follows that God must have perfect self-knowledge, since he knows his own nature as fully as possible, and his own nature is as perfectly knowable as can be.

Second, Aquinas argues that in addition to having perfect self-knowledge, God also has knowledge of things other than himself. There is an interesting wrinkle in Aquinas's argument, however. He maintains that when we come to know something, we come to know it because it acts on us. I come to know that Martha has gotten into the garbage because rays of light impinge on my eyes. I come to know that she is taking a drink of water because I can hear her lapping at (what I hope is) her bowl. Aquinas insists, however, that this model cannot be applied to God since nothing can act on God (or, if you like, because God is already fully actual). Aquinas therefore suggests that God knows other things not because they act on him, but because he acts on them. More carefully, Aquinas maintains that God knows other things because he knows his own nature perfectly, and in knowing his own nature perfectly, he knows what is produced by his own nature (see *Summa Theologica*, Part I, Question 14, article 5).

Third, Aquinas maintains that God has knowledge of future contingents. A future contingent for Aquinas is something that is not fully determined by nonfree causes. So, for example, my choosing chocolate at the ice cream store tomorrow is a future contingent provided that it is true and left up to my free choice. The core of Aquinas's account of God's knowledge of future contingents can be found in the following passage from the *Summa Theologica*:

> We can regard things as contingent in two ways: in one way as actually existing; in the second way as existing in their causes. [i] In the first way, we regard contingent things as present, not future, and as determined to one outcome, not contingent to one of several outcomes. And so we can know them with certitude. [ii] But in the second way, we regard contingent things as future and not yet determined to one outcome. And so we cannot know them with certitude, since whoever knows a contingent effect only in its cause has only probable knowledge about it. [iii] But God knows all contingent things both in their causes and in their actual existence. And although contingent things become actual successively, God knows them all at once. This is so because . . . everything in time is present to God from eternity, both because he has the natures of things present with him, and because his sight is borne from eternity over all things as they exist in their presence to him. And so God knows contingent things unerringly, since they are subject to his inspection by their presence, and yet they are future contingent things in relation to their own causes. (Part I, Question 14, article 13)

We might pause here to highlight three main points, with each point corresponding to one of the numbers inserted into the passage just quoted.

Aquinas's first point is that something being contingent is consistent with its being known with certainty. Even if my choosing chocolate ice cream is a future contingent because it is not determined independently of my free choice, you might still know with certainty that I have chosen chocolate ice cream if you happen to see me placing my order at the ice cream store. Thus, insofar as one experiences a future contingent as present, one can know it with certainty.

Aquinas's second point is that a future contingent cannot be known by us with certainty prior to its being present to us. The reason for this is simply that—although prior conditions can make a future contingent more or less likely—such conditions by definition cannot make the outcome of a future contingent determinate. Insofar as we have knowledge of future contingents prior to their being present to us, we can therefore have only probable or causal knowledge of them.

Aquinas's third point is that God has both kinds of knowledge of future contingents. God, of course, has knowledge of causal influences on future contingents. All the information that leads to my knowledge that the Packers are unlikely to win a Super Bowl anytime soon is also available to God as well. More significantly, however, Aquinas additionally maintains that God has certain knowledge of every future contingent because, with respect to God, every future contingent is experienced as present. The idea here is that since we are within the order of time, we can have certain knowledge of a future contingent only once it has occurred. God, however, standing outside of time, experiences all events within the temporal order simultaneously and thus doesn't have to wait for an event to occur within the temporal sequence in order to experience it as happening now. God can thus have certain knowledge of future contingents because all events are present to him, and his having such knowledge does not undermine their contingency, since they are nonetheless not predetermined by non-freely willed causes within the order of nature.

11.2. Divine Will

Having established that God has knowledge, Aquinas next argues that God also has a will—that God chooses things, does things voluntarily, and has volitions. In fact, Aquinas sees the conclusion that God has a will as following immediately from his having perfect knowledge. Aquinas maintains that through his omniscience, God must have knowledge of what is good. But having knowledge of what is good, Aquinas holds, necessarily involves desiring or willing the good. In short, to know the good is to will the good, and since God must know the good, he must will the good. This line of thought comes out especially clearly in a passage from the *Summa Contra Gentiles*:

> From the fact that God is endowed with intellect it follows that He is endowed with will. For, since the understood good is the proper object of the will, the understood good is, as such willed. Now that which is understood is by reference to the one who understands. Hence, he who grasps the good by his intellect is, as such, endowed with will. But God grasps the good by His intellect. For, since the activity of His intellect is perfect, as appears from what has been said, He understands being together with the qualification of the good. He is, therefore, endowed with will. (Book I, Chapter 72; see also *Summa Theologica*, Book I, Question 19, article 1)

There is, of course, a rather natural objection to Aquinas's argument. We might suppose that it is one thing to understand the good and another thing to will the good. I might understand that getting more exercise and eating less ice cream would be good. But that isn't the same as willing to get more exercise and eat less ice cream. But Aquinas stands his ground on this point. To his way of thinking, my not willing more exercise must stem from an imperfect understanding of the good of more exercise, and my not willing to eat less ice cream must similarly arise from a lack of understanding of the good of laying off the desserts. It simply makes no sense to Aquinas that one could see the good in something and not have some will for that good.

In the previous section, we saw Aquinas claim that what God *knows* first and foremost is his own nature or essence. Accordingly, Aquinas also suggests that what God *wills* first and foremost is himself. In the *Summa Contra Gentiles*, he writes,

> The understood good is the object of the will, as has been said. But that which is principally understood by God is the divine essence, as was proved above. The divine essence therefore is principally the object of the divine will. (Book I, Chapter 74)

A little further on in the same chapter, he continues,

> Furthermore, for each being endowed with a will the principal object willed is the ultimate end. For the end is willed through itself, and through it other things become objects of will. But the ultimate end is God Himself, since He is the highest good, as has been shown. Therefore, God is the principal object of His will. (Book I, Chapter 74)

Significantly, Aquinas takes his reasoning here to be perfectly general. Every intelligent being, he maintains, necessarily wills the highest good it understands. God, however, has perfect, intimate, necessary knowledge of the highest good of all, and so God necessarily wills that highest good (which, in this case, is himself). God is therefore the principal object of his own will.

While Aquinas maintains that God is the principal object of the divine will, he also grants that God wills the existence of other things. In the *Summa Theologica* he writes,

> I answer that things of nature have an inclination from nature both regarding their own good and to pour out their good into other things as much as possible. And so efficient causes, inasmuch as they are actual and perfect, produce things like themselves. And so also it belongs to the nature of the will that it as much as possible communicates to others the good it possesses. And this belongs most to the divine will, from which every perfection is derived by some likeness. And so if things of nature, insofar as they are perfect, communicate their good to other things, much more does it belong to the divine will as far as possible to communicate its good to other beings by likeness. Therefore, God wills both himself and other things to exist. But he wills himself as the end, and he wills other things as means to that end, since it befits his goodness that other things share in his goodness. (Part I, Question 19, article 2)

Central to Aquinas's argument here is again a principle that he takes to be perfectly general: things insofar as they are good, perfect, and actual have a natural tendency to share or spread their perfection. Fire spreads itself as far as it can, crocodiles produce baby crocodiles, and artists produce art. Given this general principle it follows that God—the best, most perfect, and most actual of all things—should produce as well, that he should let his excellence "pour forth." God, for Aquinas, thus creates from a superabundance of being and goodness so that the created world spills forth from God's nature with God's own nature as its fullest end.

Significantly, although Aquinas holds that God creates through an effusion of his own goodness, he denies that God, absolutely speaking, must will the existence of other things. Again, in the *Summa Theologica*, he writes,

> With respect to what God wills, it is absolutely necessary that God will one thing but not everything. His will has a necessary relationship to his goodness. And so God necessarily wills that his goodness exist, just as our will necessarily wills our happiness.
>
> But God wills other things than himself inasmuch as they are related to his goodness as their end. And when one wills an end, one does not necessarily will things that are means to that end unless the things be such that the end cannot be attained without them. But God's goodness is perfect and can exist without other things, since no perfection accrues to him from anything else. And so it is not absolutely necessary that he will other things than himself. (Part I, Question 19, article 3)

Aquinas's suggestion here might best be approached through an example. Suppose that I necessarily will my own happiness, but that there are many means through which I might obtain my own happiness. I might, say, become a Greenpeace volunteer or a corporate executive. Then, even though my willing my happiness might be said to be absolutely necessary, my willing to be a volunteer or an executive might still not be absolutely necessary. For Aquinas, God finds himself in an extreme version of this scenario. With absolute necessity God wills his own goodness, and with absolute necessity God's goodness obtains. Through a natural disposition to spread his goodness, God also wills the existence of other things, but since the existence of other things can in no way undermine or alter God's goodness, his willing them is not necessary. (Their existence is only, as Aquinas puts it, *hypothetically* necessary, that is, necessary *given*—or on the hypothesis—that God omnipotently wills them to exist.)

11.3. Divine Love

Aquinas also maintains that God is rightly said to love. And indeed, he takes this conclusion to follow straightforwardly from the fact that God wills, for Aquinas holds that to will by its nature involves love.

> I answer that the first movement of the will and every appetite is love. . . . There are some acts of the will and appetite that regard good under a special condition. For example, joy and pleasure concern a good that is present and possessed, and desire and hope concern a good not yet possessed. But love concerns good in general, whether possessed or not. And so love is by nature the first act of the will and appetite. (*Summa Theologica*, Part I, Question 20, article 1)

As we might have guessed, divine love is not an emotional or needy affair according to Aquinas. God by necessity understands his own nature as good, and therefore of necessity wills his own good in general, and therefore of necessity loves his own divine nature. Just as God's existence, goodness, and happiness are not dependent upon any other being, so too divine love is not dependent upon anything other than God's necessary nature.

Nonetheless, although Aquinas maintains that divine love is not dependent upon other beings, he does allow that God loves things other than himself. Indeed, Aquinas maintains that God loves all his creatures:

> I answer that every existing thing as such is good. But God's will causes everything. And so things necessarily have as much existing and perfection as God wills. And so God wills some good for everything that exists. But loving is willing good for something. And so God loves everything that exists. (*Summa Theologica*, Part I, Question 20, article 2)

The main idea here is simply that insofar as God wills that all things exist, he also wills their goodness, and so also loves them. That God should love all things is made clearer if we bear in mind that—like Augustine—Aquinas insists that to the extent that anything exists, it is good, and so God necessarily recognizes its goodness. Thus, although he might disapprove of a sinner to the extent that she lacks some further due perfection, God must nonetheless love her insofar as she exists with the actuality and perfection she possesses.

Finally, we might note that although God loves all of his creatures, Aquinas insists that in an important sense he does not love them all equally. And, of course, given his understanding of divine love, this stands to reason. For according to Aquinas, God loves his creatures to the extent that they are actual, perfect, or good, but creatures differ in their degrees of actuality, perfection, and goodness, and thus they vary with respect to the degree to which they are loved by God. Thus, Aquinas tells us,

> Things can be loved more or less . . . regarding the good itself that one wills for the object of one's love. And this is the way in which we love more than another one for whom we will a greater good. But God's goodness causes the goodness of things. And so nothing would be better than something else if he were not to will a greater good for one thing than for another. And so he loves some things more than others in this way. (*Summa Theologica*, Part I, Question 20, article 3)

11.4. Is God Male?

The sacred texts of the Abrahamic faiths generally refer to God in masculine terms and attribute male properties to God. God is called a "father." Jesus is held to have been incarnated as a man. He is called the son of God. Furthermore, males are disproportionately represented in the sacred texts of the Abrahamic religions. To be sure, there are important female figures such as Eve, Sarah, Mary, and Asiyah. But in number and overall significance these seem to be dwarfed by the likes of Adam, Abraham, Moses, Peter, Matthew, Mark, Luke, John, Muhammad, Abu Bakr, and more. There are, it seems, many church fathers but relatively few church mothers.

The apparent gender bias of Abrahamic texts has been, and often still is, echoed in differing treatments of male and female believers. Although men and women are both said to be created in the image of God, they have been, and continue to be, subject to different obligations and to enjoy different rights. Many Catholics (men and women) believe that men, but not women, may be ordained as priests and administer sacraments. Many Muslims (men and women) believe that women, but not men, must cover their hair or faces in public. This differing treatment of men and women, of course, strikes many secular and religious people today as inherently unfair, and persuasive cases have been made that such privileging has dramatically harmed women and—insofar as it has encouraged their own oppressive behavior—men as well.

What should we make of Western religion's apparently male bias? This is, of course, a huge and difficult question, and we won't even aspire to getting to the bottom of it here. Nonetheless, it may be helpful to mark out three different sorts of responses that have been given to this question. Those three responses, which I'll call *traditionalist*, *reformist*, and *rejectionist*, might serve as a helpful springboard for further reflection on the alleged patriarchy of Western religion.

A first, *traditionalist*, view maintains that whether we like it or not, whether we can make sense of it or not, the differing representations and treatment of men and women is written into sacred writings, and that gender bias is something that we must accept even if it is not something we can fully comprehend. Such a view is elegantly defended by C. S. Lewis in a posthumously published piece arguing against the ordination of female priests:

> The Church claims to be the bearer of a revelation. If that claim is false then we want not to make priestesses but to abolish priests. If it is true, then we should expect to find in the Church an element which unbelievers will call irrational and which believers will call supra-rational. There ought to be something in it opaque to our reason though not contrary to it. . . . And that is the real issue. The Church of England can remain a church only if she retains this opaque element. If we abandon that, if we retain only what can be justified by the standards of prudence and convenience at the bar of enlightened common sense, then we exchange revelation for that old wraith Natural Religion. (2014, 260)

Lewis acknowledges that those in favor of the ordination of female priests are "sincere and pious and sensible people." And he grants that "women can preach," that "women are [no] less capable than men of piety, zeal, learning and whatever else seems necessary for the pastoral office." Nonetheless, he insists that believers in the Church of England should not allow women to be ordained. For true believers, Lewis thinks, are bound not simply by the dictates of (mere) human reason but by revelation as well, and revelation, he thinks, is gender biased. While that fact may be puzzling to us, to the believer it is, Lewis maintains, a fact that must nonetheless be accepted. To abandon the authority of scripture is to abandon properly religious belief itself.

In making his argument, Lewis takes it for granted that sacred writings are gender biased. That is to say, he takes it for granted that accepted religious texts support, for example, the ordination of men but not women. A second, *reformist* response argues that the relevant sacred texts are not as gender biased as is often thought. In pioneering work, Elizabeth Cady Stanton and Phyllis Trible have argued, for example, that the stories of the Bible have been grossly misinterpreted in favor of men at the expense of women. There is no denying, for example, that the tale of Genesis has been used to denigrate women and to justify their mistreatment. But Stanton and Trible argue that such abuses are not just abuses of women but also abuses of the sacred texts themselves. Read more carefully, and without an interpretative bias, sacred writings often do not support the misogynist uses to which they have been put. This line of thought suggests that the problem of bias lies with us as interpreters, not with the sacred texts themselves. Reformists, insofar as they are reformists, can agree with traditionalists in maintaining that sacred texts may transcend our reason, and must be adhered to, and yet deny at least some of the gender-biased implications that have been drawn from sacred writings.

As even reformists like Trible openly acknowledge, however, it is unlikely that all sacred texts that appear to evince a male bias can be reinterpreted in such a way as to remove that bias. To some believers a more radical response is thus required. *Rejectionists* agree with traditionalists that sacred texts are shot through with a deep and pervasive gender bias. Unlike traditionalists, however, rejectionists maintain that we should reject that gender bias ourselves. One way of pursuing such a rejectionist line of thought is to argue that any gender bias in the sacred texts should be attributed to human contingencies rather than to the word of God itself. The thought here is that gender bias has snuck into the sacred texts because the divine message that they carry has been recorded, compiled, and preserved by fallible human beings. Confronting texts that are divinely inspired but humanly recorded, we should aim to purge them of the biases that have accrued due to human error.

Of course, another rejectionist line is possible. One might see the gender bias of sacred texts as clear evidence that such texts are not divinely inspired at all. On this view, the patriarchy and misogyny that we seem to find in some revered texts are to be taken as evidence that those texts are products of patriarchal, misogynist societies. Insofar as we find such attitudes utterly unacceptable, this line of thought suggests, we must also find reverence for allegedly sacred texts unacceptable as well. The most radical rejectionist line thus agrees with traditionalists in seeing a gender bias in sacred texts but sees such gender bias as a reason for rejecting sacred texts as sacred texts, rather than as a reason for submitting to the biases they encourage.

Further Study

Pamela Sue Anderson, "What Are Challenges for a Feminist Philosopher of Religion?" Video from the Center for Philosophy of Religion at Notre Dame, August 16, 2013, https://youtu.be/SgBVy7oYuK4.

Thomas Aquinas, *Summa Contra Gentiles*, 5 vols., Anton Pegis and Vernon J. Bourke. Notre Dame, IN: University of Notre Dame, 1975.

Thomas Aquinas, *The Summa Theologica of St. Thomas Aquinas*. Trans. English Dominican Fathers, 3 vols. New York: Benziger, 1947–48; reprinted, Allen, TX: Christian Classics, 1981.

Mary Daly, *The Church and the Second Sex*. Boston: Beacon Press, 1986. Pioneering work generally supportive of the rejectionist response to gender bias in sacred writings.

C. S. Lewis, *God in the Dock*. Grand Rapids: William B. Eerdmans, 2014. Collection of posthumously published essays, including "Priestesses in the Church?" which expresses a traditionalist response to gender bias in sacred writings.

Michael Rea, Pamela Sue Anderson, and Andrea White, "Roundtable Discussion on Feminist Philosophy of Religion." Video from the Center for Philosophy of Religion at Notre Dame, August 14, 2013, https://youtu.be/vcfoO8x9QVA.

Richard Regan, trans. and ed., *Thomas Aquinas, A Summary of Philosophy*. Indianapolis, IN: Hackett, 2002. A student-friendly, highly abridged edition of Aquinas's *Summa Theologica*.

Elizabeth Cady Stanton, *The Women's Bible*. Mineola, NY: Dover Publications, 2002. Pioneering work generally supportive of the reformist response to gender bias in sacred writings.

Phyllis Trible, *God and the Rhetoric of Sexuality*. Philadelphia: Fortress Press, 1978. Pioneering work generally supportive of the reformist response to gender bias in sacred writings.

12

Porete's *The Mirror of Simple Souls*

What Is Salvation?

12.1. The Setting

Many historical facts about the life of Marguerite Porete remain uncertain. We know that she spoke French and probably came from the county of Hainaut along the border of modern-day Belgium and France. She must have been well educated. Her writings indicate that she was familiar with university conventions and discussions. The writings also suggest that she was well read, not only in philosophy and theology but also in poetry and literature. Her levels of education and literacy in turn suggest that she must have come from a well-to-do family. In the medieval period, books were expensive and education a luxury. Although we don't know when she was born, her death in 1310 is reliably documented.

In official reports, Porete is described as a beguine. The term "beguine," however, was used so variously that it raises almost as many questions as it answers. Generally speaking, the beguine movement was a lay female religious movement that was especially active in the Low Countries from around the thirteenth to the sixteenth centuries. As a lay movement, beguines did not take religious vows and were free to abandon their affiliations at any time. Some beguines formed communities modeled on monasteries. Others lived solitary lives, some as recluses, some as traveling preachers. Existing outside the formal orders of the church, beguines were easily associated with heretical movements and often viewed with suspicion by church authorities.

Around the year 1300, the bishop of Cambrai condemned a book written by Porete and ordered that it be burned in the presence of its author. The bishop further ordered that Porete never mention the ideas of her book again, and warned that if she did, she would be condemned as a heretic and turned over to secular authorities for punishment. Porete seems to have been unfazed by the bishop's admonition. Around 1306 she confessed that she had retained copies of her book and was charged with continuing to circulate

Saints, Heretics, and Atheists. Jeffrey K. McDonough, Oxford University Press. © Oxford University Press 2022.
DOI: 10.1093/oso/9780197563847.003.0012

her works to both lay and ecclesiastical audiences. Refusing to even speak to her inquisitors, she was held in prison for a year and a half. An examining commission of theologians found her writings to be heretical. She was condemned as a relapsed heretic and burned at the stake in Paris on 1 June 1310.

Porete's *The Mirror of Simple Souls*, written in Old French, was translated in the medieval era into Latin, Italian, and Middle English. In spite of its associations with heresy, it circulated widely in medieval Europe. It was long thought to be the work of an anonymous French cleric. An important discovery announced in 1946, however, identified Porete as the author of the *Mirror of Simple Souls*, leading to a full edition of a surviving Middle French manuscript in 1965. Porete's masterpiece is now widely available and studied.

The Mirror of Simple Souls is both a treatise and a spiritual guidebook. It presents a dialogue between Reason, Love, and Soul. The three allegorical figures debate the proper relationship between human beings and God. In its mode of presentation, the *Mirror* clearly draws inspiration from Boethius's *The Consolation of Philosophy* as well as earlier generations of philosophical dialogues. Perhaps more surprisingly, the *Mirror* also draws on French courtly traditions. As a treatise, it outlines seven stages of spiritual progress, describes three kinds of "death," and draws a distinction between lost souls and sad souls. In effect, it presents an account of the relationship between humans and God as well as a theory of salvation. As a spiritual guidebook, the *Mirror* aims to provide its readers with a path toward a more pious, more religiously perfect life. Indeed, it aims to provide a path toward salvation itself. In the sections that follow, we focus first on Porete's account of spiritual ascent and theory of salvation. We then turn to some broader philosophical issues that arise in connection with the idea of eternal salvation.

12.2. Ascent and Annihilation

The *Mirror* presents seven stages of spiritual progress by which, as Porete puts it, "one ascends from the valley to the height of the mountain, which is so isolated that one sees nothing save God" (118; this chapter follows Babinsky's translation in Porete [1993]). In the first stage, the believer is "touched by God through grace and stripped of her power to sin." She is commanded "to love Him with all her heart, and also her neighbor as herself." When the believer reaches this stage, Porete maintains, she has died her first spiritual "death"—"the death of sin . . . by which the Soul must die completely so that there no longer remains in her color, taste, or odor of anything which God prohibits by Law" (137). For the person who has reached this first stage and passed through his first "death," Porete writes, "It is sufficient for them, that they keep themselves from doing what God prohibits, and that they be able to do what God commands."

Given Porete's description, it may seem that the believer who has made it to the first stage of spiritual progress has already achieved a very high level of piety. And perhaps Porete would even agree if we are drawing a comparison with the average person. Nonetheless, it is clear that for Porete this is merely the beginning of a demanding transformation. She chides those who would rest content with the piety of the first stage of ascent as being "cowardly" and slothful.

The second stage of ascent demands that the believer "go beyond what He [i.e., God] commands" (189). It is central to this stage that the believer should abandon all care for worldly goods. For, at this stage, Porete tells us, the Soul "fears neither the loss of possessions, nor people's words, nor the feebleness of the body, for her beloved does not fear them, and so neither can the soul who is overtaken by Him" (189). What Porete labels as "lost souls" are souls that remain stuck at this level. They are lost because, in spite of their piety—perhaps even because of their piety—they are unable to see that further—much further—progress is still required to live the divine life in this world.

The third stage begins with the soul willing only to do good. It "loves only the works of goodness, through the rigor of great enterprises of all labors by which she can nourish her spirit." To progress, however, Porete suggests, somewhat paradoxically, that the soul must be willing to abandon even its will to do good:

> For no death would be martyrdom to her except abstaining from the work she loves, which is the delight of her pleasure and the life of her will which is nourished by this. And thus she relinquishes such works from which she has such delight, and she puts the will to death which had life from this. In order to accomplish this martyrdom, she obliges herself to obey another will, in abstaining from work and from will, in fulfilling another will, in order to destroy her own will. (190)

This third stage, in which the believer passes from being a "lost soul" to being a "sad soul," is, Porete maintains, much harder than the first two stages. The believer has to give up what she loves, even though what she loves is willing the good. As becomes clearer as the work progresses, the lost soul must give up willing the good in order to lose her own will and make room for God's will. In graphic language, Porete insists that, at this stage, "it is necessary to be pulverized in breaking and bruising the self in order to enlarge the place where love would want to be" (190).

The fourth stage is marked by meditation and "the pure delight of love, by which she is singularly joyful and charmed" (190). Her delight is so great that, indeed, she "believes that there is no higher life" than the one she is enjoying. But "just as love has deceived many souls," so she is deceived. The soul awakens to a fifth stage of ascent when it "considers that God is Who is, from whom all things are, and she is not if she is not of Him from whom all things are." In her amazement, "she sees that He is total goodness who has placed free will in her who is not, except in total wretchedness" (191). The thought here, poetically expressed, appears to be that in the fifth stage the soul moves beyond the contentment of loving God and comes to recognize the gulf that still separates her from God. As an independent will—even as an independent will that wills the good, or simply loves God singularly—she is still "nothingness" insofar as her will is distinct from God's will. The fifth stage thus marks the extinction of the soul's independent will and marks the "death of the spirit."

In the sixth stage, the soul appears to lose its grip on the distinction between itself and God. It no longer sees itself as distinct from God, nor even God in his goodness. Rather "God now sees himself in her soul by His divine majesty." Porete continues,

> God shows to her that there is nothing except Him. And thus this Soul understands nothing except Him, and so loves nothing except Him, praises nothing except Him, for there is nothing except Him. For whatever is, exists by His goodness, and God loves His Goodness whatever part He has given through goodness. . . . And thus also He sees Himself of Himself in such a creature, without appropriating anything from the creature. All is properly His own, and His own proper Self. (193)

The language here again is intentionally poetic, but I think we can make out at least the general idea of the sixth stage. Having abandoned the pure pleasure of loving God singularly, and having recognized she is nothing apart from God, in the sixth stage the believer comes to see that there is no distinction between her and God. Or, rather, since she is nothing independent of God, God sees himself in the believer, and loves her as an aspect of himself. Porete says little about the seventh stage but it would appear that its defining characteristic is that it cements for all eternity the relationship of the sixth stage. Although we can "have no understanding" of the seventh stage "until our soul has left our body," it presumably constitutes full salvation for Porete.

The writings of mystics tend toward lyricism and can be obscure by philosophical standards. Porete's *The Mirror of Simple Souls* is no exception in this regard. And yet, I think, if we take a step back, we can see a coherent, interesting picture in Porete's seven stages of ascent. Creation essentially involves the production of wills that are in some respect independent of God's will. They are, of necessity, born into an essentially fallen, imperfect state. We improve our wills by aligning them with God's will. Presumably few get to even this state, and clearly Porete thinks very few get beyond it in this life. To progress, however, one must move beyond mere piety to a deeper love of God. The suggestion that one might progress beyond the mere commands of God is one aspect of Porete's writings that first brought her to the attention of church authorities. But Porete is not done. The ultimate goal, according to her, is not merely to align one's will with God's will, nor even to transcend one's will in a meditation of love, but to actually eliminate one's independent will and replace it with God's will. Salvation involves not only willing what God wills, but willing what God wills through God's will. We thus reach a conclusion that is somewhat paradoxical, but not uncommon among mystical writers, that the goal of salvation involves transcending *oneself* in order to become united with God. There is thus a sense in which, according to Porete and other mystical writers, salvation involves not just transcendence but self-annihilation.

12.3. Heaven

Porete's seventh stage of ascent points toward her—inarticulable—understanding of eternal salvation. For many believers, the idea of eternal salvation is captured by the concept of heaven. We are all familiar with various representations of heaven as a kind of place. Dante depicts heaven as a series of concentric spheres surrounding the earth. Each sphere corresponds to a celestial object and represents a different level of salvation. The first sphere, for example, is the sphere of the moon and is the resting place for the virtuous but inconstant. The eighth sphere corresponds to the fixed stars and is home to the saints. More recently, a popular television show offered (at least initially, before the twist) a colorful vision of heaven as *The Good Place* tailored to the needs and desires of each individual inhabitant. Depictions of heaven vary widely, but they all generally present heaven as a place of great joy and pleasure.

While it is natural to picture salvation as a kind of special location, more traditional accounts typically focus less on the specific surroundings in which the blessed find themselves and more on the relationship to God in which the blessed stand. For many spiritual thinkers, the essence of salvation or heaven involves a kind of spiritual absorption, an endless fascination and enjoyment of God. As Augustine puts it, God "shall be the end of our desires who shall be seen without end, loved without cloy, praised without weariness." Aquinas similarly maintains that salvation is our final happiness and essentially involves the soul's apprehension of the essence of God for eternity. For traditional thinkers, salvation—heaven—is less a place than it is a relationship between the blessed and God.

Understood either as a special place or as a special relationship, the topic of heaven raises many interesting theological and philosophical questions. Naturally, many believers have been concerned first and foremost with questions about admission. They have wanted to know more about how they can achieve salvation than about the details of what salvation is like. Fair enough. The question of how to obtain salvation, however, is most often posed as a question of theology not of philosophy. It is a question of theological standards, requirements, and doctrine. As interesting as the question of admission might be, here we focus on a more clearly philosophical issue connected to salvation. It can be put simply. Is the doctrine of heaven—the doctrine of eternal salvation—fair? In some ways, but only in some ways, this is the flip side of the problem of evil. The question asks: can it be fair that some people enjoy an eternal salvation of immeasurable happiness and bliss?

It is not hard to appreciate reasons why some people have thought that many conceptions of heaven are inherently unfair. First, in many traditions, it is suggested that salvation is determined by a freely given, but unearned gift from God, namely by grace. If, however, salvation is based on grace, and grace is unearned and unequally distributed, it is easy to conclude that the doctrine of salvation must be inherently unfair. Second, many traditions avoid the difficulties associated with unearned grace by insisting that grace is given at least in part on the basis of merit. Grace is granted to those who have led a certain kind of life, performed certain rites, or adopted certain beliefs. Heaven might be reserved for those who have lived piously, been baptized, or been purified by good deeds. But—the objection goes—the likelihood that one has merited grace, to whatever extent it can be merited, is hugely dependent upon the circumstances in which one happens to find oneself. Those born to parents of a particular religious tradition are far more likely to perform the rites of that religious tradition. The idea that the possibility of obtaining salvation might be hugely influenced by forces outside of one's control strikes many as inherently unfair. Third, the suggestion that heaven is rewarded on the basis of specific deeds or beliefs might seem particularly problematic in the especially sad cases of infant and child deaths. Indeed, such cases can seem unfair in either direction. On the one hand, it may seem unfair that infants should be denied eternal happiness given that they never had a chance to perform the requisite deeds or hold the requisite beliefs. On the other hand, it may seem unfair that infants should be granted eternal happiness given that they never had to struggle to live a good life, to find the right path, or to perform the correct acts and believe the right things. The doctrine of heaven can seem like a minefield of potential injustices.

The question of the fairness of heaven raises far more questions than we can hope to address here. Nonetheless, it may be helpful to sketch three broad strategies for arguing that the doctrine of heaven might be fair after all. The first such strategy suggests that it is not unfair—or not problematically unfair—that some people don't get into heaven, precisely because no one is entitled to eternal salvation. The thought here is that the doctrine of heaven could be problematically unfair only if there were some people who deserved to get into heaven but who nonetheless did not get into heaven. If that thought is correct, and no one deserves to get into heaven, then it follows that the doctrine of heaven is not problematically unfair. By analogy, it is not unfair that some people win the lottery even though others do not; no one is entitled to win the lottery. Those who do have gotten lucky. Those who do not have not been unlucky. One should not expect, or demand, to win the lottery. On this line of response, heaven is a supererogatory gift from God. That some are admitted is perhaps unfair in the sense that even the admitted don't deserve to be admitted, but not in a sense that is problematic. The doctrine of heaven does not entail that anyone has failed to get something that she deserves, and thus is not unjust in the most relevant sense.

A second strategy challenges the implicit assumption that admission to heaven is determined at the time of bodily death. The doctrine of purgatory—that is, an intermediary stage between bodily death and salvation—offers potential responses to many apparent charges of unfairness. Perhaps those who lived in circumstances unfavorable to obtaining salvation will be compensated in purgatory. Perhaps they will be given the same sorts of opportunities as others had in this life. The doctrine of purgatory, however, has especially direct application to the case of infant and child death, for it holds out the possibility that those who die before an age during which they could be expected to make important decisions will have time to make such decisions responsibly. The doctrine of purgatory thus promises to remove many of the obstacles that can make the doctrine of heaven seem inherently unjust.

Finally, a third strategy would challenge the assumption that only some people are admitted to heaven. This response is consistent with also adopting versions of one or both of the first two responses. That is, one might allow that no one is entitled to heaven, but still maintain that, nonetheless, in his generosity, God grants eternal salvation to all. Likewise, one might hold that purgatory is a means for granting salvation to all. Perhaps some people have—to whatever extent possible—merited eternal salvation in this life. Perhaps saints, prophets, and mystics are prepared for heaven at the time of their earthly deaths. But perhaps others must labor for some time before they are similarly prepared. Supposing that all will eventually enjoy salvation doesn't automatically entail that the doctrine of heaven is fair. It might still be the case that admission is unfair even if all are finally granted it. Nonetheless, *universalism*—as the view is often called—does seem to provide important resources to address many of the deepest worries concerning the doctrine of heaven. In particular, universalism removes the concern that the great good of salvation will be awarded to some but not all rational creatures.

12.4. Hell

Although heaven raises many interesting questions, it has been relatively neglected by philosophers in favor of its negative correlative, hell. Doctrines of hell—a place or condition of eternal suffering and alienation—raise many of same questions as doctrines of heaven. For example, just as we asked if any doctrine of heaven could be fair, we can ask if any doctrine of hell might be fair. In earlier times, Christians widely held that anyone who dies without being baptized is condemned to hell. But such a view is likely to strike many today as unjust. People might die without being baptized for any number of reasons for which they don't seem to be responsible. They might have been born in the first century in China or South America. They might have been raised by devout parents of another faith. They might have died unexpectedly on their way to their own baptismal ceremony. In all these cases, we might think that the person's failure to be baptized is not their fault, and therefore condemning them to eternal torment for having failed to be baptized would be inherently unjust.

If doctrines of hell raise many of the same philosophical questions as doctrines of heaven, they also invite many of essentially the same strategies for responding to those questions. So, for example, in responding to the apparent unfairness of hell, one might suggest that no one is unjustly condemned to hell because all rational creatures are fully deserving of hell. Or one might appeal to a doctrine of purgatory to address cases in which timing or circumstances might otherwise lend credibility to charges of injustice. Finally, one might simply maintain that hell either doesn't exist, or that it is at any rate empty. In the case of fairness, as with many other questions, heaven and hell can appear to be almost exact correlatives. Issues and answers concerning one can often be readily, if not quite mechanically, carried over to the other.

Doctrines of hell may also invite concerns about the problem of evil. Some philosophers have argued that it is impossible to reconcile the eternal damnation of finite creatures with a view of God as being wholly good, omnipotent, and omniscient. We can hear the concern first as a question of justice. Could a just god condemn finite creatures to eternal damnation? Some have thought the answer must be "no," arguing that there is simply no crime that a semi-ignorant, finitely capable creature could perform that would merit such a punishment. Others, however, have maintained that the answer is "yes." They may argue that a punishment is just if and only if it is commensurate to the crime being punished. They may argue that eternal damnation may be justified for contravening God's infinite, perfect will. Those are all good and difficult issues, and we touch upon some of them in other chapters.

We can also hear the problem of hell not as a question about justice but, second, as a question about goodness or mercy. Could a good, merciful god condemn finite creatures to eternal suffering? Perhaps one can best feel the pull of this objection by considering an analogy. A child who disobeys his parents might be fairly punished, but a loving parent might be expected to also be merciful, and, indeed, be merciful precisely in not demanding all that justice allows. It is admittedly hard to see how any loving parent could bear, much less enact, an eternal torment for their child no matter what they did. How then—if God is like a loving parent—could he possibly permit countless souls to suffer in hell for eternity?

Both the question of the fairness of hell and its consistency with a loving god point toward a third, perhaps even deeper question—namely, what might be the point of hell? Here, again, more answers have been given than we can possibly canvas. Nonetheless, it may be helpful to highlight two broad pictures. According to the first picture, the point of hell is clear. The point of hell is punishment. Sin is a wrong committed against God or one of God's creatures. Sin places the scales of justice out of balance, and punishment restores that balance. Perhaps one can begin to feel the pull of this way of thinking if one reflects on individuals who have done terrible things in their lives and yet seemed to have gotten away with it: leaders who have carried out atrocities and yet died enjoying the comforts of power, tycoons who have profited off the abuse of people and the environment and yet died happy and pampered. When we reflect on such cases, we might think that the point of hell is to right these apparent injustices; it is to assure that the guilty are punished for their sins.

A rather different picture has its roots in a different understanding of sin. It is natural to think of sin as a violation of a divine command, a violation that is wrong precisely because it is a violation of God's decree. But one can also see sin as an injury to the relationship between God and a believer. Given such a view, sin is less akin to exceeding the speed limit and more akin to not showing up for a lunch date or forgetting your best friend's birthday. At root, sin is a betrayal of trust. Such a picture does not rule out the possibility of punishment. If an adolescent betrays a trust by, say, staying out too late, punishment might represent an appropriate response. Perhaps the teenager is rightly condemned to spending the next weekend at home with her parents. In this picture, however, punishment, and even justice, is not the goal. The goal is ultimately restoring the relationship that has been undermined. The point of the punishment is to encourage conditions that are necessary for a trusting relationship to be restored and flourish.

The idea that sin is first and foremost a harm to the relationship between a creature and God in turn suggests a rather different picture of the nature of hell. In the popular imagination, hell is a place, quite possibly replete with literal fire and demons, or more imaginatively, as in Dante's *Inferno*, with levels and various kinds of carefully tailored species of torment. But if hell is the correlative of heaven, Porete's understanding of salvation invites a very different understanding. If salvation is just an especially intimate relationship with God, perhaps hell is nothing more—but also nothing less—than an estrangement from God. In this picture, hell is not a place of fire and demons but rather one of alienation from (as Porete has it) the source of all goodness and joy. Intriguingly, such a picture of the nature of hell fits well with an account of how even a loving god could tolerate hell. According to that picture, hell results from the sinner's turning away from God. Like a loving parent, God stands ready to welcome the wayward sinner back, even as he refrains from compelling the sinner to return. In this picture, hell is a self-inflicted alienation that lasts just as long as one fails to reconcile with God. From this view, one may imagine the "gates" of hell being—as C. S. Lewis famously put it—locked from the inside.

Further Study

Jonathan Kvanvig, *The Problem of Hell.* New York: Oxford University Press, 1993. An important study for an advanced audience of difficulties presented by doctrines of hell.

Marguerite Porete, *The Mirror of Simple Souls.* Trans. Ellen L. Babinsky, New York: Paulist Press, 1993. English translation of Porete's masterpiece with a helpful introduction and notes.

Thomas Talbott, "Heaven and Hell in Christian Thought." *Stanford Encyclopedia of Philosophy* (Fall 2017 edition), ed. Edward N. Zalta, https://plato.stanford.edu/archives/fall2017/entries/heaven-hell/. A helpful overview of heaven and hell with an emphasis on Christian thought. Includes an extensive bibliography.)

Wendy R. Terry and Robert Stauffer, *A Companion to Marguerite Porete and* The Mirror of Simple Souls. Boston: Brill, 2017. A collection of scholarly articles on the history, content, and influence of Porete's *The Mirror of Simple Souls.*

Jerry L. Walls, *Heaven: The Logic of Eternal Joy.* New York: Oxford University Press, 2002. A nicely written exploration of the doctrine of heaven from a broadly philosophical viewpoint.

13

Pascal's *The Wager*

Should We Bet on God?

13.1. The Setting

Blaise Pascal was born in 1623 in France. He was chronically ill throughout his relatively short life. His sister reports, for example, that from the age of eighteen he was in daily pain, and from the age of twenty-four he was forced to subsist on a liquid-only diet. Presumably because of his health, Pascal was educated at home by his father, an accomplished mathematician in his own right. Unhealthy but precocious, Pascal quickly gained a reputation for general brilliance. He excelled early in mathematics, working on projective geometry, infinitesimals, and probability. He also made significant contributions to the natural sciences, designing early experiments in hydrostatics and the study of barometric pressure. He died at the age of thirty-nine in 1662.

In his early thirties, Pascal underwent a powerful, life-changing religious experience. Following the strict interpretation of Christianity developed by Cornelius Jansen (1585–1638) and the Abbé de Saint-Cyran (1581–1643), Pascal came to see the quest for empirical knowledge and scientific learning as nothing more than human vanity and a distraction from pious reflection on religious matters. He accordingly abandoned his mathematical and scientific studies and began to pen what would become known as his *Provincial Letters*. Published serially from 1656 to 1657, Pascal's open letters ridiculed Jesuit criticisms of Jansenism and lent support to the embattled Jansenist Antoine Arnauld. Following Arnauld, and taking inspiration from Augustine, Pascal argued that people are predetermined to be saved or condemned. He insisted that in our current corrupted state we can be saved only by an arbitrary gift of divine grace.

In the final years of his life, Pascal began gathering ideas and notes for a book defending the Catholic faith. Although never completed, the edited results are known today as Pascal's *Pensées*. The subjects and writing of the

Saints, Heretics, and Atheists. Jeffrey K. McDonough, Oxford University Press. © Oxford University Press 2022.
DOI: 10.1093/oso/9780197563847.003.0013

Pensées vary widely. It includes topics ranging from the corrupting influence of the theatre to the tenability of miracles. Many entries are brief, provocative, even aphoristic. The *Pensées* is Pascal's most philosophically influential work. It continues to be carefully studied by philosophers today and anchors Pascal's ongoing influence in the philosophy of religion and existentialism. The *Pensées* also includes Pascal's most famous argument, which we explore in this chapter: his "wager." Before taking up Pascal's argument directly, however, it should be helpful to set the stage by thinking through how we might rationally approach a straightforward wager, for example, a simple toss of a coin.

13.2. A Simple Wager

Let's imagine the following game at a casino: You are asked to bet on an even coin toss. If you bet on heads and the coin shows heads, you win a million dollars. If you bet on heads and the coin shows tails, you lose a thousand dollars. If you bet on tails and the coin shows tails, you win a dollar. If you bet on tails and the coin shows heads you lose a thousand dollars. Now suppose that you have to play. What is the rational bet?

Since the coin is fair, there is no reason to think that the coin toss is more likely to be heads rather than tails. So it seems that the rational thing to do is to allow the expected payoff to determine your bet. The following table should help us calculate the expected payoff of the coin toss:

	Heads	Tails
You bet on heads	+$1 million	–$1000
You bet on tails	–$1000	+$1

We can now calculate expected utility by multiplying the probability of the payoff by the amount of the payoff:

Bet on heads: ($1 million)(.5) + (–$1000)(.5) = + $1/2 million (approx.)
Bet on tails: (–$1000)(.5) + ($1)(.5) = – $500 (approx.)

Given the expected payoff, it seems that the rational bet is heads. Heads, you effectively expect to win half a million dollars; tails, you effectively expect to lose five hundred dollars.

Two nonstartling points are worth keeping in mind here. First, although it is more rational to bet on heads, heads is no more likely to appear than tails. Second, if the coin were not fair, the likelihood of heads showing could become so small that it would be rational to bet on tails. (This, in effect, is what happens in lotteries. Receiving the large payoff for winning is so unlikely that—in terms of expected utility—you are better off not betting.)

13.3. Pascal's Wager

In *The Wager*, Pascal suggests that we might think of believing in God as analogous to betting on God's existence. He tells us,

> "Either God is or he is not." But to which view shall we be inclined? Reason cannot decide this question. Infinite chaos separates us. At the far end of this infinite distance a coin is being spun which will come down heads or tails. How will you wager? Reason cannot make you choose either, reason cannot prove either wrong. (This chapter follows Krailsheimer's translation of *The Wager* in Pascal [1966].)

At root, Pascal's suggestion is that the same reasoning that makes betting on heads rational in our simple wager makes believing in God rational. To bring Pascal's thought out more clearly, suppose that if God exists and you believe in God, then you will enjoy everlasting paradise after your earthly death. Furthermore, suppose that if God exists and you don't believe in God, then you will suffer eternal torment after your earthly life. Finally, suppose that if you believe in God and God doesn't exist, you lose some finite amount of earthly pleasure that you would experience if you don't believe in God and God doesn't exist. Quantifying that finite amount of earthly pleasure as "ten pleasure units (p.u.)," we can summarize the payoff structure for Pascal's wager as follows:

	God exists	**God doesn't exist**
Believe	$+\infty - 10$ pleasure units	$- 10$ pleasure units
Don't Believe	$-\infty + 10$ pleasure units	$+ 10$ pleasure units

Assuming for now that the odds of God's existing are fifty-fifty, we can calculate the expected payoff for each bet just as we did in our simple wager:

Believe in God: $(+\infty - 10\text{ p.u.})(.5) + (-10\text{ p.u.})(.5) = +\infty$
Don't believe: $(-\infty + 10\text{ p.u.})(.5) + (+10\text{ p.u.})(.5) = -\infty$

In this case, the potential infinite payoffs swamp the potential finite payoffs. As determined by expected payoff, it looks like "betting" on God is obviously the rational choice. The expected payoff of believing in God seems to be infinitely positive, while the expected payoff of not believing in God seems to be infinitely negative.

Although students are often taken aback by Pascal's talk of "wagering" on God and the mathematical formulation of his argument, the sentiment that underlies Pascal's wager is, I think, quite common. We don't know whether or not God exists. Given that we are uncertain, and the stakes are so high, perhaps it is best to believe in God just in case. In believing, we've got, as it were, everything to win and nothing (well, hardly anything) to lose. Best then to "bet" on God.

13.4. Background Assumptions

All philosophical arguments make some background assumptions—they all take some general views or points for granted. We might pause here to consider four important background assumptions made by Pascal's argument, beginning with the assumption that the odds are evenly balanced as to whether or not God exists. After all, one might think that even if we can't know for certain whether or not God exists, we can nonetheless have strong evidence one way or the other. Perhaps you are impressed by Aquinas's argument from motion and think that it is almost certain that God exists. Or perhaps you are struck by the problem of evil and think that it is almost certain that God does not exist. But, of course, this is one of the neat features of Pascal's argument. It doesn't seem to matter how small the odds are that God exists (as long as they aren't zero, or infinitesimally small). As long as there is some chance that God exists, and the payoff structure remains the same, it will turn out that the expected payoff for believing in God is always higher than not believing in God.

Second, it might seem that Pascal takes for granted that belief is under our voluntary control, and this might be thought to be problematic. After all, even if you were to offer me a lot of money to believe that Martha is a cat, I still couldn't do it. (Although I'd certainly give it a try!) In fact, however, Pascal seems to be onto this worry, and suggests that the wager is only supposed to win your rational assent. With that done, you might then decide to do things that are under your control—go to services, hang out with religious folks, and so on—and those habits might eventually lead you to wholehearted belief:

> "I am being held fast and I am so made that I cannot believe. What do you want me to do then?" That is true, but at least get it into your head that, if you are unable to believe, it is because of your passions, since reason impels you to believe and yet you cannot do so. Concentrate then not on convincing yourself by multiplying proofs of God's existence but by diminishing your passions. You want to find faith and you do not know the road. You want to be cured of unbelief and you ask for the remedy: learn from those who were once bound like you and who now wager all they have. These are people who know the road you wish to follow, who have been cured of the affliction of which you wish to be cured: follow the way by which they began. They behaved just as if they did believe, taking holy water, having masses said, and so on. That will make you believe quite naturally, and will make you more docile.

Pascal explicitly denies that his wager turns on our beliefs being under our voluntary control. The wager is only supposed to convince us that belief in God is rational. Once we are convinced that we should believe in God, we may follow other steps in order to engender that belief.

Third, the argument as we have presented it makes some assumptions about the assignment of finite values. Perhaps some will think that Pascal has greatly underestimated the value of not going to services or the pleasure of sinful activity. In fact, there is a nice little wrinkle here in that Pascal actually argues that the virtuous life will be *more* pleasurable than the sinful life on the whole:

> Now what harm will come to you from choosing this course? You will be faithful, honest, humble, grateful, full of good works, a sincere, true friend. . . . It is true you will not enjoy noxious pleasures, glory and good

> living, but will you not have others? I tell you that you will gain even in this life, and that at every step you take along this road you will see that your gain is so certain and your risk so negligible that in the end you will realize that you have wagered on something certain and infinite for which you have paid nothing.

Pascal's minor point is a nice one. Many people would prefer a religiously oriented life even in the absence of a deep conviction that God exists. Whether or not you think that Pascal has correctly estimated the costs and benefits of leading a virtuous life, however, it is clear that as long as those assignments are finite, they won't matter given the structure of the argument.

Fourth, Pascal seems to take for granted that we must either believe that God exists or believe that God doesn't exist. But might we not decide at all? Couldn't we be agnostic? Pascal's response to this point is not entirely clear. In a relevant, but somewhat opaque passage, he writes,

> How will you wager? Reason cannot make you choose either, reason cannot prove either wrong. Do not then condemn as wrong those who have made a choice, for you know nothing about it. "No, but I will condemn them not for having made this particular choice, but for any choice, for, although the one who calls heads and the other one are equally at fault, the fact is that they are both at fault: the right thing is not to wager at all." Yes, but you must wager. There is no choice, you are already committed. Which will you choose then?

Perhaps Pascal's thought is that one must either positively believe that God exists or fail to believe that God exists. On this division there is no third option. The agnostic and the atheist, for Pascal, are essentially in the same boat. The fundamental choice is between believing and failing to believe, and that, Pascal insists, is a choice we are committed to making.

13.5. Objections and Replies

Having reviewed at least some of the assumptions that Pascal takes for granted in presenting his wager, we should be in a better position to consider possible objections. To begin with, one might object that Pascal's wager offers a poor reason to believe in God. That is, one might imagine that God wouldn't want us to believe in his existence for the sorts of reasons Pascal offers. Perhaps God would be offended to find you believing in him because it seemed the best "bet." Pascal's response to the worry about voluntary belief, however, seems relevant here as well. Even if conversion on the basis of the wager does not engender belief in God for the right sorts of reasons, it might nonetheless be sufficient to get you to mend your ways and arrange your life so that you will eventually come to believe in God for the right sorts of reasons.

One might also object that Pascal has misrepresented the relevant payoff structure in suggesting that one faces only two possible outcomes, namely, that either God exists or does not exist. To get the feel for what has been called the "many gods objection," consider the seemingly possible God "Jealous." Jealous, as his name suggests, is exceptionally jealous, and so he punishes with eternal damnation people who believe in any other god, and rewards with eternal salvation people who do not believe in other gods. (This, of course, is not such an outlandish suggestion from a historical perspective—many religious traditions insist on a thou-shall-believe-in-no-other-god clause.) Now—if we set aside epistemic considerations—should we still believe in Pascal's God?

To help us think through this new scenario, let's once again arrange the proposed payoff structure with a table:

"Many Gods"	Pascal's God exists, not Jealous	Jealous exists, not Pascal's God
Believe in Pascal's God and Not Jealous	Infinite Reward	Infinite Punishment
Believe in Jealous and Not Pascal's God	Infinite Punishment	Infinite Reward

In our previous scenario, we assumed that Pascal's God is, as it were, the only game in town. In our current scenario, we are assuming that there is at least one other, rival God in which we could believe.

If we keep things simple by assuming that Pascal's God and Jealous are equally likely, mutually exclusive and collectively exhaustive, we might hope to calculate the expected payoff much as we did before:

Believe in Pascal's God (and not Jealous): $(+\infty)(.5) + (-\infty)(.5) = ?$
Believe in Jealous (and not Pascal's god): $(-\infty)(.5) + (+\infty)(.5) = ?$

When we try to calculate the infinite positive and negative sums, however, we run into a difficulty. What are the values of $(+\infty)(.5) + (-\infty)(.5)$ and $(-\infty)(.5) + (+\infty)(.5)$? Perhaps the most intuitive answer is that $(+\infty)(.5) + (-\infty)(.5)$ and $(-\infty)(.5) + (+\infty)(.5)$ both equal zero. Technically that is wrong. Mathematicians generally maintain that the addition of positive and negative infinities is undefined (in much the way that division by zero is generally held to be undefined). Viewed intuitively or technically, however, the lesson is the same. The many gods objection suggests that the payoff structure for believing in any particular god is importantly different from a coin toss. Once we recognize that there are many possible gods, the possibility of many different, mutually exclusive, cross-rewarding, and mutually undermining payoffs threatens to spoil Pascal's sure bet.

One might reasonably reply to the many gods objection that the existence of any traditional God is more likely than the existence of Jealous. And, indeed, Pascal himself argues that his Christian god is the most likely god to exist, in part because he thinks the story of the Fall helps to explain the imperfections we find in ourselves and our fellow human beings. But once epistemic considerations enter back into the story, the argument presented in *The Wager* changes fundamentally since we will now have to take into account the *evidence* we have for our beliefs (whereas the original argument implied that such evidence is really beside the point).

Finally, one might object to the assumption that it is always rational to do what promises the greatest expected payoff. One way of developing this strategy would be to draw a distinction between two kinds of rationality, namely, practical and theoretical rationality. Intuitively, practical rationality could be thought of as reasoning proper to governing action. And perhaps the golden rule of practical rationality is to follow paths with the greatest expected payoff. When confronted with the simple wager, bet on heads. When confronted with Pascal's wager, bet on God. In contrast, theoretical rationality might be thought of as reasoning proper to governing belief. And perhaps the golden rule of theoretical rationality is to proportion one's beliefs to one's evidence. When confronted with the simple wager, believe that the coin has a 50 percent chance of landing heads and a 50 percent chance of landing tails. When confronted with Pascal's wager, believe that God exists to the extent that you have evidence that God exists. By distinguishing between two kinds of rationality, one could challenge Pascal's suggestion that it is straightforwardly rational to do what promises the greatest expected payoff. Perhaps it is practically rational to believe in God but epistemically irrational.

Yet another way of challenging the assumption that it is always rational to do what promises the greatest expected payoff draws support from paradoxes that suggest that, where infinities are involved, maximizing expected payoffs can lead to intuitively suboptimal practical strategies. Consider, for example, a case known as the St. Petersburg Paradox, introduced by Nicolaus Bernoulli in the eighteenth century. Bernoulli imagined a game in which a fair coin is flipped until it comes up tails, and in which the prize of the game is determined by the number of times the coin is flipped. More specifically, if n is the total number of flips, the prize paid out is $\$2^n$. So, if the coin lands tails on the first flip, the payout is \$2. If the coin lands tails (for the first time) on the second flip, the payout is \$4. If the coin lands tails on the third flip (for the first time), the payout is \$8. And so on. The interesting thing about this game is that its total expected payoff is infinite. (The expected payoff of each possible flip is \$1 and there are infinitely many possible flips.) If it is always rational to do what promises the greatest expected payoff, then a rational gambler (interested only in money) should be willing to pay any finite amount to play Bernoulli's game. But that seems crazy. (If you don't think so, I've got a game for you!) Over the centuries there has been a great deal of discussion by mathematicians and philosophers about paradoxes such as the St. Petersburg Paradox. We needn't worry about those details here. The important point for our purposes is just that it is possible to challenge the assumption that it is always rational to do what promises the greatest expected payoff, especially where infinite payoffs are involved.

Further Study

Desmond Clarke, "Blaise Pascal." *Stanford Encyclopedia of Philosophy* (Fall 2015 edition), ed. Edward N. Zalta, http://plato.stanford.edu/archives/fall2015/entries/pascal/ . Helpful overview of Pascal's life, works, and his philosophical views with an extensive bibliography.

Gary Gutting, "Pascal's Wager 2.0." *New York Times*, 28 September 2015, https://opinionator.blogs.nytimes.com/2015/09/28/a-new-wager/?_r=0. An engaging and accessible attempt to "update" Pascal's wager.

Alan Hájek, "Pascal's Wager." *Stanford Encyclopedia of Philosophy* (Winter 2012 edition), ed. Edward N. Zalta, http://plato.stanford.edu/archives/win2012/entries/pascal-wager/. An extremely helpful overview of Pascal's wager with laudatory attention given to Pascal's text; also includes an extensive bibliography.

Blaise Pascal, *Pensées*. Trans. A. J. Krailsheimer. New York: Penguin Books, 1966. An elegant translation of Pascal's *Pensées*, includes *The Wager*.

14
Spinoza's *Ethics*
Is God Nature?

14.1. The Setting

We noted in chapter 6 that medieval philosophy had flourished in Andalusia in the twelfth century with luminaries such as Averroes. As the Islamic Empire began to recede from what is today Spain and Portugal, however, Jews living there became increasingly subject to persecution. Pogroms led many Jews to convert, at least ostensibly, to Christianity. Suspicion and resentment of recent converts, known as "conversos," however, quickly led to laws intended to limit the roles of converted Jews in both church and state. Concerns over the enforcement of those laws soon inspired the infamous Spanish Inquisition. Finally, in 1462, by decree of King Ferdinand and Queen Isabella, Jews were banished from the Iberian Peninsula altogether. In the diaspora that followed, many Jews resettled in the relatively tolerant Netherlands, where they eventually established successful and thriving communities, especially in Amsterdam.

Baruch Spinoza was born into the Jewish community in Amsterdam on 24 November 1632. At roughly the age of twenty-five, however, he was expelled from it for his "wrong opinions" and "horrible heresies." His resulting excommunication forced him to abandon his career as a merchant and break with his former friends and associates. He soon found a new trade in grinding lenses and formed social ties with members of some minor Christian sects that shared his interest in the philosophy of René Descartes.

After leaving Amsterdam, Spinoza took up residence in the village of Rijnsburg near Leiden and later in the village of Voorburg just outside The Hague. He wrote a short treatise on philosophical method followed by an exposition of the first two parts of Descartes's *Principles of Philosophy.* For years he was best known as a Cartesian and as an expositor of Descartes's philosophy. Around 1670, he published his *Treatise on Theology and Politics*. Its

Saints, Heretics, and Atheists. Jeffrey K. McDonough, Oxford University Press. © Oxford University Press 2022.
DOI: 10.1093/oso/9780197563847.003.0014

stated aim was to defend the freedom to philosophize and think freely. It was a highly controversial work and sent shockwaves throughout Europe.

While the *Treatise* was being discussed, Spinoza was busy working on what would later be recognized as his philosophical masterpiece, *The Ethics*. Imposingly written in the geometric style of Euclid's *Elements*, the *Ethics* lays out Spinoza's own philosophical system beginning with a discussion of God and ending with a difficult account of eternality. In the mid-1670s Spinoza's political situation worsened with the rise of conservative Dutch Calvinists. In July 1674 his *Treatise on Theology and Politics* was banned in Holland, and a draft of his *Ethics* that he had prepared for publication was delayed. Spinoza's health, however, was already in decline. He passed away in 1677. His *Posthumous Writings*, including the *Ethics* and his philosophical correspondence dating back to 1661, appeared shortly thereafter.

14.2. Substance Monism

The driving force behind Spinoza's radical philosophy is a conviction that we have become entangled in numerous religious and philosophical puzzles as a result of a deeply mistaken and anthropomorphic metaphysics. Spinoza suggests that if we take a sober look at our most basic metaphysical ideas and assumptions, we can clear away the most pressing difficulties that have plagued religion and philosophy in the Western tradition. The cost of this clean slate will be the removal of many traditional theological views. The reward will be a truer perspective on the world and our place in it, as well as a program for living the best lives available to us.

Perhaps the most important concept in traditional metaphysics is that of *substance*. A substance is something that is a basic constituent of the world. It is what, at the end of philosophical analysis, is shown to exist most fundamentally. So, for example, one might suppose, like the ancient philosopher Thales, that everything in the world is fundamentally made of water and thus that water is the only substance. Alternatively, one might imagine, as Democritus did, that at its most basic level the world comprises nothing but atoms and space. Or, perhaps, following contemporary physics, one might suppose that the foundations of the world comprises , say, fields, quarks, strings, and so on.

In thinking about substance, philosophers have typically focused on two defining criteria. The first criterion is that a substance is something that does not depend essentially on other things in order to exist. If you're an atomist, for example, you might think that a table is not a substance because its existence depends on the existence of atoms, and that atoms are substances because they don't require anything else in order to exist. The second criterion suggests that things are predicated of substances, but that substances are not predicated of other things. So, for example, Aristotle maintains that "being tan" is predicated of the substance Socrates, while "Socrates" is not predicated of the nonsubstance "being tan." Socrates is tan. His tan isn't Socrates.

Throughout the history of philosophy there has been a great deal of dispute over whether these two criteria are exhaustive, how to understand them, and how to apply them. These disputes were often entangled with, and exacerbated by, various theological disputes. It was hard to see, for example, how any creature could truly be independent if all created things are dependent upon God. And yet, we don't typically predicate things like Socrates, atoms, or fields of God himself. We don't say, for example, that God is Socratic or atomistic. Such tensions had led Descartes to simply stipulate that the concept of substance is applied equivocally to God and to creatures. On Descartes's view we mean one thing when we say that God is a substance and another thing when we say that some created things are substances.

Spinoza boldly rejects Descartes's equivocal account of substance and argues that, strictly speaking, there is only one substance and that that one substance may be identified with God. He proposes that finite things like minds, brains, boats, and boots are all merely "modes" or "modifications" of the one divine being. My mind, for example, according to Spinoza, may be identified with a particular modification of the divine intellect, while my body may be identified with a particular modification of divine matter. Spinoza identifies more general things, like thought-in-general, and extension-in-general, with what he calls "attributes" of God. Such attributes are the most general expressions of the divine nature, according to Spinoza. The upshot of all this is a kind of radical metaphysical monism according to which there is, strictly speaking, only one thing, and everything else is merely an aspect, modification, or attribute of that one being.

14.3. The Master Argument

Spinoza offers an elegant argument in support of his substance monism, which—following tradition—we'll call his Master Argument. It appears in the *Ethics* at 1p14d (that is, in Part 1, Proposition 14, in the demonstration):

> Since God is an absolutely infinite entity of which no attribute that expresses the essence of substance can be denied (by Def. 6), and since God necessarily exists (by Prop. 11), then if there were some substance besides God, that substance would have to be explained through some attribute of God. So there would exist two substances of the same attribute, which (by Prop. 5) is absurd. Therefore, no substance besides God can exist, and consequently it cannot also be conceived. For if it could be conceived, it would necessarily have to be conceived as existing; but this (by the first part of this demonstration) is absurd. Therefore, besides God no substance can exist or be conceived. QED.

Like much of Spinoza's work, his Master Argument is dense and difficult, but repays careful consideration. In this chapter we won't have the chance to look at all the bends and twists in Spinoza's argument, but we can try to get a feel for its general structure and why Spinoza thinks that there can be only one substance, which he contentiously calls "God or Nature."

Spinoza's Master Argument might be thought of as having two main premises and one primary conclusion:

> (Premise 1) No two substances can have the same attribute. (1p5)
> (Premise 2) A substance with every possible attribute exists. (1p11)
> (Conclusion) There can be only one substance. (1p14)

The gist of the argument is that since there must be a substance with every possible attribute, and no two substances can have an attribute in common, the substance with every possible attribute must be the only substance. If it is assumed that every substance must have at least one attribute, and the two premises are granted, it looks like the conclusion follows. So, the real challenge for Spinoza is to defend his two premises. Let's therefore look briefly at Spinoza's arguments for each of his main premises.

In support of his first premise, Spinoza argues that if there were two substances, they would have to be distinct from one another in virtue of something. That is to say, it couldn't be the case that they are exactly similar in every respect and yet are not the same thing. We can get a feel for Spinoza's idea by supposing that there are two dogs. If they are really two dogs, then we might suppose that there must be something that distinguishes the two of them. In the context of Spinoza's metaphysics, however, this implies that if there were two substances they would have to be distinct in virtue of either having different attributes or in virtue of having different modes. To return to our dog analogy, our two dogs would have to be distinct from one another either in virtue of being different kinds of dogs or in virtue of having different particular properties. So, for example, one dog might be a Labrador, the other a poodle, or one might be neatly trimmed, the other one shaggy.

Spinoza argues that no two substances could be different in virtue of their modes alone. His deepest reasons for holding this view are most likely rooted in his understanding of the order of dependence between modes and substances. Very roughly, if two substances differed only in virtue of their modes, then the existence of those substances would be dependent upon their modes, whereas Spinoza thinks that modes must be dependent upon the existence of their substances. At any rate, we can get an intuitive feel for why one might think that substances shouldn't be distinct solely in virtue of their modes. Suppose that our two dogs were distinct solely in virtue of one's being neatly trimmed and the other's being shaggy. Then trimming the one dog would leave the two dogs identical to one another. But it seems absurd that two dogs should be made into one dog simply with a haircut!

Spinoza also argues that no two substances can have the same attribute and be different in virtue of having different attributes. His thought here seems to be that if two substances differed in their attributes, then they couldn't have the same attribute. This makes good sense with respect to our dog example. If my two dogs differ from one another in virtue of one being a Labrador and the other being a poodle, then clearly they do not have an attribute in common. So, two dogs cannot be the same kind of dog—have the same "attribute"—and yet be different in virtue of being different kinds of dogs—having different "attributes." (There is a worry here, originally pointed out by Spinoza's contemporary Gottfried Wilhelm Leibniz, that we won't address. The worry, in short, is that two *substances* might share one or more attributes, and still differ from one another in virtue of their having *other* attributes. If cuteness were an attribute, perhaps our two dogs could differ in the fact that one is a Labrador and the other a poodle, and yet be the same in their both being cute. In that case, they would differ in virtue of their attributes and yet have an attribute in common.)

Spinoza's defense of his second premise is fairly straightforward (although there are puzzles in the details here as well). We might think of it as having two steps. First, Spinoza, in effect, argues that a substance having every possible attribute must be *possible*, since a substance's having one attribute can't preclude it from having any other attribute. Second, essentially following along the lines of Anselm's argument, Spinoza maintains that the greatest possible substance must exist, and so a substance with every possible attribute must exist. And with that, his conclusion is secured, since any other substance would have to share an attribute with the "absolutely infinite" substance of Premise 2, a possibility that is supposed to be ruled out by Premise 1.

14.4. "*Deus sive Natura*" (God or Nature)?

Spinoza provocatively calls his one substance "God or Nature." His readers, however, have long wondered where the emphasis should be placed in his identification. That is to say, should we take Spinoza to be someone who deifies existence, making everything divine, or should we take him to be someone who would make God mundane? Is he, in the words of the German poet Novalis, "a man drunk on God" or is he, in the words of Antoine Arnauld, "the most impious" philosopher of the early modern period? Although I don't think we should expect a decisive answer to the question of whether Spinoza is a pantheist or an atheist, the question itself is worth considering. In that spirit, we might briefly address a couple of things that can be said in support of both sides of this dispute.

There are grounds for seeing Spinoza as deflating traditional theism and making God more mundane. It is clear that Spinoza means to deny that God is a transcendent being that creates an independent world with independent creatures. His pantheism, however, goes even further than this in its departure from traditional conceptions of the divine. In his Appendix to Part I of the *Ethics*, Spinoza rails against anthropomorphizing God in general, arguing that those who seek to explain events in terms of God's intentions take refuge in ignorance. Likewise, Spinoza denies that God acts for the sake of ends, arguing that such a "doctrine takes away God's perfection. For if God acts for the sake of an end, he necessarily wants something he lacks." And in Part V of the *Ethics*, Spinoza famously asserts, "He who loves God will not try to get God to love him back" (5p19). In insisting that Nature lacks traditional personal attributes of God, Spinoza takes an important step away from many traditional conceptions of God and effectively makes God less divine, more mundane.

Nonetheless, there are also grounds for thinking that Spinoza's identification of Nature with God is not wholly vacuous. And in particular, we might be struck by two reasons for seeing Spinoza as deifying nature rather than making God mundane. First, although Spinoza denies that many traditional personal attributes are rightfully ascribed to God, he does allow that God is, in perhaps an unexpected way, omniscient and omnipotent. Furthermore, he consistently maintains that many of the traditional impersonal divine attributes may be ascribed to Nature. He maintains, for example, that Nature as a whole is infinite, eternal, and unique. Finally, as the contemporary philosopher Jonathan Bennett has noted, on the basis of these attributes, Spinoza seems to have genuinely felt a kind of "awe and reference and fear and a kind of love" for Nature that many traditional theists feel toward God. Second, it's also notable that Spinoza's God fits quite well with Anselm's traditional definition of God as that which nothing more perfect can be imagined. Insofar as Anselm's definition is accepted as capturing something deep and central about God's nature, Spinoza seems to be in a good position to insist that his Nature really does deserve to be called "God." Spinoza could see himself as agreeing that God is the most perfect being, even if that most perfect being turns out to be somewhat different from what more traditional religious thinkers have supposed.

Further Study

Jonathan Bennett, "Glimpses of Spinoza." *Syracuse Scholar* 4, no. 1 (1983): 43–56 https://www.earlymoderntexts.com/assets/jfb/glimpses.html. A lovely introduction to Spinoza's life and thought by a distinguished Spinoza scholar.

Steven Nadler, "Baruch Spinoza." In *Stanford Encyclopedia of Philosophy* (Spring 2011 edition), ed. Edward N. Zalta, http://plato.stanford.edu/archives/spr2011/entries/spinoza/. Helpful overview of Spinoza's life, works, and philosophy with an extensive bibliography.

Steven Nadler, *A Book Forged in Hell: Spinoza's Scandalous Treatise and the Birth of the Secular Age*. Princeton, NJ: Princeton University Press, 2011. Entertaining introduction to Spinoza's *Theological-Political Treatise* and its impact.

Steven Nadler, *Spinoza: A Life*. Cambridge: Cambridge University Press, 1999. An authoritative yet accessible biography of Spinoza in English.

Baruch Spinoza, *The Ethics*. Ed. Feldman Seymour; trans. Samuel Shirley. Indianapolis, IN: Hackett, 1992.

Baruch Spinoza, *Theological-Political Treatise*. Trans. Samuel Shirley. Indianapolis, IN: Hackett, 2001.

15

Spinoza's *Ethics*

Are We Modes of God?

15.1. Substance, Attributes, Modes

In the previous chapter, we saw Spinoza defend substance monism, that is, the view that there is only one substance, which Spinoza calls "God or Nature." For Spinoza this implies that God, as the only substance, is also the only independent thing. Let's look back quickly at Spinoza's definition of *substance*:

> By substance I understand what is in itself and is conceived through itself, i.e., that whose concept does not require the concept of another thing, from which it must be formed. (1def3; this chapter follows Curley's translation of *The Ethics* in Spinoza [1994])

This is couched a bit idiosyncratically, but Spinoza's thought here is just that God doesn't require anything else in order to exist. Spinoza, however, doesn't mean to deny that, in some sense, other things exist too. In particular, he allows for two kinds of dependent entities, namely, attributes and modes.

Spinoza's understanding of attributes was discussed briefly in chapter 14 in connection with his Master Argument. His official account of attributes is provided in a short definition in his *Ethics* at Book 1, definition 4:

> By attribute I understand what the intellect perceives of a substance, as constituting its essence. (1d4)

Readers have long disagreed over how exactly to interpret this definition. A couple of things, however, seem reasonably clear. First, an attribute is something like a very general way of being. Second, although Spinoza maintains that God must have infinitely many attributes, he really only ever

Saints, Heretics, and Atheists. Jeffrey K. McDonough, Oxford University Press. © Oxford University Press 2022.
DOI: 10.1093/oso/9780197563847.003.0015

talks about two attributes, namely, thought and extension-or-matter. Third, he thinks that attributes are conceptually and causally distinct from one another. Pulling these points together, Spinoza suggests that we can think of God or Nature in either of two very different, general, and all-encompassing ways. We can think of God or Nature as something that is thinking or as something that is material. He insists, however, that there aren't any interesting explanatory relations holding between God as a thinking thing and God as a material thing or vice versa. We can think of God in either mental terms or in material terms, but not in both ways at the same time.

Spinoza's official account of modes is also extremely brief. It is given at Book 1, definition 5:

> By mode I understand the affections of a substance, or that which is in another through which it is also conceived.

This is perhaps even more opaque than the definition of an attribute! It nonetheless becomes clear that Spinoza holds that modes must be conceived through attributes, so that there will be a distinct kind of mode corresponding to each attribute. And in particular, there will be modes of body and modes of thought. Since these modes must be conceived through attributes that are themselves conceptually distinct from one another, modes of thought will be conceptually distinct from modes of extension. Spinoza nonetheless maintains that there is a parallelism between modes of thought and modes of body: every thinking mode has a corresponding mode of body, and every mode of body has a corresponding mode of thought. Modes may be considered finite manifestations of God that can be thought of either from a bodily perspective or a mental perspective.

15.2. Human Beings

We are now in a better position to see how human beings fit into Spinoza's metaphysics. Since we are finite things, we can't be substances, and since we aren't general ways of being, we can't be attributes. We must therefore be modes of the one substance. And, put very generally, that is exactly what Spinoza thinks we are. More specifically, he thinks that our minds are modes of thought and that our bodies—including our brains—are modes of extension. Since modes of different attributes are conceptually distinct from one another, there should be no way to understand our minds in material terms, and no way to understand our bodies (including our brains) in mental terms. Neuroscience can tell us a great deal about the brain but can never provide us with an analysis of what it is like, from a mental standpoint, to be in love or to taste a pineapple. Conversely, psychology might tell us all sorts of things about the nature of mental states, but it can never teach about the physical nature of the brain or the body. Nonetheless, in light of Spinoza's parallelism thesis, it must be the case that our minds as mental modifications of God correspond to our bodies as physical modifications of God and vice versa. So, to be explicit, my mind, according to Spinoza, is a mental mode that corresponds to my body, which is a physical mode. The same is true, of course, of your mind and your body.

If we now ask, "How exactly are our minds—or, if you like, our souls—related to our bodies?" we enter into a vexed topic of early modern metaphysics that is still very much with us today. It seems like our minds can cause changes in the physical world through our volitions. I will to raise my hand, and lo and behold my hand goes up. It also seems like bodies can cause changes in our mental states. I touch a hot stove and all of a sudden, I have a mental sensation of pain. Spinoza's contemporaries offered very different accounts of the apparent interaction of minds and bodies. Let's consider two, one by René Descartes (1596–1650) and one by Nicholas Malebranche (1638–1715).

Descartes suggested that although the mind and body are two fundamentally different kinds of substance, the mind and the body can nonetheless *causally* interact. Just as one billiard ball might move another billiard ball, or one thought give rise to another thought, a pinprick might cause my mental pain, and my mental pain might cause me to yell, "Ouch!" Although straightforward in its own way, this account seemed unacceptable even to many of Descartes's followers, and worries were soon raised over its compatibility with conservation principles in the domain of physics. (If my will can directly cause changes in the physical world, it might seem that the amount of energy in the world could be increased if we all, for example, decided to raise our arms at the same time.)

Nicholas Malebranche defended a solution that might seem to be as far removed from Descartes's as possible. He suggested that the mind and body do not directly interact at all. On Malebranche's view, my willing my arm to move merely serves as an "occasion" for God to move my arm. Likewise, my hand touching something hot merely serves as an "occasion" for God to give my mind a sensation of heat. The appearance of causal interaction is an illusion that arises because God correlates mental and physical states in a lawful way. This account gained a perhaps surprisingly favorable reception in the seventeenth century as a general theory of creaturely causation. Not everyone, however, was convinced. Some objected, for example, that Malebranche's proposal would commit God to performing perpetual miracles and undermine creaturely freedom and autonomy.

Spinoza's metaphysics of substance, attributes, and modes allows him to offer an elegant solution to the traditional problem of mind-body interaction. As we've just seen, for Spinoza, my mind and my body are not two distinct substances, but rather two distinct ways of understanding a finite aspect of God. My mind and body are really just different expressions of me—one under the attribute of thought, and one under the attribute of extension. Strictly speaking there is neither direct nor indirect causal interaction between the states of my mind and the states of my body. Changes in my mind and my body are, as it were, the very same changes viewed in two different ways. When I will my hand to go up, a change takes place not only in my mind but also in my body, and that change in my body may be used to explain (in bodily terms) my arm's going up. Likewise, when I touch a hot stove, a change takes place not only in my hand, but also in my mind, and that change in my mind may be used to explain (in mental terms) my subsequent fear of hot stoves. What appear as causal interactions—or regular correlations—between mental and physical states are, in fact, parallel manifestations of a single underlying order viewed through the guise of two different attributes.

15.3. Against Libertarian Freedom

Spinoza thinks that his account of human beings as modes of God is not mere metaphysical speculation. It has deep and important practical implications. One particularly important implication concerns the nature of human freedom. As we've seen, many philosophers and theologians ascribe to what we've called a "libertarian" conception of freedom, according to which our free decisions are not constrained by any external factors (for example, laws of nature and antecedent events). If we could go back in time and face exactly the same options under exactly the same circumstances, we could freely choose to do otherwise.

Spinoza denies that humans have libertarian freedom, and his rejection of libertarian freedom may be seen as following directly from his metaphysics. Conceived of as bodies, we follow the same laws as every other body, and we are just as determined in our next action as any other body. Spinoza's parallelism doctrine, however, implies that our thoughts and our minds must be equally determined by past thoughts and laws of nature. If we could go back in time, and face exactly the same options under exactly the same circumstances, we would have to choose exactly the same thing. We are no more free in a libertarian sense than is a dog, a cat, or a stone flying through the air.

Spinoza's denial of libertarian freedom is part of a more general tendency on his part to see human beings as belonging to the same natural order as other modes. He denies that human beings are inherently special or are subject to a fundamentally different set of principles than other modes. Thus, in the preface to Part III of the *Ethics*, he denounces the tendency of philosophers to treat human beings as if they were things "outside nature" and to view human beings as "a dominion within a dominion," supposing that "man disturbs, rather than follows, the order of nature, that he has absolute power over his actions, and that he is determined only by himself" (III, Preface).

Spinoza's commitment to viewing human beings as obeying the natural order of things is often referred to as his "naturalism." *Naturalism* has meant lots of different things to lots of different people, but in Spinoza's hands it means that humans are continuous with other things in the natural world. They are not a group singled out with nonnatural powers, powers like libertarian free will. Naturalism and its limitations are important themes in philosophical discussions of religion, and many people have seen Spinoza's commitment to naturalism as a hallmark of his being a transitional figure from a premodern religious worldview to a modern secular worldview. As later chapters note, Spinoza's embrace of naturalism is something he shares with both Hume and Nietzsche.

15.4. For Compatibilist Freedom

As we've just seen, Spinoza denies that anything could possibly have libertarian freedom. He nonetheless insists that we can be more or less free in a nonlibertarian or compatibilist sense of freedom. In order to understand

Spinoza's positive account of freedom, it will be helpful to begin with his notion of *conatus*. According to Spinoza, all finite things have an innate tendency, striving, or power to preserve and increase their own being. He calls that innate tendency a "conatus." It is formally introduced in Book 3, proposition 6 of the *Ethics*:

> Each thing, in so far as it is in itself, endeavors to persevere in its being.

Although Spinoza's statement leaves important questions unanswered (such as whether conatus is a tendency to merely preserve being, or rather to increase being), the main idea is fairly intuitive. According to Spinoza, everything tries to stay in existence as best as it can. People take care of their health and avoid dangerous situations. Animals defend themselves against attackers. And even rocks resist being crushed into smaller rocks. (Suicides, bombs, and candles are all prima facie difficult cases for Spinoza. He must argue that these are not really cases where an entity contains within itself the seeds of its own destruction.)

With his notion of conatus in the background, Spinoza offers an account of human "affects" such as love, anger, hate, pride, jealousy, and the like. Such affects, according to Spinoza, can be divided into two types. He calls affects that have their origins in the agent's own nature, and in particular in the agent's inner knowledge, *actions*. He calls affects that have their origins in other modes, which act upon the agent, *passions*. Such passions, Spinoza maintains, can be further subdivided into various kinds. He thus proposes, for example, that *joy* or *pleasure* is a very general term used to denote any "passion by which the Mind passes to a greater perfection," while *sadness* or *pain* is any passion by which the Mind passes to a lesser perfection. *Love* may then be defined as joy accompanied by an awareness of the external cause that brings about that transition to greater perfection within the agent. *Hate* is defined as sadness with a similar awareness of the external object that brings about that transition within the agent (see IIIp11s).

Spinoza suggests that it follows from his views on conatus and the affects that we have a natural tendency to pursue passions that increase our conatus and to avoid passions that decrease our conatus. In short, we are naturally disposed to pursue joys and avoid sorrows. While natural, this tendency is, according to Spinoza, the root of our being unfree. In the Preface to Part IV of the *Ethics*, tellingly titled "On Human Servitude, or, The Powers of the Affects," Spinoza informs us,

> Human lack of power in controlling and restraining the emotions I call "servitude." For a man who is subject to the emotions is not his own master, but is mastered by fortune, whose power over him is such that he is often compelled, even though he sees what is better for himself, to follow what is worse.

Spinoza's dim view of the passions is *not* based on the idea that passions are always bad in themselves. Joy is an increase in one's conatus and is rightfully counted as a good by Spinoza. Rather, the difficulty with the passions is that they lie outside of our control. Joy in itself is a good thing, but we can't guarantee that we will experience joy, and our pursuit of joy often results in our experiencing a decrease of power, which is bad. The very uncertainty of the passions is a source of misery and servitude. The thought that you may at any time lose your joy and become sad may be enough by itself to spoil your current joy. To be free, according to Spinoza, is therefore to be free from affects. Since we can never do that completely, it might be better to say that, for Spinoza, one is more free to the extent that one is not determined by affects and therefore acts from one's own nature.

15.5. Moderating the Passions

Spinoza's account of freedom implies that we are freer the more we are determined by actions and the less we are determined by passions. But how are we supposed to increase our freedom—to become more active and less susceptible to our passions? Spinoza's solution is, at the end of the day, not so different from Augustine's, and has a common root in ancient Stoicism. Spinoza maintains that no matter how powerful a person might become, she can never fully control the external causes that give rise to passions in her. The only way that she can hope to moderate the passions is to moderate her evaluation of external goods and harms. By modifying our perspectives on external influences, we can hope to minimize their control over us and thereby become both more tranquil and (in Spinoza's special sense of acting from our own natures) more active.

So the next question is: how are we to gain such a freeing perspective on external causes? Spinoza's own account winds through his difficult treatment of knowledge. What is most important for us, however, is simply the idea that we are capable of obtaining what Spinoza calls "adequate" ideas—that is, thoughts that are clear and distinct (to borrow Descartes's terminology). By means of adequate ideas, we are able to see particular causes from an eternal perspective—we are able to better grasp their deepest nature and see how they follow inexorably from God's divine nature. If we had an adequate idea of, say, Socrates, we would be able to understand his essential nature and see how his existence followed inevitably from God in something like the way that we are able to grasp the essence of the number 4 and see how it follows from summing 2 and 2.

Adequate ideas, which reveal the necessity of things to us, are, according to Spinoza, the key to lessening the grip of our passions. At Book 5, proposition 6 (in the scholium), he writes,

> The more this knowledge—namely, the knowledge that things are necessary—concerns particular things which we imagine more distinctly and more vividly, the greater is this power of the mind over the emotions. This is also supported by experience. For we see that pain at the loss of some good is mitigated as soon as the man who has lost it considers that that good could not in any way have been preserved. So also we see that no one pities an infant because it cannot speak, walk, or reason, and finally because it lives for so many years as if it were unconscious of itself. But if most people were born adult, and only one or two were born infants, then each person would pity infants, because he would regard infancy not as a natural and necessary thing, but as a defect or error of Nature. We could note several other things of this kind.

Spinoza's thought here, I suggest, has some psychological plausibility. Much of what is so problematic about the passions, he thinks, is our inability to control them, the way they buffet us about. Outside forces can determine whether we feel sudden joys and sudden sorrows, and so we anxiously anticipate what will happen to us next. But if we came to recognize that all events must follow from the absolute necessity of God's perfect nature, then we would recognize that it is impossible to control external events. We'd see that everything happens as it must happen. That thought might result in our feeling resigned to whatever does happen and in our ceasing to feel anxiety over what is, in fact, inevitable.

In keeping with his understanding of the passions, Spinoza suggests that the ideal person—the "freeman" as he puts it—is, well, essentially chill. She's not an ascetic, since joys, including bodily joys, are good. But she's not chasing after fleeting pleasures or running scared from goblins and priests. She makes the most of what she has and calmly endures what she must. This is, I think, a common ideal for Stoically inspired philosophers like Spinoza. The central idea is that our lives should be ruled by reason and that our passions are to be suppressed and overcome. While clearly enticing in some respects, not everyone will agree that this is a full picture of human flourishing. It is often objected that Spinoza's ideal leaves out an important dimension to human life: that while the passions expose us to forces beyond our control, they are also essential to a life worth living. The objection is that while it is true that we don't want to be constantly buffeted about with fits of mania and depression, we also don't want to live a life devoid of emotional love or even appropriately felt sorrow.

Further Study

Isaac Bashevis Singer, "The Spinoza of Market Street." 1944. Widely available online. A deservedly famous fictional story about a devotee of Spinoza's philosophy. The ending of the story is, I think, intended to make the case that Spinoza's "freeman" is not an ideal to which we should fully aspire.

Baruch Spinoza, *The Ethics*. Ed. Seymour Feldman; trans. Samuel Shirley. Indianapolis, IN: Hackett, 1992). A good and affordable edition of Spinoza's *Ethics*.

Baruch Spinoza, *A Spinoza Reader*. Ed. and trans. Edwin Curley. Princeton, NJ: Princeton University Press, 1994. An excellent selection of Spinoza's writings by the leading translator of Spinoza's works in English.

Jason Waller, "Benedict de Spinoza: Metaphysics." *Internet Encyclopedia of Philosophy*, ed. James Fieser and Bradley Dowden, https://iep.utm.edu/spinoz-m/. Helpful overview of Spinoza's metaphysics with extensive references for further reading.

16
Spinoza's *Ethics*
Good without God?

The previous chapter looked at Spinoza's suggestion that we are modes of God and the implications of that suggestion for freedom and the sort of lives we ought to live. This chapter turns to Spinoza's understanding of goodness and its relation to his understanding of God.

16.1. Two Accounts of Goodness?

Spinoza offers two accounts of goodness that are at least prima facie at odds with one another. In Book III of the *Ethics*, he suggests that traditional views of goodness have misunderstood the relationship between what we desire and what we call "good." Earlier thinkers like Aquinas maintained that we recognize things as good and so pursue them. Indeed, they plausibly maintain that we pursue things because we think they are good, and that when we act we always do what seems best to us at the time. (Why else would we do it?) Spinoza, however, thinks this story gets things the wrong way around. He suggests that we pursue and desire things by our very nature and that we call those things "good" that we pursue and desire. On Spinoza's first account, I don't eat Wisconsin cheese because I think it is good, I think Wisconsin cheese is good because I'm strongly inclined to eat it.

In Book IV of the *Ethics*, Spinoza returns to the topic of goodness. There, however, he seems to offer a very different picture. He suggests that when we evaluate things, we first form a standard or a model. We then compare other things to that model. Those things that compare well we call "good"; those that don't compare well, we call "bad." So, for example, I might hold up Martha as the ideal dog. I might then compare other dogs to Martha in order to evaluate them. I might think that Benji is too small because he's

Saints, Heretics, and Atheists. Jeffrey K. McDonough, Oxford University Press. © Oxford University Press 2022.
DOI: 10.1093/oso/9780197563847.003.0016

smaller than Martha. I might think that Marmaduke is too big because he's bigger than Martha. As mentioned in the previous chapter, for Spinoza the most important model for a well-lived life is the dispassionate "freeman" or freeperson. If that is our model too, then we can evaluate things and actions by asking whether they will lead us to be more or less like the freeperson or not. Those that lead us to be more like the freeperson will be good. Those that lead us to be less like the freeperson will be bad.

It is, I think, an open question whether Spinoza's Book III account of goodness is consistent with his Book IV account. Suppose that I have a strong, innate inclination to read Agatha Christie's detective stories. By the Book III account, it seems that I should call those stories "good" since I have a strong inclination to read them. But suppose that those stories also give rise to passions in me. If I hold up Spinoza's freeperson as a model for myself, by the Book IV account it seems that I should count such stories as "bad," since the freeperson avoids strong passions as much as he can. Whether this is a real tension in Spinoza's system or merely the appearance of a tension is difficult to say and remains a topic of debate among scholars. (One possible way of attempting to resolve the tension is by seeing the Book III account as an account of our evaluative practices insofar as they are based on inadequate knowledge, and the Book IV account of our evaluative practices insofar as they are based on adequate knowledge.)

Spinoza's Book IV account of Goodness also raises another natural concern. We've seen Spinoza argue that we all have a natural inclination to self-preservation—that we all strive to persevere in being as far as we are able. This is his conatus doctrine. Spinoza also makes it clear that he thinks that it would be nonsense to suppose that we shouldn't be that way—he thinks it is literally impossible for anything not to strive to persevere in its being. But how is Spinoza's conatus doctrine supposed to jibe with his ideal of the freeperson? The freeperson is essentially rational and contemplative. We can imagine many scenarios in which such a person might indeed be well positioned to persevere in her being. Sometimes a cool, rational head is just what is needed to survive. But it's not clear that this is a recipe for human endurance in general. We can imagine plenty of scenarios in which a person with a very different character is better positioned to persevere in her being. Sometimes, it seems, a passionate soul—or a strong body—is just what is needed to persevere. This is a second prima facie objection to Spinoza's Book IV account of Goodness and his ideal model of the freeperson. Spinoza seems to be suggesting that in at least some circumstances we both should and should not strive to persevere in our being. Again, I think it is an open question as to whether this is a real tension or merely the appearance of a tension. Perhaps a better understanding of what exactly Spinoza understands by persevering in our being would help to resolve this apparent impasse as well.

16.2. Beyond Egoism?

Egoism is the doctrine that we do, or should, act only in our own self-interest. There are passages in which Spinoza appears to embrace egoism. So, for example, at Book 4, Proposition 18 (in the scholium), he writes,

> Since reason demands nothing contrary to Nature, it demands that everyone love himself, seek his own advantage, what is really useful to him, want what will really lead a man to greater perfection, and absolutely, that everyone should strive to preserve his own being as far as he can. (This chapter follows Curley's translation of *The Ethics* in Spinoza [1994].)

Such passages naturally suggest that Spinoza is a thoroughgoing egoist—that he thinks people do, and should, act only for the sake of benefiting themselves, and never for the sake of benefiting others.

In fact, however, Spinoza argues that pursuit of self-interest should lead us to support others as well. The key to moving from self-interest to common interest, according to Spinoza, is to be found in the fact that we share a common nature with other human beings. Thus, for example, at Book 4, Proposition 31, Spinoza writes,

> Insofar as a thing agrees with our nature, it cannot be evil (by P30). So it must either be good or indifferent. If the latter is posited, namely, that it is neither good nor evil, then (by A3) nothing will follow from its nature which aids the preservation of our nature, that is (by hypothesis), which aids the preservation of the nature of the thing itself. But this is absurd (by 3P6). Hence, insofar as it agrees with our nature, it must be good, q.e.d.

Although characteristically dense, I think Spinoza's suggestion here can be unpacked as follows: We share a nature with other human beings, so anything that benefits the nature of our fellow human beings must also benefit our nature. If we call things that benefit our nature "good," we should also call things that benefit the nature of our fellow human beings "good." To do otherwise would be contradictory or absurd.

It is, I think, a clever argument, although I'm not sure that it works. There is an ambiguity in Spinoza's understanding of the nature that each of us is supposed to share with other humans. To understand this point better, consider two copies of the same textbook. We recognize that there's a sense in which they are the same book and a sense in which they are not the same book. In the sense that they are the same book, philosophers say that the two books are of the same type, that is, that they are *type-identical*. In the sense that they are two different books, philosophers say that they are different tokens of the same type, that is, that they are *distinct tokens*. Applying this distinction to Spinoza, we can ask if benefiting others is supposed to support my own existence or the existence of things like me, that is, is it supposed to further my token-existence or my type-existence?

It is not hard to see how altruistic behavior might further my type-existence. Insofar as something shares my nature—is same type of thing as I am—promoting that thing's nature is just promoting my (type) nature. The hitch is that it is not clear why the conatus doctrine would necessarily lead us to promote our type-existences. It was natural to understand the conatus doctrine as suggesting that I strive to persevere in my token-existence, not my type-existence. And it is hard to see how promoting the existence of things with the same type-existence as me will necessarily promote my token-existence. To be sure, there are many cases in which promoting the existence of things like me might also promote my (token-) existence. We all derive tremendous benefits from the collaborative work of humans, including collaborative work aimed specifically at benefiting human beings. Roads, fire departments, and penicillin are all the result of the work of other creatures that share our nature. But Spinoza seems to think that there is a conceptual connection between our helping others that share our natures and helping ourselves, and that is a much tougher case to make if our token-natures are at stake. If the plane is going down, and there's only one parachute left, promoting your token-nature would seem to come at the cost of promoting my token-nature (even if promoting your token-nature would promote my type-nature). If I'm motivated only to promote my token-nature—as the conatus doctrine seemed to imply—then giving you the parachute seems like a bad idea. And of course, the same goes for all sorts of conflicts that arise in less fanciful cases as well. Paying taxes, telling the truth in court, and so on all might promote human nature without promoting my own personal survival.

Spinoza, I think, recognizes this difficulty (see the definition in Book IV, Proposition 34) and thinks that he can address it. This isn't the place to get deeply into his proposed solution, but perhaps we might note that Spinoza does offer a different basis for our altruistic behavior as well. In his account of the passions, Spinoza suggests that we naturally have sympathy with things that are similar to ourselves. When we see something similar to ourselves get hurt, we hurt too. Likewise with respect to joy. Indeed, Spinoza maintains that this carries over even to objects that cause pain and pleasure in things like us. Since we hurt when we see things similar to us hurt, we naturally come to hate those things that cause things like us to hurt. Spinoza is not, I think, interested in grounding morality or altruism in this sort of natural sympathy, since natural sympathy of this sort is ultimately rooted, for Spinoza, in the passions, and thus—according to him—ultimately in intellectual confusion. Nonetheless other naturalistically inclined philosophers—including Hume—would later seek to ground morality and altruism in our natural and shared emotions, feelings, or "sentiments."

16.3. Good without God?

Spinoza's discussion of morality may remind us of a perennial question in the philosophy of religion: can we be good without God? There are at least two ways to hear the question. First, one can understand it to be asking if it is possible to act morally—to do the things that moral people do—without believing in God. Second, one can understand the question as asking if it is possible for anyone to act morally—for morality itself to be well founded—if God doesn't exist. It is this second sense that Dostoevsky has in mind, for example, when he has Ivan Karamazov claim that if God doesn't exist, then everything is permitted.

If taken in the first sense, the question has an easy answer: of course. Many atheists lead perfectly admirable, moral lives. They care for their family, friends, and strangers. They are honest and honorable. They aren't liars, cheats, or sociopaths. And, of course, belief in God is no guarantee of moral probity. As we all know, there are plenty of scoundrels among theists and atheists alike.

If taken in the second sense, the question is much harder. Part of what makes the question harder is that it is unclear what sort of foundation we are demanding for morality. As a rough start, let us distinguish between two broad sorts of moral foundations: naturalist and nonnaturalist.

Naturalists think that morality may be founded in naturally occurring properties or facts. One possible candidate for such foundations is our naturally occurring emotional reactions (or "sentiments"). One might suppose that the deepest foundation for morality is the way we respond to certain events. We see someone hurt unnecessarily, and it bothers us. We feel a negative sentiment and disapprove. We see someone justly rewarded, and it pleases us. We feel a positive sentiment and approve. Another possible candidate is practical reason. One might suppose that the deepest foundation for morality is our ability to solve certain problems of cooperative behavior. Perhaps prohibitions on lying are rooted in our collectively recognizing that we need to cooperate and that we can't cooperate without some such prohibition. Still another possible candidate is pleasure and pain. One might think that pleasures—including higher pleasures, like taking a philosophy course—are intrinsically good, while pains are intrinsically bad. And one might suppose, for example, that that being the case, it follows inexorably that promoting overall pleasure must also be good and increasing overall pain must be unavoidably bad.

If morality can have naturalistic foundations, then there seems to be no reason why we can't have moral goodness without God. If morality is grounded in the sentiments, practical reason, or pleasure and pain, then our actions can be right or wrong regardless of whether or not God exists. Of course, such naturalistic views about ethics are also consistent with belief in God. A theist could similarly accept that the foundations of ethics are naturalistic and maintain that God commands that we do what is right. This would in effect be to take one horn of the *Euthyphro* argument: God exists, and commands us to do what is right, but what is right is not right *because* God commands us to do it.

Some philosophers have maintained that morality cannot have naturalistic foundations. Perhaps the most famous advocate of such a view is G. E. Moore. In the early twentieth century he argued that we cannot explain what goodness is by appeal to natural properties, such as what is pleasant or desirable. His thought is that natural properties are properties of the world as it is, whereas moral properties are properties of the world as it should be. We can't infer how the world should be from the way the world in fact is. For any natural property—say, pleasure—we can ask: Is that property (in these circumstances) good? Is that property (in these circumstances) bad? According to Moore, moral properties must be nonnatural properties, knowable only through nonempirical means.

Some theists maintain that God provides the grounds for such nonnatural, moral properties. The reason why pleasure is good in this situation and bad in that situation is ultimately to be explained by appeal to divine properties, whether those properties are divine commands or the divine nature itself. Perhaps pleasure is good in this situation because it is the result of an action that God commands. Perhaps pleasure is bad in that situation because it is the result of an action that God forbids. If one holds such a view, then one can consistently maintain that, without God, there would be no morally distinct goodness or badness. There would just be the way that things are, and there may be smarter or dumber moves in life, but there wouldn't be morally good or morally bad actions.

Does that mean that if Moore is right, the atheist must allow that we cannot be good without God? Not necessarily. For the atheist could also grant that morality is ultimately grounded in nonnatural properties or facts while denying that those properties or facts are divine. Indeed, Moore himself seems to have held such a view. On such a view, there are ethical facts in addition to natural facts. It is as evident to me that murder is wrong as that grass is green. It is as evident to me that hurting someone for no reason is wrong as it is that snow is white. It is not the case—so this story goes—that natural facts ground ethical facts. Rather the correct picture is that ethical truths are simply on a par with natural facts. This brand of atheist may therefore insist that theists are not uniquely entitled to transcendent, ethical facts, and thereby insist that even if goodness is not naturally grounded, we can nonetheless be good without God.

Further Study

Louis Anthony and William Lane Craig, "Is God Necessary for Morality?" *Veritas Forum*, April 24, 2012, https://youtu.be/6wKkbquUDSM.

Fyodor Dostoevsky, *The Grand Inquisitor*, from *The Brothers Karamazov*. 1880. Widely available online.

Greg M. Epstein, *Good without God: What a Billion Nonreligious People* Do *Believe*. New York: Harper, 2010. An engaging introduction to secular humanism.

Robert Shaver, "Egoism." *Stanford Encyclopedia of Philosophy* (Spring 2015 edition), ed. Edward N. Zalta, http://plato.stanford.edu/archives/spr2015/entries/egoism. A helpful overview of egoism with an extensive bibliography.

Baruch Spinoza, *The Ethics*. Ed. Seymour Feldman; trans. Samuel Shirley. Indianapolis, IN: Hackett, 1992. A good, inexpensive edition of Spinoza's *Ethics*.

Baruch Spinoza, *A Spinoza Reader*. Ed. and trans. Edwin Curley. Princeton, NJ: Princeton University Press, 1994. An excellent selection of Spinoza's writings by the leading translator of Spinoza's works in English.

17

Hume's *Dialogues Concerning Natural Religion*

Is the Universe Designed?

17.1. The Setting

David Hume was born in Edinburgh, Scotland, on 26 April 1711. He was raised in the strict Calvinism of the Presbyterian Church of Scotland, and as a young man was taught doctrines such as original sin, predestination, and the depravity of human nature. Hume reports that he lost his religious faith while still a teenager. Having turned his back on the church, Hume became deeply suspicious of organized religion in general. He strongly disapproved of the strict Calvinism in which he was raised, thought that Catholicism was a superstition, and once remarked that "when he heard a man was religious, he concluded he was a rascal, though he had known some instances of very good men being religious."

In his late teens, Hume conceived of a fundamentally new system of philosophy to introduce experimental reasoning into the study of human nature. The theory as presented in his *Treatise of Human Nature* (1739) and *Enquiry Concerning Human Understanding* (1748) suggests that humans are to be understood less as creatures of reason than as creatures of feeling and habit. This was a radical proposal at the time, as it implies that our beliefs, behaviors, and convictions flow more from custom, habit, and disposition than from reflection, wisdom, and insight. Much to Hume's disappointment, the early *Treatise* was a publishing failure, leading him to declare famously, "Never was a literary attempt more unfortunate than my *Treatise of Human Nature*. It fell *dead-born from the press*; without reaching such distinction, as even to excite a murmur among the zealots."

Saints, Heretics, and Atheists. Jeffrey K. McDonough, Oxford University Press. © Oxford University Press 2022.
DOI: 10.1093/oso/9780197563847.003.0017

In the early 1750s Hume began circulating a draft of his *Dialogues Concerning Natural Religion* to his friends. They advised him not to publish it. He took up the manuscript again a decade later and revised it shortly before his death. Among his final requests, he asked that the *Dialogues* be published within two years of his passing. And so it was done. The fruits of Hume's reflections on religion for more than twenty-five years finally appeared in 1779.

The *Dialogues* depict a discussion about religion involving five characters—two minor and three major. The minor characters are Pamphilus and Hermippus, with the former relating the discussion of the major characters to the latter. The major characters are Cleanthes, Philo, and Demea. Cleanthes is described as having "an accurate philosophical turn," holds that reason sheds light on faith, and is declared the winner at the end of the dialogue. Philo is described as "a careless skeptic." He comes around to a very weak deism by the end of the dialogue. He is awarded second place. Philo most closely represents Hume's own perspectives on religion—although, as we'll see, it is difficult to pin down Hume's exact views, and it is probably a mistake to assume that any one character represents his outlook precisely. Finally, Demea is described as having a "rigid inflexible orthodoxy" and espouses an unwavering fideism throughout the dialogue. He is awarded third place at the end of the discussion.

In this chapter, we explore the ways in which Hume takes up the so-called argument from design—that is, the argument that would have us infer the existence of a designing god from the apparent design of the universe. In chapters 18 and 19 we consider some of Hume's most famous objections to that argument and the lessons he would have us draw from the apparent existence of evil in the world. We conclude our exploration of Hume's *Dialogues* by asking what sort of picture of religion they might support as a whole. Hume clearly thinks that a sober weighing of the evidence does not support many traditional religious views. Whether he thinks that the evidence supports atheism, deism, or something else altogether, however, remains an open, difficult question.

17.2. The Limits of Reason

Hume's *Dialogues* opens with the first of several unlikely alliances. The orthodox Demea joins the careless skeptic Philo in emphasizing our limited ability to understand the nature of the divine. Although they agree on this point, they presumably have very different motivations in emphasizing it. Demea seeks to use pessimism about our ability to understand God's nature to support his fideism—that is, his view that religious beliefs should be based on faith rather than evidence. Philo, in contrast, sees pessimism about our ability to understand God as a specific instance of his general skepticism. For Philo, our inability to know much about God fits into a larger pattern of our inability to know much about anything. Demea and Philo are thus both eager to underscore the limitations of human reason even though they do so to very different ends.

The philosophical Cleanthes pushes back against the skepticism that Demea and Philo share. Cleanthes argues that unmitigated skepticism is impossible to live by. When we eat, we have to believe that food will nourish us. When we leave by the stairs rather than by the window, we have to believe that our bodies are heavy and that a fall would harm us. Cleanthes suggests that the skepticism of Demea and Philo is phony. They can't really accept the radical position they are espousing.

Philo responds to Cleanthes's objection by suggesting that Cleanthes has drawn the wrong lesson from the unlivability of unmitigated skepticism. The real lesson to be drawn from Cleanthes's objection, Philo suggests, is that we should embrace not unmitigated skepticism but a more limited, mitigated skepticism. We should hold that we must accept many things not on the basis of hard evidence, but rather on the basis of habit, custom, and disposition. More specifically, we should allow that in many day-to-day matters we have no choice but to proceed on the basis of habit, custom, and disposition. When our thoughts turn to abstract topics like metaphysics and religion, however, we should be duly aware of the limitations of our epistemic—that is, knowledge-seeking—capacities. Significantly, the mitigated skepticism that Philo espouses in response to Cleanthes's objection closely mirrors Hume's own views as expressed in his *Treatise of Human Nature* and *Enquiry Concerning Human Understanding*.

In responding to Philo, Cleanthes in turn suggests that there is no significant difference between unmitigated and mitigated skepticism. In doing so, he makes two important charges that recur throughout the dialogue. The first charge is that Philo does not hold scientific theories to the same skeptical standards to which he holds religious beliefs. This is, I think, a deep charge that ultimately receives a subtle answer from Hume. Very briefly, Hume holds that there are two ways in which a belief might lack justification.

First, it might rest on foundations that are not epistemically justified but that human nature nonetheless compels us to accept. If the skeptic is right, I may not have good evidence that the stove will burn my hand if I touch it again. Nonetheless, I might find it literally impossible to suspend my belief that the stove will burn my hand if I touch it again. Second, a belief might rest on foundations that are not epistemically justified but that we are not compelled by human nature to accept. Again, if the skeptic is right, I do not have good evidence that my horoscope is inaccurate. Unlike the stove case, however, I find it easy to suspend my belief in astrological predictions. With his distinction in hand, Hume can consistently argue that while religious and scientific beliefs both lack justification in the first way, only religious beliefs (and not foundational scientific beliefs) falter in the second way.

Cleanthes's second charge is that Philo is guilty of the fallacy of division. The charge, in short, is that it doesn't follow from the fact that our faculties do not in general support our claims to knowledge, that they do not support specifically our claims to religious knowledge. (Analogously, the fact that I generally drive too fast doesn't entail that I'm driving too fast now.) As will become clearer as we go along, this technical point is important to Cleanthes precisely because he thinks that the situation is indeed better in the case of religious belief than in the case of scientific belief since he thinks that while science presents us with paradoxes at every turn, "the religious hypothesis . . . is founded on the simplest and most obvious arguments" (40; unless otherwise indicated, all references in this chapter are to Hume [1998]). Cleanthes's second charge thus not only offers a response to Philo's skepticism but also serves as a springboard for his own positive account of our evidence in favor of religious beliefs.

17.3. Cleanthes's First Design Argument

Cleanthes's positive account in support of religious belief is most deeply rooted in a pair of design arguments. The first of those arguments attempts to show that the existence of an intelligent deity can be proved by experience:

> Look around the world: Contemplate the whole and every part of it: You will find it to be nothing but one great machine, subdivided into an infinite number of lesser machines. . . . The curious adapting of means to ends, throughout all nature, resembles exactly, though it much exceeds, the

> productions of human contrivance; of human design, thought, wisdom, and intelligence. Since therefore the effects resemble each other, we are led to infer, by all the rules of analogy, that the causes also resemble; and that the Author of nature is somewhat similar to the mind of man; though possessed of much larger faculties, proportioned to the grandeur of the work, which he has executed. By this argument . . . do we prove at once the existence of a Deity, and his similarity to human mind and intelligence. (15)

Cleanthes is clearly trying to draw an analogy between human artifacts and the "machine" of the universe in order to establish the existence of a designing god. Cleanthes's analogy might be thought of as having three main points. First, we find examples of means-end ordering throughout the domain of artifacts that we attribute to intelligent design. The parts of my watch, for example, are arranged in just the sort of way necessary for it to keep time, and I attribute that means-end ordering to an intelligent watchmaker. Second, it is a fundamental principle of analogical reasoning that similar effects should be assigned similar causes. If I know that all the parts of my watch have been designed so that it keeps good time, and I see that your watch also keeps good time, I should infer by analogy that all the parts of your watch have also been designed so that it keeps good time. Third, we find examples of means-end ordering throughout the domain of nature: the earth is positioned in just the right way to support human life, the plant has exactly the cells and dispositions it needs to live in its environment, and so on. Taking the three points together, Cleanthes is suggesting that we ought to attribute the means-end ordering that we find in the universe to an intelligent being or divinity.

Not surprisingly Philo and Cleanthes skirmish over how strong Cleanthes's particular analogy is. A more general issue, however, lurks in the background: what makes for a good argument by analogy? We may see Hume as suggesting two principal criteria. First, analogical arguments presuppose that similar effects are likely to have similar causes. Drawing on that criterion, Philo is quick to point out that any dissimilarity of effect will raise some doubt about the intended analogy. As he puts it,

> Unless the cases be exactly similar, [just reasoners] repose no perfect confidence in applying their past observation to any particular phenomenon. Every alteration of circumstances occasions a doubt concerning the event. (18)

Second, in the *Enquiries*, Hume suggests that in analogical reasoning we are generally only entitled to infer a cause minimally sufficient for an effect:

> When we infer any particular cause from an effect, we must proportion the one to the other, and can never be allowed to ascribe to the cause any qualities, but what are exactly sufficient to produce the effect. (Hume 1748, [14G]136)

In this context, this second principle implies that from an analogous effect we may only infer an analogous cause that is minimally sufficient for producing that effect. Although both principles seem reasonable, it is worth noting that in certain cases we may see a tension between them. I see a dam in the river and infer by the principle of like-effects–like-causes that it was built by a beaver. But by the principle of a minimal sufficient cause, perhaps I should only infer that the dam is the result of the river's current and some branches that happen to be floating down it in just the right way.

In addition to raising general questions about arguments by analogy, Philo also raises two important direct objections to Cleanthes's initial design argument. First, Philo suggests that it is rash to move from the apparent design of parts of the universe to the conclusion that the whole universe is designed (19). His point seems to be that Cleanthes's argument slides from a comparison between one part of the universe and other parts of the universe to the conclusion that the universe as a whole is designed. Philo's objection is that this slide isn't valid. From the fact that a bunch of the parts in a trash heap are well designed, it doesn't follow that the trash heap itself is well designed. Philo seems to have a valid point, although it is less clear how it fits into the dialectic between theists and atheists. There are simply not many defenders of the view that large-scale parts of the universe are designed, but that the universe itself is not designed.

Second, Philo suggests that even if the universe is thought to be analogous to one of its parts, it might not be analogous to one of its apparently designed parts (19). Here I think Philo is best understood as suggesting that if we are to move by analogy from parts to whole, there is something perverse about modeling the whole universe upon one of its apparently designed parts. After all, many parts of the universe seem chaotic. Why should we suppose that the universe as a whole is more like one of the apparently designed parts than one of the apparently not-designed parts?

17.4. Cleanthes's Second Design Argument

Cleanthes is unfazed by either of Philo's main objections, which he thinks could only be accepted by an unmitigated skeptic. To Cleanthes, the analogy between the means-end ordering of nature and the means-end ordering of human artifacts is so obvious and compelling that only a thoroughgoing skeptic could deny it. Convinced that Philo cannot be persuaded by reason, Cleanthes changes tack and tries to get Philo to share in the same feelings of conviction that he himself has and that he assumes are natural to most people. His efforts in this regard are capped by a pair of provocative thought experiments.

The first of Cleanthes's thought experiments runs as follows:

> Suppose, therefore, that an articulate voice were heard in the clouds, much louder and more melodious than any which human art could ever reach: Suppose, that this voice were extended in the same instant over all nations, and spoke to each nation in its own language and dialect: Suppose, that the words delivered not only contain a just sense and meaning, but convey some instruction altogether worthy of a benevolent Being, superior to mankind: Could you possibly hesitate a moment concerning the cause of this voice? And must you not instantly ascribe it to some design or purpose? Yet I cannot see but all the same objections (if they merit that appellation) which lie against the system of theism, may also be produced against this inference. (23)

Cleanthes's suggestion is that if we were to hear such a voice in the clouds, we would naturally infer that an intelligent being is the cause of the sound. Nonetheless, the same skeptical doubts that Cleanthes takes Philo to have been raising against his original design argument might be raised in this case as well. We could imagine that the sound is just an unlikely breeze blowing, unusual birds that we can't see, and so on. Cleanthes takes this to show that Philo's doubts about the original design argument are unfounded, and that he is skeptically denying an obvious analogy. Unless we can find some strong reason to overturn our natural view, Cleanthes thinks, the analogy must be granted.

Cleanthes's first thought experiment raises a real challenge for Hume, a challenge that contemporary philosophers of religion have echoed. The thought runs like this: Look, you can raise skeptical doubts about almost any epistemically basic practice—logical inference, induction, sense perception, and so on. (And, indeed, in other works Hume raises skeptical worries about all these practices.) But we don't just abandon those practices in the face of such skeptical objections. We continue to use them and refine them even though we recognize that we have no wholly independent grounds for thinking them to be reliable. But why then shouldn't we say the same thing about those epistemic practices that underpin religious belief? If skeptical worries don't undermine our nonreligious beliefs, why should they be allowed to undermine our religious beliefs? (It is perhaps worth noting that Hume's own answer might be simply pragmatic: religious beliefs are dangerous, they lead to intolerance and war; our other beliefs typically have less dire consequences. Whether this is true or not is, of course, a further question.)

Cleanthes makes essentially the same point with a second thought experiment. This time, Cleanthes imagines a library full of self-propagating "natural volumes, containing the most refined reason and most exquisite beauty." He asks Philo,

> Could you possibly open one of them, and doubt, that its original cause bore the strongest analogy to mind and intelligence? When it reasons and discourses; when it expostulates, argues, and enforces its views and topics; when it applies sometimes to the pure intellect, sometimes to the affections; when it collects, disposes, and adorns every consideration suited to the subject: could you persist in asserting, that all this, at the bottom, had really no meaning, and that the first formation of this volume in the loins of its original parent proceeded not from thought and design? Your obstinacy, I know, reaches not that degree of firmness: Even your skeptical play and wantonness would be abashed at so glaring an absurdity. (24)

Cleanthes suggests that faced with a library of such "natural volumes," one could hardly doubt that their "original cause bore the strongest analogy to mind and intelligence," even though such volumes would nonetheless be less refined in their ordering and less amazing in their capacities than the living organisms of everyday experience.

With his second thought experiment, Cleanthes is, in effect, attempting to shift the burden of doubt in his own favor. In the natural volumes case, he thinks it is clear that we naturally suppose that there is a strong enough analogy to warrant the inference to design (even though it is possible to raise skeptical objections even in this case). But, he maintains, unless we are utter skeptics, we should have the same natural reaction to the order and structure of the world. Our familiarity with the marvelous organization of the world may dull our surprise, but the prima facie case remains and strong evidence—not just skeptical worries—should be demanded if we are to overturn our initial conviction. To Cleanthes's way of thinking, the inference to the design of the universe and the belief in an intelligent god are utterly natural and can be denied only by those who would have us believe almost nothing.

Is the belief in religion really "natural" in the sense Cleanthes suggests? From Hume's perspective, the case for the naturalness of religious belief seems mixed. On the one hand, it can hardly be denied that the belief in an intelligent, designing divinity is widespread among humans, and that philosophical arguments over thousands of years seem to have had little impact on the general beliefs of ordinary people. Furthermore, many people have held that religious belief plays an essential role in the functioning of human society, and even in the everyday lives of individuals.

Nonetheless, the case for the naturalness of religious belief is not one-sided. In his *Natural History of Religion*, Hume notes that while the belief in a god-like power is widespread, it is not uniform or universal. Unlike other beliefs that Hume takes to be natural, such as the belief in induction and enduring objects, religious beliefs vary considerably across societies and times. Furthermore, while there are at least a fair number of agnostics and atheists around, there are very few skeptics about induction or the external world. Such considerations suggest that religious belief is at least not as deeply entrenched in our natures as some other epistemically basic beliefs.

17.5. Is the Universe Fine-Tuned?

Although Hume's discussion of the argument from design remains a classic touchstone even today, his treatment has of course not been the last word. In an interesting development, contemporary cosmologists have recently argued that if various features of the universe had been even slightly different, life as we know it would be impossible. If, for example, gravity had been a bit stronger, or had there been slightly more matter, or slightly less energy, the universe would be in such a state that it could not support plants, animals, and humans.

Some philosophers have seen in these scientific conclusions grounds for an updated version of the argument from design. The central thrust of the updated argument is that the fact that just the right conditions necessary for life exist is best explained by the hypothesis that the world was created by an intelligent being. For on the assumption that there is an intelligent creator, the fact that the world is "fine-tuned" for life is perfectly understandable. Indeed, that is just what we might expect if we believe in an intelligent creator. But on the assumption that the world has come about by blind forces or sheer luck, the fact that the world is fine-tuned for life becomes astoundingly improbable. Proponents of the updated argument conclude that the world's fine-tuning gives us good reason to suppose that the world was designed by an intelligent creator.

Many people have found the fine-tuning argument intuitive and convincing—but, of course, not everyone. One strategy for resisting its line of thought may be viewed as having two steps. The first step is rooted in speculative cosmology. Some cosmologists have argued that our universe is just one of very, very many universes. This multiverse hypothesis implies that it is not, after all, so improbable that there exists a universe capable of supporting life. If you buy a million lottery tickets, it's not so unlikely that you hold a winning ticket. Even granting the first step, however, one might think that it is incredibly lucky that we inhabit a universe that happens to support life. Even if I buy a million lottery tickets, I might find it astonishing that *this* ticket happens to be the winner. The second step of the multiverse strategy aims to address this residual worry. It suggests that no one should be surprised that they live in a universe that supports life because living in a universe that supports life is a necessary condition for raising that sort of worry to begin with! You can be surprised that there is a world that supports life—the first step is supposed to address that surprise; you can't be surprised that the world you live in supports life. No one lives in a world that doesn't support life!

A second response suggests that we have no good way to assign the relevant probabilities involved in the fine-tuning argument. Suppose it is true that if the gravitational constant had been varied by one-tenth of 1 percent, the universe would be incapable of supporting life. That sounds dramatic, but we should want to know how likely it is for the gravitational constant to vary by one-tenth of 1 percent. And it is not clear that we have any good sense of that likelihood at all. To illustrate the point, consider the fact that if I had only been a couple of feet taller, I might have been a very good basketball player.

On a cosmic scale, a couple of feet is very little indeed. Is it therefore miraculous that I'm not a very good basketball player? Not at all. Although there are people a couple of feet taller than me, it is very, very unusual. And although things might have been very different for me had I only been slightly different on a cosmic scale, my current height is actually unremarkable and much more likely than my being eight feet tall. The point is that we seem to have no good way to assess the probability of the conditions appealed to in fine-tuning arguments. The existence of life in the universe may be a lucky throw of the die, but it is hard to know how likely it is without knowing how many sides the die actually has.

Further Study

David Hume, *Dialogues Concerning Natural Religion*, 2nd ed., ed. Richard H. Popkin. Indianapolis, IN: Hackett, 1998. A good, inexpensive edition of Hume's *Dialogues*.

David Hume, *The Natural History of Religion*. In *Dialogues and Natural History of Religion*, ed. J. A. C. Gaskin. New York: Oxford University Press, 1993. Hume's attempt to offer a "naturalistic-historical" account of the origins of religion. Widely available in many contemporary editions and online.

David Hume, *Philosophical Essays Concerning Human Understanding*. London: A. Millar, 1748; 1777. Hume's revised attempt to present the epistemological and metaphysical themes of his philosophical system. Widely available in many contemporary editions and online.

David Hume, *A Treatise of Human Nature*. London: John Noon, 1739–40. Hume's first book-length presentation of his philosophical system. Widely available in many contemporary editions and online.

Neil Manson, "The Fine-Tuning Argument." *Philosophy Compass* 4, no. 1 (2009): 271–86. A clear and helpful discussion of the fine-tuning argument.

William Edward Morris and Charlotte R. Brown, "David Hume." *Stanford Encyclopedia of Philosophy* (Spring 2016 edition), ed. Edward N. Zalta, http://plato.stanford.edu/archives/spr2016/entries/hume/. Helpful overview of Hume's philosophical system with an extensive bibliography.

Paul Russell, "Hume on Religion." *Stanford Encyclopedia of Philosophy* (Winter 2014 edition), ed. Edward N. Zalta, http://plato.stanford.edu/archives/win2014/entries/hume-religion/. Helpful overview of Hume's treatment of religion and religious belief with an extensive bibliography.

18
Hume's *Dialogues Concerning Natural Religion*

Design without a Designer?

18.1. The Regress Objection

In the last chapter, we saw Hume—via the character Cleanthes—present two arguments from design. Both arguments suggest that we should infer the existence of a designing god from the apparent design of parts of the universe. Just as we infer that a watch was designed by some intelligent agent because it is so well ordered, we should infer that the universe was designed by some intelligent agent because it is so well ordered. Cleanthes argued that attempts to block such an inference violate customs of analogical reasoning, swim against our natural sentiments and opinions, and must ultimately rest on a thoroughgoing and unlivable skepticism.

In Part IV of his *Dialogues Concerning Natural Religion*, Hume has the character Philo introduce an important objection to Cleanthes's design arguments. The reasoning of the design argument merely pushes back a step the felt need for an explanation of apparent design.

> How, therefore, shall we satisfy ourselves concerning the cause of that Being whom you suppose the Author of Nature, or, according to your system of anthropomorphism, the Ideal World into which you trace the material? Have we not the same reason to trace that ideal world into another ideal world or new intelligent principle? But if we stop and go no farther, why go so far? Why not stop at the material world? How can we satisfy ourselves without going on in infinitum? . . . If the material world rests upon a similar ideal world, this ideal world must rest upon some other, and so on

Saints, Heretics, and Atheists. Jeffrey K. McDonough, Oxford University Press. © Oxford University Press 2022.
DOI: 10.1093/oso/9780197563847.003.0018

> without end. (31; unless otherwise indicated, all references in this chapter are to Hume [1998])

Philo further develops his central objection by pointing out that there are many phenomena that have order for which there is no apparent or known cause, "as in all instances of generation and vegetation where the accurate analysis of the cause exceeds all human comprehension" (31). Likewise, there are countless examples of disorder that seem to arise without any apparent or known cause—for example, cases of madness and corruption. Why, then, should we think that all of these things can be, or need be, explained? And if such things *in* the universe needn't be explained, why should we think that the universe itself must be explained?

Although this is sometimes treated as an absolutely devastating objection to the design argument, I think Cleanthes actually makes a pretty good reply here. While acknowledging that explanations must come to an end somewhere, he suggests that that is no reason to stop sooner rather than later:

> Even in common life, if I assign the cause for any event, is it any objection, *Philo*, that I cannot assign the cause of that cause, and answer every new question which may incessantly be started? And what philosophers could possibly submit to so rigid a rule? . . . You ask me what is the cause of this cause? I know not; I care not; that concerns not me. I have found a Deity and here I stop my inquiry. Let those go farther who are wiser or more enterprising. (32)

The situation, Cleanthes implies, is the same wherever we look, including in natural philosophy or science. We may, for example, explain the orbits of the planets by appealing to the laws of gravity. And perhaps we may explain the laws of gravity by appealing to even deeper laws of physics. But at some point, we must appeal to principles for which we do not have further explanations. Only a skeptic, Cleanthes suggests, would maintain that the threat of explanatory regress must undermine the explanations that we can give.

Philo adopts a good strategy in his response to Cleanthes's reply insofar as he argues that religious and scientific cases are importantly different. Granting that explanations must come to an end somewhere, he suggests that natural philosophers seek to subsume more specific phenomena under more general phenomena, while Cleanthes's design argument offers an explanation that stands in need of exactly the same kind of explanation as what it is supposed to explain. He suggests that God, as "an ideal system, arranged of itself, without precedent design, is not a whit more explicable than a material one which attains its order in a like manner; nor is there any more difficulty in the latter supposition than in the former" (33).

While Philo's strategy is indeed a sensible one, it is far from clear that he wins this argument, or that Hume thinks that he does. After all, there is a sense in which the theist is offering a more general explanation subsuming many specific phenomena under it. A single designer might explain the order we find in plants, animals, and the universe as a whole. Granted that some features of the design argument make it significantly different from features of scientific arguments—How, for example, could it be confirmed by experiment? How could it be falsified?—it is not a trivial matter to say why Philo's regress concern is applicable more to the former than the latter.

18.2. The Design Argument and Traditional Theism

Having raised his infinite regress objection, Philo next presses a line of attack that looks back to one of Cleanthes's own objections to Demea's fideism. At its heart is the thought that to the extent that God is supposed to be analogous to a human creator, we should suppose that he is finite, imperfect, and collaborative.

Pressing the point with respect to imperfection, Philo notes, "There are many inexplicable difficulties in the works of Nature which, if we allow a perfect author to be proved *a priori*, are easily solved, and become only seeming difficulties from the narrow capacity of man, who cannot trace infinite relations. But according to your method of reasoning, these difficulties become all real; and, perhaps, will be insisted on as new instances of likeness to human art and contrivance" (36).

The same point can easily be made with respect to finitude and collaboration. All the designers that we know about are finite, and indeed embodied, so it is not clear how we can argue by analogy to an infinite, immaterial designer. Likewise, all the large-scale design projects of which we have experience are typically collaborative affairs involving many designers and implementers. So, if we are to argue by analogy, why shouldn't we arrive at the conclusion that there are many gods with different skills all working together? Philo concludes that any analogy between a divine creator and human creators will be of little help to the traditional theist.

Interestingly, Cleanthes, for his part, seems untroubled by Philo's objection. He of course denies that the divine creator is defective or limited in any of the ways Philo suggests, and maintains that such worries are themselves strained and ridiculous. Indeed, Cleanthes appears to be encouraged by the fact that Philo's objection seems to take for granted that his argument does imply a divine intelligence, and he tells us, "This I regard as a sufficient foundation for religion" (38).

18.3. An Immanent Designer?

In the arguments between Cleanthes and Demea, it has been a shared assumption up to this point that the order, or apparent design, of the world needs explaining in terms of something independent of the world. That is, it has been assumed that the design of the world calls out not just for an orderer, but for a distinct, independent orderer. In Part VI of the *Dialogues*, Philo begins to challenge that assumption by raising the possibility that the world might be self-organized, or immanently designed, and thus might more closely resemble an organism than a machine.

> Now, if we survey the universe, so far it falls under our knowledge, it bears a great resemblance to an animal or organized body, and seems actuated with a like principle of life and motion. A continual circulation of matter in it produces no disorder; a continual waste in every part is incessantly repaired: The closest sympathy is perceived throughout the entire system: And each part or member, in performing its proper offices, operates both to its own preservation and to that of the whole. The world, therefore, I infer, is an animal; and the Deity is the *Soul* of the world, actuating it, and actuated by it. (39–40)

The suggestion here is that the argument from design supports at least as well the postulation of a kind of animated pantheism as it does an independent designer. That is to say, Philo is suggesting that the argument offered by Cleanthes leads at least as quickly to a view like Spinoza's (or to the views of the ancient Stoics) as it does to the sort of traditional theism Cleanthes intends to defend.

Cleanthes initially responds to Philo's new proposal (in part) by suggesting that it "seems to imply the eternity of the world." That inference is hardly obvious, but probably Cleanthes is thinking that, in the most natural way to understand Philo's proposal, the world wouldn't be created at all, but rather would have always existed with everything it needs to bring about its current well-ordered state. Cleanthes maintains, however, that the eternity of the world is highly improbable. He notes that there are many large-scale events that have occurred in the world relatively recently—cherry trees, for example, were introduced into Europe from Asia in Roman times; grapevines didn't grow in France more than two thousand years ago, and so on. Cleanthes reasons that if the world were eternal, it is highly unlikely that such events would have occurred in relatively recent history. The thought here, apparently, is that if cherry trees, for example, had existed for eternity and could grow in Europe, they would have started growing there long before Roman times. Cleanthes concludes that these considerations "seem convincing proofs of the youth, or rather infancy, of the world" (42).

Not surprisingly, Philo is not terribly impressed with Cleanthes's initial response, noting that "matter [may] be susceptible of many and great revolutions, through the endless periods of eternal duration" (42). Nonetheless, Philo takes his own proposal a step further in a way that would circumvent Cleanthes's concern. He argues that, to the extent that the world more closely resembles an organism rather than a machine, we might suppose that the present world has come into being through a process of generation. If the world resembles more closely a plant or an animal than a machine or an artifact, its present existence might be attributed to a process of generation rather than to design. Again, it is important to recognize that Philo's point is not that we should accept such a hypothesis as true. His point is rather a (moderately) skeptical one. The argument from design supports a wide variety of nontraditional theological views at least as well as it supports traditional theism. The appropriate response, according to Cleanthes, is to conclude, "No one [of these systems] has any advantage over the others" (43).

18.4. No Designer at All?

In Part VIII of the *Dialogues*, Philo continues to press his view that the hypothesis that the world has been designed by an independent deity is no better supported than countless other hypotheses. He sketches two further possibilities that have their roots in Epicurean cosmogony.

The first such possibility has two main postulates, namely, that the world (i) has a finite number of particles as well as active principles capable of generating and sustaining motion, and (ii) lasts for an infinite period of time. Philo suggests that if these postulates—which seem to be at least possible—are granted, then:

> It must happen, in an eternal duration, that every possible order or position must be tried an infinite number of times. This world, therefore, with all its events, even the most minute, has before been produced and destroyed, and will again be produced and destroyed, without any bounds and limitations. No one who has a conception of the powers of the infinite, in comparison to the finite, will ever scruple this determination. (49)

Again, Philo's point is not that we should accept this hypothesis, which he says is justly esteemed "the most absurd system that has yet been proposed." His point is rather that the apparent design of the universe does not allow us to infer the existence of a transcendent designer. It is worth noting, however, that the argument here is slightly different, slightly more ambitious than before. Whereas Philo had argued previously that the apparent design of the universe is equally consistent with an immanent designer as it is with an independent designer, he is now arguing that the apparent design of the universe is equally consistent with there being *no designer at all.*

The second hypothesis that Philo entertains involves the possibility of a naturally emerging self-sustaining system. Where the earlier account turned on the idea that, given enough time, matter might take on every possible arrangement, including ones that appear well designed, the second hypothesis turns on the idea that matter might take on different arrangements until it settles into one that is self-sustaining. On this account, matter is essentially arranged by chance, but some arrangements are self-sustaining, and those arrangements persist and give the impression of being designed to persist. (This picture is, of course, very much in the spirit of evolution's account of the apparent design of creatures, and indeed, Philo goes on to suggest explicitly that the same idea might be applied in explaining the well-adapted features of organisms [51–53].) Here again, Philo's hypothesis seems to go beyond his earlier suggestion in holding that the appearance of design is consistent with there being no designer at all.

Cleanthes's response in some ways simply goes back to the original intuitions that motivate the design argument to begin with. The design argument, after all, needn't deny the mere possibility of apparent order without design. It need only insist that apparent order makes design more likely than not. At this stage of the dialectic, however, Cleanthes does introduce one new wrinkle that will become important in subsequent parts of the *Dialogues*. He suggests that although evolutionary-style stories might explain features absolutely requisite for subsistence, they cannot explain the abundance of benefits that are not strictly necessary for survival: delicious fruits, domesticated animals, and scientific marvels are all wonderful but seem unnecessary for our mere existence. Cleanthes concludes,

> Though the maxims of nature be in general very frugal, yet instances of this kind are far from being rare; and any one of them is a sufficient proof of design, and of a benevolent design, which gave rise to order and arrangement of the universe. (52)

What is novel in Cleanthes's response is his emphasis on the thought that the absence of design cannot explain the abundance of beneficial features in the world. Cleanthes seems willing to grant that self-sustaining systems could emerge from relative chaos, and exhibit merely apparent design, but he thinks that that is an implausible explanation of the apparent design of a system as beneficial as ours. This somewhat subtle shift in emphasis from general means-end ordering to robustly benevolent ordering marks an important change in Cleanthes's strategy and effectively sets up Hume's discussion of evil in Parts X and XI of the *Dialogues*.

18.5. Contemporary Criticisms

The next chapter shifts gears to turn to Hume's presentation of a causal argument for the existence of God and the problem of evil. Before leaving the design argument, however, it may be helpful to briefly sketch three arguments against intelligent design that have been raised by contemporary thinkers.

18.5.1. The Panda's Thumb

The first argument comes from Stephen Jay Gould (1941–2002), a renowned paleontologist and evolutionary biologist, and a prolific science writer. Gould argued that intelligent design and evolution both do a good job of explaining examples of good or near optimal design. Both intelligent design and evolution, for example, can explain why we have eyes, a heart, ears, and so on. They are all things that both a good, benevolent designer might bestow upon us and that might be selected for because they confer evolutionary advantages.

Gould maintained, however, that evolution offers a better explanation of poor or "jury-rigged" adaptations. His most famous example of such a jury-rigged adaptation is the panda's "thumb." What looks like a sixth digit on the panda's paw isn't really a thumb at all, but rather an extended bone belonging to its wrist. Gould reasoned that from an evolutionary perspective, the panda's thumb makes good sense. Pandas that developed elongated wrist bones would plausibly enjoy a selection advantage in being able to better grip stalks of bamboo. But, Gould maintained, the panda's thumb makes no sense from an intelligent design perspective. If God were designing a panda from scratch, there'd be no reason to fashion an extra digit from a wrist bone.

Note, by the way, the relevance here of an objection that Philo made. Someone like Demea who defends the existence of God on a priori grounds might, in effect, reply to Gould: well, how do we know? Maybe the design of actual pandas really is the best design after all, even if it looks jury-rigged to us. But Philo would insist that such a reply would undercut the argument from design. If we are going to argue from the apparent design of the universe to the existence of God, we should, Philo would insist, follow the argument where it leads—perhaps, in this case, concluding that the designer of the world prefers ingenious to optimal designs, or recycling parts to following established patterns, and so on.

18.5.2. God's Utility Function

Drawing on work by the philosopher Daniel Dennett (1942–), Richard Dawkins presents a different argument against the intelligent design of the natural world. Dawkins suggests that if there is a designer, it should make sense to ask what it is trying to accomplish. What is it seeking to optimize? Dawkins argues that often we can offer a plausible answer to this question when we consider particular species. It seems that the gazelle, for example, is optimized to run fast and escape cheetahs. But if we suppose that God designs all creatures, Dawkins maintains, then God's utility function must seem baffling, for the apparent utility functions of different species seem to be at odds with one another. If the apparent utility function of gazelles is to run fast to escape cheetahs, the apparent utility function of cheetahs seems to be to run fast in order to catch gazelles. This sort of natural arms race is just what we should expect, Dawkins maintains, if evolutionary biology is correct. He argues that it is completely unintelligible, however, if the world as a whole has been designed by a single intelligent creator.

18.5.3. Nature's Indifference

A third argument has also been articulated by Richard Dawkins (1941–). Dawkins points out that competition among animals leads to extraordinary suffering in the world. Here's Dawkins in his own words:

> The total amount of suffering per year in the natural world is beyond all decent contemplation. During the minute it takes me to compose this sentence, thousands of animals are being eaten alive; others are running for their lives, whimpering with fear; others are being slowly devoured from within by rasping parasites; thousands of all kinds are dying of starvation, thirst and disease. (1995, 131–32)

As with the previous case, Dawkins thinks this all makes perfectly good sense from an evolutionary perspective. Nature itself is indifferent to suffering, and so suffering is only minimized to the extent that it has evolutionary payoff, which, unfortunately, isn't often enough. But, Dawkins argues, the tremendous suffering of animals doesn't make any sense given a benevolent, traditional designer. We should expect that a benevolent, traditional designer would minimize, or at least reduce, the suffering of the world. And that thought brings us back once again to the issues raised at the end of Part VIII of Hume's *Dialogues*. In the next chapter, after a few preliminaries, we look in some detail at Hume's presentation of the problem of evil.

Further Study

Richard Dawkins, *River Out of Eden: A Darwinian View of Life*. New York: Basic Books, 1995.

Stephen Jay Gould, "The Panda's Peculiar Thumb." In *The Panda's Thumb*, 19–26. New York: W.W. Norton and Company, 1980.

Kenneth Einar Himma, "Design Arguments for the Existence of God." *Internet Encyclopedia of Philosophy*, ed. James Fieser and Bradley Dowden, https://iep.utm.edu/design/#SH2c. A helpful overview of design arguments for the existence of God with an extensive bibliography.

David Hume, *Dialogues Concerning Natural Religion*, 2nd ed., ed. Richard H. Popkin. Indianapolis, IN: Hackett, 1998. A good, inexpensive edition of Hume's *Dialogues*.

Alvin Plantinga, "What Is the Evolutionary Argument against Naturalism?" *Closer to the Truth*, interview with D. P. Mosteller, available online. Plantinga has very cleverly argued that belief in nondirected, evolutionary naturalism is self-undermining. This interview offers a concise overview of Plantinga's position.

Del Ratzsch and Jeffrey Koperski, "Teleological Arguments for God's Existence." *Stanford Encyclopedia of Philosophy* (Spring 2015 edition), ed. Edward N. Zalta, http://plato.stanford.edu/archives/spr2015/entries/teleological-arguments/. A helpful overview of the argument from design with an extensive bibliography.

19

Hume's *Dialogues Concerning Natural Religion*

True Religion?

19.1. The Causal Argument

At the beginning of Part X of the *Dialogues Concerning Natural Religion*, Hume has the character Demea present a new argument that Demea claims "cuts off at once all doubt and difficulty" (54; unless otherwise indicated, all references in this chapter are to Hume [(1998]). Although there are some subtle differences between Demea's causal argument and Aquinas's first way (see chapter 9 in this volume), the general drift is much the same: The existence of a contingent thing like a planet or a person presupposes a cause. That cause must either be a necessary being or a contingent being. If it is a necessary being, then we have discovered something we may identify with God. If it is a contingent being, then we are launched on a regress. An infinite regress of contingent causes is supposed to be nonviable, so the regress must ultimately terminate in a necessary being that we may identify with God.

Cleanthes (not Philo) quickly raises a series of powerful objections against Demea's causal argument. Let's consider three. First, Cleanthes argues that the existence of no being can be proved a priori (that is, without appeal to experience):

> I shall begin with observing that there is an evident absurdity in pretending to demonstrate a matter of fact, or to prove it by any arguments a priori. Nothing is demonstrable unless the contrary implies a contradiction. Nothing that is distinctly conceivable implies a contradiction. Whatever we conceive as existent, we can also conceive as non-existent. There is no being, therefore, whose non-existence implies a contradiction. Consequently

Saints, Heretics, and Atheists. Jeffrey K. McDonough, Oxford University Press. © Oxford University Press 2022.
DOI: 10.1093/oso/9780197563847.003.0019

> there is no being whose existence is demonstrable. I propose this argument as entirely decisive, and am willing to rest the whole controversy upon it. (55)

The objection is somewhat difficult to assess because it bundles together two seemingly distinct considerations. On the one hand, it implies that no a priori argument can prove a matter of fact such as that God exists. But this might well seem misdirected as a criticism of Demea's argument, for although Demea himself characterizes his argument as a priori, it has a manifestly a posteriori premise, namely, that contingent things exist. Demea's argument thus does not appear to even attempt to derive a matter of fact—God's existence—from purely a priori considerations, but rather from reasoning together with matters of fact. On the other hand, Demea does take his argument to establish not just a first cause, but a necessarily existing first cause. And Cleanthes's suggestion that "whatever we conceive as existent, we can also conceive as non-existent" is a legitimate argument against the postulation of any necessarily existing being, whether the grounds offered in support of that being's existence are a priori or a posteriori.

Cleanthes argues next that even if a necessary being could be proved in the way that Demea proposes, nothing would rule out it being a nonanthropomorphic god or even identical to the universe itself. The point is well taken, albeit with a grain of salt. Cleanthes seems right in insisting that the causal argument does not establish the existence of a personal God. The argument taken by itself seems to be consistent with the existence of an impersonal first cause. But, in Demea's defense, the causal argument—if sound—might be thought to establish an important foothold for further arguments that might establish the existence of a personal god. And indeed, as discussed in chapter 9, that was precisely Aquinas's strategy. Aquinas argued that a version of the causal argument was a crucial first step in establishing first the existence of a being with the impersonal attributes canonically associated with God, and then for establishing that that being must also have the personal attributes canonically associated with God. So, although Demea has a point, it is a point to which there already is a well-known reply.

Finally, Cleanthes offers a famous objection to the causal argument often associated with Hume. The gist of the objection is simply that once a cause has been assigned to every member of a series, there are no grounds for demanding a further cause of the series itself. Suppose, for example, I have a collection of twelve baseball cards that you very much admire. You ask me where I acquired this fantastic collection, and I explain to you how I came to acquire each of the twelve cards. It would seem unreasonable to complain that you still want to know how I acquired not just each card but also the whole *collection*. Cleanthes is suggesting, analogously, that if every effect of a series—even an infinite series—has a cause, it is unreasonable to insist on there being a cause of the series-as-a-whole as well. Cleanthes's point is that we should not be troubled by an infinite regress of contingent causes, since in such a series there is an explanation for every effect in the series, namely, its antecedent cause, and any demand for a further explanation—for example, for an explanation of the series-as-a-whole—is unwarranted.

19.2. The Problem of Evil

Part X of Hume's *Dialogues Concerning Natural Religion* opens with Demea and Philo effectively agreeing that there is evident misery and suffering in the world. Hume eloquently suggests that such suffering is deeply and inextricably woven into every aspect of the world and life:

> Demea: The whole earth, believe me, *Philo*, is cursed and polluted. A perpetual war is kindled amongst all living creatures. Necessity, hunger, want stimulate the strong and courageous: fear, anxiety, terror agitate the weak and infirm. The first entrance into life gives anguish to the new-born infant and to its wretched parent: weakness, impotence, distress attend each stage of that life, and it is, at last, finished in agony and horror. (59)

The strong and the weak, humans and animals, the insulated and the exposed—all, according to Demea, suffer alike. Any attempt to dismiss the existence of misery, suffering, and evil must therefore run against "the united testimony of mankind, founded on sense and reason."

Demea and Philo agree that suffering is the principal root of religious belief. They disagree, however, about what should be made of this fact. Demea holds that our recognition of suffering in the world helps us to appreciate the truth of religious belief. That is, he maintains that misery leads us to a true belief in God, since each person, as he puts it, "from a consciousness of his imbecility and misery rather than from any reasoning, is led to seek protection from that Being on whom he and all nature are dependent." From Demea's viewpoint, the very wretchedness of our lives rightfully leads us to seek repose and atonement in religion (58). Philo, on the other hand, thinks that our fears and anxieties explain our irrational, unjustified belief in God. Our understandable desire to escape the misery of the world leads us to accept without any good epistemic reason the existence of an omnipotent being that might save us from our inevitable suffering. Whereas Demea sees suffering as a true path to God, Philo sees it as an all-too-understandable path to delusion.

Philo seizes on Demea's partial agreement to renew his attack on Cleanthes's belief in a traditional anthropomorphic God:

> And is it possible, *Cleanthes*, said *Philo*, that after all these reflections, and infinitely more which might be suggested, you can still persevere in your anthropomorphism, and assert the moral attributes of the Deity, his justice, benevolence, mercy, and rectitude, to be of the same nature with these virtues in human creatures? His power, we allow, is infinite; whatever he wills is executed: But neither man nor any other animal is happy; therefore, he does not will their happiness. His wisdom is infinite; He is never mistaken in choosing the means to any end; But the course of nature tends not to human or animal felicity: Therefore, it is not established for that purpose. Through the whole compass of human knowledge there are no inferences more certain and infallible than these. In what respect, then, do his benevolence and mercy resemble the benevolence and mercy of men? (63)

Here we see Philo returning to a theme he pursued in more detail in Parts V through VII of the *Dialogues*, namely, that the attribution to God of many personal attributes such as goodness, mercy, and justice are especially unjustified. This theme plays an important, perhaps central, role in the last two parts of the dialogue as well.

19.3. Consistency, Evidence, and Evil

Part XI of the *Dialogues* opens with Cleanthes essentially trying to steer a middle course between Philo's antianthropomorphism and Demea's fideism. Thus, he maintains, on the one hand, that we do have sound evidence that God is benevolent, intelligent, and powerful, but, on the other hand, we have no reason to suppose that he is omnibenevolent, omniscient, or omnipotent. By limiting God's attributes, Cleanthes suggests, we can reconcile an anthropomorphic theism with the problem of evil. In his own words, he suggests that by "supposing the Author of Nature to be finitely perfect, though far exceeding mankind, a satisfactory account may then be given of natural and moral evil, and every untoward phenomenon be explained and adjusted" (67).

Philo's interesting response to Cleanthes's limited theism is effectively framed by two arguments. The first argument itself relies on a pair of thought experiments. The first thought experiment asks us to imagine a person born into the world already convinced that "it were the production of a very good, wise, and powerful being" (67). Such a person, Philo conjectures, "might, perhaps, be surprised at the disappointment, but would never retract his former belief if founded on any very solid argument; since such a limited intelligence must be sensible of his own blindness and ignorance, and must allow that there may be many solutions of those phenomena which will forever escape his comprehension" (68). We might say that the existence of evil, according to Philo, is not, for all we know, *logically* inconsistent with the existence of a finite, but nonetheless very good, wise, and powerful being.

The second thought experiment asks us to consider another man born into the world "not antecedently convinced of a supreme intelligence, benevolent, and powerful, but [who] is left to gather such a belief from the appearances of things" (68). "This," Philo says, "entirely alters the case." Such a man, aware of his ignorance, may allow that the world *might* be well designed for all he knows, but he will find no reason to think that it is, "since he must form that inference from what he knows, not from what he is ignorant of" (68). If, according to Philo, the existence of evil is logically consistent with the existence of a benevolent deity, nonetheless, he maintains, the state of the world does not provide us with convincing evidence for the existence of a perfect, anthropomorphic creator.

Philo's second argument begins with a listing of the "four circumstances on which depend all or the greatest part of the ills that molest sensible creatures," including (i) that animals are spurred to action not only by pleasure but also pain (69); (ii) the world is governed by general laws rather than more specific laws that accommodate particular volitions (70); (iii) the susceptibility of creatures to suffering and death (71); and (iv) the lack of precision and reliability in natural teleology, for example, sometimes it rains too much, sometimes too little, sometimes an itchy sensation is helpful, sometimes simply an irritant (73). He dramatically concludes,

> Look round this universe. What an immense profusion of beings, animated and organized, sensible and active! You admire this prodigious variety and fecundity. But inspect a little more narrowly these living existences, the only beings worth regarding. How hostile and destructive to each other! How insufficient all of them for their own happiness! How contemptible or odious to the spectator! The whole presents nothing but the idea of a blind nature, impregnated by a great vivifying principle, and pouring forth from her lap, without discernment or parental care, her maimed and abortive children! (74)

Although Philo's stance is generally skeptical—maintaining that given our limited faculties we cannot know for certain whether the world is benevolently designed or not—he significantly closes, in Part XI of the *Dialogues*, by suggesting that the most likely hypothesis is that "the original source of all things is entirely indifferent to all these principles, and has no more regard to good above ill than to heat above cold, or to drought above moisture, or to light above heavy" (75).

19.4. "True Religion"

Hume brings his discussion of religion to an end in the twelfth part of the *Dialogues*. But what view would he have us take away? After all the back and forth between Demea, Cleanthes, and Philo, what conclusions are we meant to draw? Hume's readers have often wondered about what view of religion Hume himself would have us endorse. To bring the concern into better focus, we can see Part XII of the *Dialogues* as presenting four prima facie puzzles to its readers.

First, although Philo seems to have been attacking religion throughout the *Dialogues*—and nowhere more so than in its eleventh part—the chapter begins with him loudly emphasizing his piety, declaring, "You, in particular, Cleanthes . . . are sensible that, notwithstanding the freedom of my conversation and my love of singular arguments, no one has a deeper sense of religion impressed on his mind, or pays more profound adoration to the Divine Being" (77).

Second, although in earlier parts Philo had assailed Cleanthes's design argument, he now suggests that the inference to a deity on the basis of design is irresistible, declaring, "A purpose, an intention, a design strikes everywhere the most careless, the most stupid thinker; and no man can be so hardened in absurd systems as at all times to reject it" (77).

Third, although he earlier appeared to be advocating a cautious skepticism throughout the dialogue, in the twelfth part Philo implies that a skeptical view is indefensible, suggesting that "the whole face of nature" presents the strongest proof possible of the existence of God, so that a Divine Being wishing to refute the skeptic could do no better than "copy the present economy of things" (78–79).

Finally, fourth, the dialogue famously concludes with the suggestion that it is Cleanthes, rather than Philo, who has presented the most compelling case. Hume wraps up his entire discussion by having Pamphilius "confess that, upon a serious review of the whole, I cannot but think that Philo's principles are more probable than Demea's, but that those of Cleanthes approach still nearer to the truth" (89).

An important clue for making sense of these four puzzles, and thus for understanding what is going on in Part XII of the *Dialogues*, is to be found in the positive picture of "true religion" that Philo appears to settle upon by the end of the dialogue.

> If the whole of natural theology, as some people seem to maintain, resolves itself into one simple, though somewhat ambiguous, at least undefined, proposition, *That the cause or causes of order in the universe probably bear some remote analogy to human intelligence:* If this proposition be not capable of extension, variation, or more particular explication: If it affords no inference that affects human life, or can be the source of any action or forbearance: And if the analogy, imperfect as it is, can be carried no further than to the human intelligence, and cannot be transferred, with any appearance of probability, to the other qualities of the mind: If this really be the case, what can the most inquisitive, contemplative, and religious man do more than give a plain, philosophical assent to the proposition, as often as it occurs, and believe that the arguments on which it is established exceed the objections which lie against it? (88)

The positive picture suggested here is one of a very weak, naturalistic deism. Its conception of God is vague and admits of a wide range of understandings. It allows some analogy between the organizing principles of the world and human minds but insists that such analogies are too weak to support an inference to an anthropomorphic deity. Philo implies that as long as such a conception of God is embraced, the existence of God is beyond doubt.

Although Philo's positive picture does not remove all the mysteries of the twelfth part of the *Dialogues*, it does, I think, help to shed some light on the four puzzles just mentioned.

First, although Philo's theism is admittedly very thin, he does think that God—properly understood—truly exists. While his conception of God may be somewhat nontraditional, there is no reason to assume that he is being disingenuous about his piety.

Second, although Philo has vigorously challenged Cleanthes's design argument, as we noted earlier, it is not clear that he ever succeeds in refuting the "natural," intuition-driven design arguments of Part III. Hume may therefore have been convinced that the order that we find in nature does indeed naturally and perhaps irresistibly engender a belief in us of some kind of ordering principle that is at least weakly analogous to a human mind. Such a view is, as we've noted, perfectly consistent with Philo's more deeply entrenched conviction that such an analogy in no way supports the attribution of canonical "personal" attributes to God.

Third, if he is indeed convinced by Cleanthes's design argument from Part III, Philo can and should grant that, as long as the content of religious belief is properly constrained, belief in the existence of God may be irresistible and not open even to cautious skepticism. Such a position, it should be emphasized, is still perfectly consistent with cautious skepticism, or even something stronger, with respect to many traditional theological and nontheological beliefs.

Finally, fourth, we can see that there is a perfectly good sense in which Philo really does lose the overall debate, and that Cleanthes's "approach is still nearer to the truth." Philo's original skepticism has been undermined, and Cleanthes's attempt to defend religion by experience and reason has been vindicated. Of course, the full results of the dialogue are subtler than can be captured by a simple division into winners and losers (a fact that might itself be suggested by Hume's speaking of Cleanthes's principles as being merely "nearer to the truth"). The real intended winner, perhaps, is the picture of "true religion" sketched by Philo. It is a view of religious belief that might best be characterized as falling between the starting points of both Cleanthes and Philo.

19.5. The Problem of Evil Today

Having considered Hume's presentation of the problem of evil, it will come as no surprise to learn that other philosophers have developed the problem of evil in different ways. (The old joke goes: five philosophers, seven opinions!) In this last section, then, we pause to consider two more recent developments of the problem of evil, the first by J. L. Mackie, the second by Marilyn McCord Adams.

19.5.1. The Logical Problem of Evil

We saw Hume in one of his thought experiments concede that nothing in the world rules out the existence of a benevolent creator. I suggested in passing that Hume thinks there is no *logical* problem of evil. That was a reference to a famous presentation of the problem of evil by the philosopher J. L. Mackie. Mackie argued that the existence of evil does present a logical, or at least a quasi-logical, problem for traditional theists.

In developing his case, Mackie claims that the following propositions can't all be true at the same time:

(1) God is omnipotent.
(2) God is wholly good.
(3) Evil exists.

To bring out the tension between these claims, Mackie introduces two "quasi-logical principles." These are, I think, supposed to be obvious and convincing to anyone who gives them any thought. They are as follows:

(4) Good is opposed to evil in such a way that a good thing always eliminates evil as far as it can.
(5) There are no limits to what an omnipotent thing can do.

It is easy to see how the argument from these starting points might go:

(2) God is wholly good
(4) So, God tries to eliminate evil. But
(1) God is omnipotent. And
(5) There are no limits to what an omnipotent being can do.

So evil shouldn't exist, but

(3) evil exists.

As Mackie recognizes, there are many subtle responses and counter-responses to be thought through here. Might God allow evil to exist so that we can know what goodness is? But couldn't an omnipotent being make us know what goodness is without creating evil? Might God allow evil to exist as a byproduct of human free will? But couldn't an omnipotent being make us free and yet bound to never sin? There are many good issues to consider here. Perhaps the most useful thing about Mackie's discussion, however, is the framework itself. By framing the problem of evil as a logical, or quasi-logical, problem, Mackie's setup makes it easier to see some of the most crucial points to be faced in thinking through the problem of evil.

19.5.2. Horrendous Evils and the Goodness of God

Marilyn McCord Adams was a philosopher, Episcopal priest, and, from 2004 to 2009, canon of Christ Church Cathedral in Oxford. Although a theist herself, she maintains that atheists and theists alike have often let themselves off the hook too easily in thinking through the problem of evil. Atheists, she maintains, must be careful not to saddle theists with views they simply do not hold. She cautions, for example, that atheists should not bother showing that the problem of evil is inconsistent with a God who seeks to maximize pleasure, since traditional theists typically do not believe that God aims to maximize pleasure. On the other hand, however, Adams insists that theists like herself should not rest content with showing—against philosophers like Mackie—that "the power, knowledge and goodness of God could coexist with some evils or other"; rather, she claims, "a full account must exhibit the compossibility of divine perfection with evils in the amounts and of the kinds found in the actual world" (298).

Adams proposes, in particular, that theists must face what she calls the problem of horrendous evils. She defines *horrendous evils* as "evils the participation in (the doing or suffering of) which gives one reason prima facie to doubt whether one's life could (given their inclusion in it) be a great good to one on the whole" (299). She offers a list of examples all too readily drawn from history, literature, and contemporary events:

> I offer the following list of paradigmatic horrors: the rape of a woman and axing off of her arms, psychological torture whose ultimate goal is the disintegration of personality, betrayal of one's deepest loyalties, cannibalizing one's own offspring, child abuse of the sort described by Ivan Karamazov,

> child pornography, parental incest, slow death by starvation, participation in the Nazi death camps, the explosion of nuclear bombs over populated areas, having to choose which of one's children shall live and which be executed by terrorists, being the accidental and/or unwitting agent of the disfigurement or death of those one loves best. (252)

Adams suggests that these are all cases in which if one were involved in some way—as victim or perpetrator—one could reasonably doubt that one's life is in fact a good thing. Adams insists that in responding to the problem of evil, the theist must not "merely" show how the existence of evil is consistent with the existence of an omnipotent, omniscient, wholly good God, she must face a higher bar. She must, Adams insists, explain how in the face of horrendous evils, human life could seem a good prospect and how it can be that "each created person will have a life that is a great good to him/her on the whole" (305).

At first pass, it might well seem as if Adams is out to argue that the problem of evil is, indeed, insurmountable. But Adams's intent is, in fact, quite the contrary. She makes two points in particular that are worth noting. First, Adams maintains that theists do have resources for responding to the problem of horrendous evils. In particular, she maintains that the theist may see divine goods, goods such as "the good of beatific, face-to-face intimacy with God," as "simply incommensurate with any merely non-transcendent goods or ills a person might experience" (306). Her idea is that the goods promised by God are so good that they might overcome even the horrendous evils we bear witness to in this world. That idea, she concedes, may not move the atheist. The atheist who does not share her faith may not allow that there are transcendent goods capable of swamping even horrendous evils. But, Adams maintains, the theist needn't convince the atheist on this point. In responding to the problem of evil, the theist need only show that her own view is internally coherent. She needn't show that it is coherent to someone who does not accept the resources that she takes herself to have as a theist.

Second, Adams puts an interesting twist on the problem of evil. Our vulnerability to horrendous evils should lead us all to question the value of human life itself. The fact that our lives could be engulfed at any time by horrendous evil should lead us to ask if human life is worthwhile. If one is to remain optimistic in the face of horrendous evil—if one is to see value in the human condition and life on earth—one must, she suggests, suppose that this is all part of a divine plan and that there will somehow be due rewards and punishments. Putting the point conversely, she suggests that we could not—should not—remain optimistic in the face of horrendous evils absent the belief in a benevolent god. Her overarching thought would thus, in the end, turn the problem of evil on its head. The value of our lives depends on our believing that the problem of evil can be addressed. But the problem of evil can only be addressed if God exists. According to Adams, the problem of evil, in fact, gives us a (practical) reason to believe in the existence of God.

Further Study

Marilyn McCord Adams, "Horrendous Evils and the Goodness of God." *Proceedings of the Aristotelian Society*, Supplementary Volumes 63 (1989): 297–310. Advanced presentation of Adams's argument concerning horrendous evils.

James R. Beebe, "Logical Problem of Evil." *Internet Encyclopedia of Philosophy*, ed. James Fieser and Bradley Dowden, https://iep.utm.edu/evil-log/. A helpful overview of the logical problem of evil with an extensive bibliography.

David Hume, *Dialogues Concerning Natural Religion*, 2nd ed., ed. Richard H. Popkin. Indianapolis, IN: Hackett, 1998. A good, inexpensive edition of Hume's *Dialogues*.

J. L. Mackie, "Evil and Omnipotence." *Mind* 64 (1955): 200–212. Seminal discussion of the logical problem of evil. Now available widely online.

Michael Tooley, "The Problem of Evil." *Stanford Encyclopedia of Philosophy* (Fall 2015 edition), ed. Edward N. Zalta, http://plato.stanford.edu/archives/fall2015/entries/evil/. A relatively advanced overview of the problem of evil with an extensive bibliography.

20
Shepherd's *The Credibility of Miracles*
May We Believe in Miracles?

20.1. The Setting

Mary Shepherd was born in 1777 at Barnbougle Castle in Scotland near Edinburgh. While her brothers attended university, she and her sisters were taught at home by a private tutor. She learned geography, history, Latin, and mathematics and discussed philosophical topics. In 1808 she married Henry John Shepherd, an English barrister, and moved to London. There she was involved in the leading intellectual circles of the London elite. She counted as her acquaintances the likes of Charles Lyell, Charles Babbage, Mary Somerville, William Whewell, Sydney Smith, Thomas Malthus, and David Ricardo. Although her works were neglected in the years following her death, she was highly regarded in her day. Charles Lyell reported that she was an "unanswerable logician, in whose argument it was impossible to find loop-hole or flaw," and the great philosopher of science William Whewell assigned one of her books in his courses at Cambridge University (Boyle 2018, 1). She died in London in 1847.

In addition to a popular exchange with her contemporary John Fearn, Shepherd published two major books in philosophy as well as several essays. Her first book, *An Essay upon the Relation of Cause and Effect*, was published in 1824. The principal aim of the work is to refute David Hume's account of causation as presented in his *Treatise Concerning Human Nature* and *An Enquiry Concerning Human Understanding.* Hume had argued that we have no knowledge of necessary causal connections in the world. We come to think that one event causes another event when we repeatedly see the first kind of event followed by the second kind of event. In reply, Shepherd argues that we can know from reasoning alone that "a Being cannot begin its existence of itself," and that "like causes necessarily have like effects." Armed with

Saints, Heretics, and Atheists. Jeffrey K. McDonough, Oxford University Press. © Oxford University Press 2022.
DOI: 10.1093/oso/9780197563847.003.0020

these two principles drawn from pure reason, she maintains that we can—contra Hume—have a priori knowledge about causal relations and even leverage that a priori knowledge in our thinking about the natural world.

Shepherd's second book, *Essays on the Perception of an External Universe*, was published in 1827. It begins with a long essay targeting doctrines expounded by Hume, as well as by George Berkeley and Thomas Reid. As the title of the book hints, the central aim of the first essay is to establish that we have good reason to believe in the existence of an external world of enduring, mind-independent objects. Shepherd argues that although our sensations are interrupted, private, and dependent on the mind, they are caused by objects in the world. Through reasoning, we can establish that those objects exist continuously, externally, and independently of our perceiving minds. She concedes that objects in the external world do not resemble our sensations. My perception of a greasy burger isn't itself greasy. Nonetheless, we have reason to suppose that there is a structural similarity between our sensations and objects in the world—that there is, for example, a causal relation between smoke and fire that is parallel to the relation between our sensations of smoke and fire.

In addition to its first long essay, Shepherd's *Essays on the Perception of an External Universe* also contains eight shorter essays addressing specific philosophical arguments made by her near contemporaries. In one of those essays—titled "That Human Testimony Is of Sufficient Force to Establish the Credibility of Miracles"—Shepherd takes aim at Hume's influential critique of the credibility of miracles that he had published in his *Enquiry Concerning Human Understanding*. Later in the chapter, we consider Shepherd's arguments that Hume misconstrues the nature of miracles and is wrong about their credibility. First, however, it may be helpful to briefly review Hume's core argument against believing reports of miraculous events.

20.2. Hume's Critique of Miracles

Almost all religious traditions encourage belief in at least some miracles. Sacred texts in the Jewish-Christian-Muslim tradition are no exception. The Old Testament, for example, relates the famous story of the parting of the Red Sea. According to the account in the book of Exodus, the Israelites, led by Moses, were fleeing an Egyptian army when they arrived at the shores of the Red Sea. At that point, Moses raised his staff and—with God's assistance—parted the sea, revealing a dry path of escape. According to Exodus, when the Israelites arrived on the opposite shore, Moses raised his staff once again and the sea closed, drowning the pursuing Egyptian soldiers. Another famous miracle is related in the New Testament. The Gospel of John tells the story of Lazarus, who died of an illness and was entombed for four days in the village of Bethany. According to the Gospel, when Jesus arrived at the village he was greatly disturbed and called Lazarus to arise from the dead. Lazarus is said to have emerged from his tomb, still wearing his burial garments, and was received by an awestruck crowd that had gathered to mourn his death.

In his *Enquiry Concerning Human Understanding*, Hume offered a compact argument to the effect that we should not believe reports of such miracles. We can think of Hume's argument as having four main steps. The first step clarifies norms of belief for matters of fact. Hume suggests:

> A wise man . . . proportions his belief to the evidence. In such conclusions as are founded on an infallible experience, he expects the event with the last [i.e. highest] degree of assurance, and regards his past experience as a full proof of the future existence of that event. In other cases, he proceeds with more caution: He weighs the opposite experiments: He considers which side is supported by the greater number of experiments: To that side he inclines, with doubt and hesitations; and when at last he fixes his judgment, then, supposes an opposition of experiments and observations; where the one side is found to overbalance the other, and to produce a degree of evidence. (1999, section 10, paragraph 4)

Although it's a bit wordy, Hume's proposal is quite straightforward. His suggestion is simply that in matters of fact—that is, with respect to questions about contingent events or existences—we should proportion our beliefs to the evidence we have. If I'm looking at a tree in broad daylight under normal conditions, I may be very confident that a tree exists. If I think I just saw a lion walking down Massachusetts Avenue at twilight—an unprecedented event, in epistemically challenging circumstances—I should be considerably less certain in my belief. So far, so reasonable.

The second step insists that the same norms apply in cases of testimony. In many situations, people are quite reliable. If I ask a colleague what time it is, I am very likely to get a correct answer. Note: very likely, not guaranteed. My colleague might be mistaken for any number of reasons, or she might even wish to deceive me. In other circumstances, we have good reason to be less confident in the testimony of others. We know that people who are uninformed or dishonest may give false testimony. We know that people make mistakes, get confused, and may be motivated to lie. We give more weight to the testimony of many over few, to unanimity over disagreement. We take into account the manner and circumstances of delivery—the witness's sweaty palms, his timid or overly confident speech patterns. It is clear that we thus instinctively, and rightfully, weigh any number of considerations in adjusting our confidence in the reliability of the testimony of others. As Hume puts it, "A man delirious, or noted for falsehood and villainy, has no manner of authority with us" (section 10, paragraph 5). Furthermore, we also take into account what testifiers are telling us. If someone tells me in January that it is going to snow tomorrow in Massachusetts, I am very likely to believe her. If someone tells me the same thing in August, I'm more likely to think that she's off her rocker.

The third step of Hume's critique of the credibility of miracles suggests that since a miracle must involve a violation of the laws of nature, and we have maximally strong evidence for the laws of nature, we have maximally strong evidence against the existence of miracles. Here's Hume:

> A miracle is a violation of the laws of nature; and as a firm and unalterable experience has established these laws, the proof against a miracle, from the very nature of the fact, is as entire as any argument from experience can possibly be imagined. Why is it more than probable, that all men must die; that lead cannot, of itself, remain suspended in the air; that fire consumes wood, and is extinguished by water; unless it be, that these events are found agreeable to the laws of nature, and there is required a violation of these laws, or in other words, a miracle to prevent them. . . . But it is a miracle, that a dead man should come to life; because that has never been observed, in any age or country. There must, therefore, be a uniform experience against every miraculous event, otherwise the event would not merit that appellation. (1999, section 10, paragraph 12)

We can see Hume's point. What we take to be laws of nature are the most confirmed empirical generalizations we have. An event might be thought to be a miracle precisely because it violates those generalizations. If we have the strongest possible empirical evidence for the laws of nature, and miracles must contradict the laws of nature, we must have the greatest possible empirical evidence against miracles.

Finally, the fourth step effectively brings together the second and third steps and draws the conclusion that any report of a miracle, understood as a violation of the laws of nature, should not be believed. It is more likely that the report is false than that the laws of nature have been violated. We should not therefore believe, for example, that Moses parted the Red Sea or that Lazarus was raised from the dead. For, on the one hand, we know that testimony—especially distant testimony under unknown circumstances—does not provide extremely strong evidence. Indeed, it is clear that Hume thinks that the evidence of biblical reports is especially weak. They are stories from long ago. They are reported by a small, motivated group. They traffic in the sorts of spectacular events that entice the credulous. Hume thinks that testimony concerning miracles is weak evidence indeed. On the other hand, the laws that would be contravened by such miraculous events are extremely well established. We have more than abundant evidence that the seas do not part on command, that the dead do not rise. If we reason justly, we must therefore pit the high level of confidence that we place in the laws of nature against the low level of confidence that should be attached to attestations of ancient miracles. When we do that, Hume claims, we can see that the evidence supporting the laws of nature is much stronger than the evidence supporting the existence of miracles. In a contest between the two, we are forced to abandon our beliefs in reported miracles.

20.3. What Is a Miracle?

In a two-pronged response to Hume's critique of miracles, Shepherd first presses on Hume's understanding of what a miracle is. She argues that "a miracle . . . is ill defined by Mr. Hume, when he would express it as 'a violation of the laws of nature,' because there is always understood to be a power in some superior influence in nature, in the presiding energy of an essential God, acting as an additional cause, equal to the alleged variety of effects" (LoLordo 2020, 166). The specific thrust of Shepherd's objection here is likely to be lost on many contemporary readers. In earlier eras, it was widely held that natural events never occur independently of God's activity. According to the doctrine of *divine concurrence*, when, for example, fire burns a piece of paper it does so not by its own activity alone, but with the assistance of God's concurring activity. Without God's active assistance, a blowtorch could not even burn a tissue. Shepherd is suggesting that the doctrine of divine concurrence is somehow inconsistent with Hume's definition of a miracle as a violation of the laws of nature.

But how exactly? Perhaps Shepherd is thinking that God's concurrence is itself miraculous but doesn't violate the laws of nature. If that's the proposal, Hume's definition would fail to account for the miraculousness of divine concurrence. A parallel brief could be made for other cases. Creation, for example, might not be thought to violate any laws of nature—before creation, there were no laws of nature!—but would presumably be counted as miraculous, nonetheless. Furthermore, if divine concurrence is itself miraculous and widespread, many events that are in accordance with the laws of nature might also be said to be at least somewhat miraculous themselves. Consider, for example, the moon orbiting the earth. The moon's orbiting of the earth obviously doesn't violate a law of nature. But if the doctrine of divine concurrence is right, and if divine concurrence is itself miraculous, then the moon's orbiting of the earth does involve a miracle. Shepherd's complaint on this line of thought would be that Hume's definition gets things wrong because it fails to recognize some miraculous events as being miraculous.

Shepherd raises a second objection that will perhaps strike contemporary readers as more intuitive. She objects that "the word miracle, in its derivation, signifies only a wonderful thing; that is, something at which we wonder, because contrary to our usual experience, or in other words, an interruption to that we conceive the course of nature" (LoLordo 2020, 168, fn 5). The thought here, I think, is that it is essential to miraculous events that they are not the sort of thing that happens all the time. The parting of the Red Sea was a miracle in part because seas do not usually divide on command. The raising of Lazarus was a miracle in part because the dead usually stay dead. These are events at which anyone would marvel. They strike us as extraordinary and may affirm in us the belief that God has directly intervened in the world.

Interestingly, Hume anticipates, and explicitly rejects, Shepherd's suggestion that a miracle must strike us as being wondrous or unusual. In the *Enquiry*, he writes,

> A miracle may either be discoverable by men or not. This alters not its nature and essence. The raising of a house or ship into the air is a visible miracle. The raising of a feather, when the wind wants ever so little of a force

requisite for that purpose, is as real a miracle, though not so sensible with regard to us. (Hume 1999, section 10, paragraph 12, footnote 23)

An event might not surprise us for any number of reasons. We might simply not notice. Perhaps the Red Sea parted in prehistoric times and no one was around to witness it. Or we might just grow accustomed to it. Perhaps the very possibility of life involves a continuous supernatural act even though we take it for granted. Hume is insisting that it is important not to confuse the conditions under which we recognize an event as being miraculous with an event actually being miraculous. A mountain defying the laws of gravity would be no more miraculous than a tiny leaf defying the laws of gravity, even though we would likely marvel at the former and overlook the latter.

Many contemporary philosophers of religion nonetheless agree with Shepherd that miracles needn't involve a violation of the laws of nature. Building further on the spirit of her suggestion that miracles should incite wonder, many contemporary philosophers have proposed that what is most central to our notion of a miracle is that the event is explicable, or especially explicable, in terms of some divine objective. The contemporary philosopher George Schlesinger has called attention to an illustrative example, reported in the *LIFE* magazine issue of 27 March 1950. According to the story, fifteen choir members were scheduled to meet for practice in Beatrice, Nebraska, at 7:20 p.m. Although usually punctual, each member of the group was at least ten minutes late for independent, utterly ordinary reasons—and good thing too, for the building in which the practice was scheduled to take place, in fact, exploded at 7:25 p.m. There is no reason to suppose that the tardiness of any choir member involved a violation of the laws of nature. But it is not hard to imagine the choir members thinking that a miracle had nonetheless taken place. Even though the behavior of the individual choir members needn't have violated any laws of nature, their collectively being saved might well seem to be explicable, or especially explicable, in terms of a rather obvious divine objective.

Tying miracles to what is explicable, or especially explicable, in terms of divine objectives, however, can be tricky. One worry that can be raised is that we might suppose that an event could be miraculous without being the least bit explicable in terms of divine objectives. If some random person, or group of people, were to suddenly rise from the dead after an extended period, we might well be inclined to think that a miracle had occurred, even if we could see no reason why these particular people should defy death. Another worry that can be raised is that standards for explanation may vary from person to person. Suppose a person suddenly regains her sight after having been blind for many years. Given the right circumstances, a religiously minded person might see evidence in this case of a miracle—she might think that the person regaining her sight can be part of a divine objective. But given the very same circumstances, a scientifically minded person might see no evidence of a miracle at all. The scientist might hold that the restoration of the person's vision should be explicable entirely in accordance with the laws of nature and that no appeal to divine objectives is warranted. Insofar as standards of explanation vary from person to person, an account of miracles anchored in the thought that miracles are explicable, or especially explicable, in terms of divine objectives will leave the status of many cases unresolved.

The appeal to divine objectives might nonetheless help to address a worry that naturally lingers in connection with Hume's account of miracles. Throughout history we have found events that seem to violate the known laws of nature. It was well known, for example, that Mercury's orbit around the sun did not follow quite the path predicted by Newton's laws. But few scientists attributed Mercury's unusual orbit to a miracle. Why not? Well, perhaps because there was little temptation to see any divine objective in the deviations of Mercury's orbit from the trajectory Newton's laws predicted. In contrast to the church choir, it is hard to see any divine end in Mercury's unusual orbit. Acknowledging a role for the thought that miracles are at least often held to be for the sake of some divine objective may help to open up some space for distinguishing between violations of known laws of nature that might be counted as miraculous and violations of known laws of nature that might be better viewed as signs that our understanding of the laws of nature is incomplete. Because it involves no discernible objective, the case of Mercury's orbit could be thought to belong to the second class, and, in fact, later played a significant role in the scientific community's abandoning of Newton's law of gravity in favor of Einstein's theory of general relativity.

20.4. Believing in Miracles?

Having made her case that Hume has not properly captured the true nature of miracles, Shepherd goes on to argue that—contra Hume—we may have good reason for accepting the existence of miracles on the basis of testimony. Her core thought is that experience shows us that people generally tell the truth unless they have some motive to do otherwise. When I ask my colleague what time it is, she will very likely tell me the truth unless she has some strong reason to lie. Given that people are generally inclined to speak the truth, however, Shepherd thinks that unless we find some reason to suppose that a witness is lying, we should take the witness at her word. In short, as Shepherd puts it, "If the testimony to marvelous events be made under such circumstances, that no sufficient motive can be imagined to tempt the witnesses to falsehood; if the events be such as would rather induce a cowardice of assertion concerning them than the contrary, then the evidence should be considered as worthy of confidence, and the facts honestly related" (337).

Hume and Shepherd disagree about whether we should think that biblical witnesses had an incentive to lie. Hume, I suspect, thinks that they did. Scottish folklore reports that the great hero of Scottish independence William Wallace once rose from the dead. But the Scots had powerful incentives for presenting Wallace as a larger-than-life hero, and those incentives would seem to give us good grounds for doubting the veracity of their claims. Hume evidently thinks that, for example, the reports of early Christians should be viewed as being no less motivated and thus no more credible than fabulous tales of Scottish folk heroes. Shepherd on the other hand thinks that early witnesses to miracles had strong motivations to deny miracles. Early witnesses often belonged to persecuted minorities. They could literally be executed for their testimony. Her thought is that early reports of miracles should be held to be all the more credible because early witnesses had incredible incentive to keep silent. Although they are effectively on exactly opposite sides of this issue, I think we can feel the pull of both Hume's thought and Shepherd's thought. We can feel the pull of the thought that early adherents of a religion might be strongly motivated to exaggerate events and deeds that might support their cause. We can also feel, however, the pull of the suggestion that the terrible price paid by many early martyrs certainly speaks to their own personal conviction.

Even if we suppose that the question of the motivations of early witnesses is a draw, there is a more technical point that Hume could press against Shepherd's argument. Shepherd is suggesting that unless we have reasons to the contrary, we should assume that people are being honest in their testimonial reports. But Hume's argument doesn't exactly require that we suppose that people are being dishonest. First, they could be simply (honestly) mistaken in their initial reports. If we are being exact, we should say that when I ask my colleague what time it is, she will very likely tell me what she takes to be the truth. After all, her watch might be wrong, she might misread it, and so on. Analogously, some reports of miracles might be honest mistakes. Perhaps Lazarus was in a coma and didn't rise from the dead at all even though people at the time honestly thought that he had. Second, mistakes—honest mistakes—might occur in transmission. Many reports of miracles were first recorded long after the alleged fact took place. They were passed down from generation to generation, language to language, preserved orally, and then by often semiliterate scribes copying by hand. One needn't imagine that all errors of transmission were deceitful. Anyone who played the game of telephone as a child can recognize how even mundane accounts can be transformed into fabulous tales as they are passed from honest person to honest person.

Hume's case is probably strongest with respect to the sorts of reports of long-ago miracles that one finds in many sacred texts. Nonetheless, it is hard not to think that Shepherd must be on to something in suggesting that Hume overstates his case. We can remove the complication introduced by problematic lines of transmission by focusing on contemporary testimony. The core of Hume's argument, appropriately updated, would be that we should accept no testimony of a violation of the laws of nature, even if that testimony is contemporary. But that's too strong, right? Suppose all the leading astronomers in the world today collectively testified to the existence of an anomaly that stood in violation of the known laws of nature. Even given what we know about the potential weaknesses of testimonial accounts, it seems like we would have very good reason to think that an event that violated the known laws of nature had occurred. And, as the Mercury case intimated, this is not even a fanciful thought experiment. We regularly get reports of phenomena that seem to defy the laws of nature. We check those reports. Sometimes those reports are found to be fraudulent or—more often—mistaken or not reproducible. But sometimes they are found to be convincing. While such aberrations may not lead us to believe that a miracle has occurred, they may nonetheless be added to the long list of things we can't at present explain or they may point us—as with the case of Mercury—toward revisions in our understanding of the laws of nature themselves. At any rate, Shepherd does seem to have a strong point that at least in some cases we seem warranted in accepting testimony even if that testimony reports a violation of known (or thought to be known) laws of nature.

Furthermore, Hume's focus on testimony introduces an intriguing, difficult wrinkle into his discussion. For there is room for philosophical disagreement over how we should best think about testimony itself. One view—a view I think Hume tacitly embraces—would see testimony as a more or less reliable indicator of the truth. On this view, a witness is not so different from a clock or Geiger counter. The clock tells us what time it is. The Geiger counter tells us if material is radioactive. We should proportion our beliefs in accordance with the reliability of the clock, of the Geiger counter. We should trust a reliable clock. We should not trust an unreliable Geiger counter. Another view thinks that this gets things quite wrong in at least a range of important cases. Perhaps if your son tells you what time it is, you should make a cold calculation about the reliability of his time telling. But if he tells you that he didn't cheat on the test or that he really will try harder next time, perhaps you should believe him regardless of his reliability. The most basic thought here is that testimony might be special and might require a more permissive attitude on our part. It might require us to treat acceptance as a default, and to doubt only with good reason. This view is, I think, certainly intimated by Shepherd, and might well be expected to resonate with other religious people. On this view, one might suppose, for example, that sacred texts and early witness reports should be accepted not because their reliability has been compared favorably against other reliabilities, but because the believer stands in a special relation to those texts and reports, a relation of prima facie acceptance, even of faith.

Finally, it should be noted, that even if Hume were entirely right in his critique of miracles, even if he were entirely right that testimony can never give us justified belief in the existence of miracles, it wouldn't follow that we could never have justified belief in the existence of miracles. For testimony seems to be only one of many ways in which one might come to acquire a justified belief. Someone might think that they have directly experienced a miracle. Many believers report having undergone a palpable religious awakening that they count as an instance of direct, divine intervention. Many report that they can feel God's immediate presence or hear God speaking directly to them. In such instances, it seems that someone might believe that a miracle has taken place without drawing any evidence from testimony. Likewise, someone might believe that a miracle has occurred as the result of an inference "to the best explanation." We use such reasoning all the time. I can't find my car keys in their usual place. I check the bowl on my wife's dresser and find them there. I infer that she borrowed my keys and left them in her bowl. This is a case of justified belief, but not a case involving testimonial evidence. It seems possible that one might make a similar inference to the existence of a miracle. A sick person might pray for an improbable recovery and be convinced that a miracle has taken place when that recovery occurs. More grandly, a believer might see in the incredible expansion of the Islamic Empire in the decades after the death of Muhammad evidence of the miraculous nature of his teachings. The point, of course, is simply that Hume's brilliant but tightly focused argument, even if it were entirely successful, would leave open the possibility that we might gain evidence for miracles through means other than testimony.

Further Study

Margaret Atherton, "Reading Lady Mary Shepherd." *Harvard Philosophy Review* 13, no. 2 (2005): 73–85. An excellent overview of the philosophy of Lady Mary Shepherd written by a leading scholar of the period.

Martha Bolton, "Mary Shepherd." *Stanford Encyclopedia of Philosophy* (Winter 2017 edition), ed. Edward N. Zalta, https://plato.stanford.edu/archives/win2017/entries/mary-shepherd/. Helpful, more advanced overview of Shepherd's philosophical thought with an extensive bibliography.

Deborah Boyle, "Introduction." In *Lady Mary Shepherd: Selected Writings*, 1–26. La Vergne, TN: Ingram Book Company, 2018. A helpful overview of Shepherd's life and works arranged by topic.

David Hume, *An Enquiry Concerning Human Understanding*. Ed. Tom L. Beauchamp. New York: Oxford University Press, 1999. Classic essay including Hume's argument against miracles.

Antonia LoLordo (ed.), *Mary Shepherd's Essays on the Perception of an External Universe*. New York: Oxford University Press, 2020. A helpful edited edition of Mary Shepherd's essays, including her essay on miracles.

Timothy McGrew, "Miracles." *Stanford Encyclopedia of Philosophy* (Spring 2019 edition), ed. Edward N. Zalta, https://plato.stanford.edu/archives/spr2019/entries/miracles/. Helpful, more advanced overview of contemporary thinking about miracles, includes an extensive bibliography.

Mary Shepherd, *An Essay upon the Relation of Cause and Effect*. London: T. Hookham, 1824. The first of Shepherd's main philosophical works, includes her response to Hume's treatment of causation.

Mary Shepherd, *Essays on the Perception of an External Universe and Other Subjects Connected with the Doctrine of Causation*. London: John Hatchard and Son, 1827. The second of Shepherd's main philosophical works, including her response to Hume's critique of miracles.

21

Mill's *Essays on Religion*

Is Religion Useful?

21.1. The Setting

John Stuart Mill was born just outside of London in 1806 to a large family of four sons and five daughters. He received a famously formidable education from his father, James Mill. John Stuart began to study Greek at the age of three, Latin at the age of eight. Soon afterward, he took up the study of mathematics and logic. By the time he was a teenager, he was studying history, politics, and philosophy. At the age of twenty, however, he suffered an acute mental crisis, which he attributed to his overly narrow education and others have attributed to exhaustion. Whatever the reason, Mill found remedy in the Romantic poets, and especially in the writings of Wordsworth. The notion that human development requires not only the cultivation of reason but also of emotions became a mainstay of his philosophical outlook.

In 1823 Mill began working for the East India Company at a junior-level position and rose through the ranks to the position of chief examiner, a post his father formerly held. In 1830 he met his future wife, Harriet Taylor. Taylor would exert a tremendous influence on Mill's life and work and helped to shape his efforts on behalf of women's rights, suffrage, and educational access. In 1843 Mill published his *System of Logic*, followed by a series of influential works, including *The Principles of Political Economy* (1848), *On Liberty* (1859), and *Utilitarianism* (1861). In 1858 Mill retired from the East India Company and was elected to the House of Commons seven years later. He published his suffragist work *The Subjection of Women* in 1869. He died four years later in 1873 in Avignon, France, and was buried beside his wife.

Mill's *Three Essays on Religion* were published posthumously in 1874. The first essay, "On Nature," examines whether nature itself might not serve as a guide to morality. The second, "The Utility of Religion," examines the

Saints, Heretics, and Atheists. Jeffrey K. McDonough, Oxford University Press. © Oxford University Press 2022.
DOI: 10.1093/oso/9780197563847.003.0021

social and personal value of religion. Both were completed by 1858. The third, "Theism," written a decade later, is generally more concessive to traditional religion. Whereas his earlier essays cleared the grounds for a positive humanism, his final essay suggests that the argument from design provides some, albeit limited, evidence for the existence of an intelligent creator. "Theism" likewise argues that while there is no evidence supporting the immortality of the soul, there is also no evidence against it. Mill suggests that one is at least permitted to hope for an existence beyond bodily death. Mill's essays on religion predictably drew criticism from both sides. Some disparaged him as being a godless atheist while others expressed their disappointment in his late-in-life concessions to religious belief.

21.2. "On Nature"

Mill's "On Nature" opens with the thought that the words "Nature, natural, and that group of words derived from them" have taken on broad connotations beyond their original meaning. We can spy those broader connotations in moralistic claims about various behaviors and practices—for example, in claims that homosexuality, polygamy, and incest are unnatural. In taking on these broader connotations, the terms associated with "nature" have become, Mill maintains, "copious sources of false taste, false philosophy, false morality, and even bad law" (65; unless otherwise noted, all references in this chapter are to Mill [2009]). Mill's central aim in "On Nature" is to distinguish two main views concerning the meaning of the term "nature," and to argue that in either of those senses, nature is a poor guide to morality. Whether an act, habit, or practice is natural or not, Mill suggests, tells us nothing about whether it is morally good or bad.

According to the first main sense of "nature" identified by Mill, nature "means all the powers existing in either the outer or the inner world and everything which takes place by means of those powers" (68). The thought here is that what is natural is just anything that happens in nature, where nature includes everything in the world—say, its elements, powers, and laws. Can nature in this sense confer moral obligation? Mill argues that many philosophers have thought so, from the ancient Stoics to modern deists. But he thinks this is obviously absurd. For if nature just connotes whatever happens in the world, it cannot distinguish between what should and what shouldn't happen in the world. As Mill puts the point, "In this signification, there is no need of a recommendation to act according to nature, since it is what nobody can possibly help doing, and equally whether he acts well or ill" (73). Lying, cheating, and stealing are no doubt wrong, but given that they are evident aspects of the world, they aren't unnatural in Mill's first sense.

The second main sense of nature identified by Mill casts a narrower net. Rather than referring to everything that happens in the world, nature in this narrower sense captures only those things that occur absent human intervention. Intuitively, whatever happens in a pristine wilderness is natural in this sense, while whatever happens due to human contrivance and law is unnatural. I think we can see an echo of this sense of nature in certain dietary recommendations. Foods are often presented as being "natural" with the intended implication that they are therefore good for you. At any rate, Mill thinks that nature in this sense "is not merely, as it is in the other sense, superfluous and unmeaning, but palpably absurd and self-contradictory" (75). For, in this sense, all human action would be against nature and thus count as immoral. As Mill puts the point, "To dig, to plough, to build, to wear clothes are direct infringements of the injunction to follow nature" (76). Indeed, Mill suggests that our most obviously moral actions—for example, laws against violence and murder—are against nature in this sense. There is no point, Mill concludes, in saying that humans should act according to nature, where "nature" means whatever happens in the absence of human action.

One might, of course, suppose that the injunction to "follow nature" should be understood as urging us to follow some but not every aspect of nature. It is an exhortation to follow what is good in nature and not what is bad—to follow, for example, our instincts of affection, sympathy, and caring while neglecting, or battling against, our instincts for hatred, selfishness, and cruelty. Mill anticipates this response:

> But even though unable to believe that Nature, as a whole, is a realization of the designs of perfect wisdom and benevolence, men do not willingly renounce the idea that some part of Nature, at least, must be intended as an exemplar, or type; that on some portion or other of the Creator's works, the image of the moral qualities which they are accustomed to ascribe to him, must be impressed; that if not all which is, yet something which is, must not only be a faultless model of what ought to be, but must be intended to be our guide and standard in rectifying the rest. (89)

Mill maintains, however, that this strategy must be utterly useless at best. For how are we to decide what portions of creation are worthy of emulation and what portions are not? If our efforts are not to be arbitrary or worse, we'll have to appeal to a moral principle in order to decide what natural impulses and behaviors are good and what natural impulses and behaviors are bad. But if we have such principles, then we don't need exemplars derived from nature in order to distinguish good from bad after all. Once we abandon—as Mill thinks we must—the notion that everything natural is good, we must also abandon the notion that nature itself is a guide to morality.

21.3. Raising the Question

In his *Utility of Religion*, Mill nominally raises the question of whether religion is *useful* or not. Mill is aware that some argue that religion on the whole has been worse than not useful, that it has had a pernicious influence on human beings. He notes that those opposed to religion have drawn attention to the "more obvious and flagrant of the positive evils which have been engendered by past and present forms of religious belief," and concedes that people have been "unremittingly occupied in doing evil to one another in the name of religion, from the sacrifice of Iphigenia to the Dragonnades of Louis XIV" (108). No one today will be hard pressed to find more familiar examples, from the Crusades, to religious extremism, to abuses of authority.

Mill himself, however, does not draw on such considerations to argue that religion is not useful. On the contrary, he argues that religion has evolved over the ages so that "the worst of these evils are already in a great measure extirpated from the more improved forms of religion; and as mankind advanced in ideas and in feelings, this process of extirpation continually goes on: the immoral, or otherwise mischievous consequences which have been drawn from religion, are, one by one, abandoned" (108).

Perhaps that is too optimistic. Perhaps one might argue that religion has improved in some respects and regressed in others. But it doesn't really matter for Mill's position, for he goes on to maintain that such evils are, at any rate, in no way essential to religion. People have been doing terrible things to one another throughout the course of human history. If many of those terrible things have been done in the name of religion, an egregious number of them have also been done in the name of other causes, including secular causes. Mill seems inclined to think that where people have done evil in the name of religion, it is not religion that is to blame, but people.

Indeed, it quickly becomes evident that Mill's real question is not whether religion is useful but whether it plays an *essential* role in obtaining important social and private goods. Many thinkers down through the ages have certainly thought so. In the *Republic*, Plato infamously suggests that the leaders of the state should promote a false creation story—a noble lie—that would lend support to stratifying society into three social classes. Others have argued that, without religion, the foundations of morality or meaningful existence would be undermined. Indeed, Mill's own argument in "On Nature" might be thought to lend some support to such a view insofar as it argues that nature is not itself a source of morality or meaning. In order to explore more carefully the questions of whether religion plays an essential role in good human lives, Mill divides the question in two. We'll follow his lead in asking if religion plays an essential role in public goods, and then if religion plays an essential role in private goods.

21.4. Is Religion Publicly Useful?

Mill first takes up the question of the *public* utility of religion. He clearly thinks that religion has in fact been tremendously useful in promoting social goods:

> Undoubtedly mankind would be in a deplorable state if no principles or precepts of justice, veracity, beneficence, were taught publicly or privately, and if these virtues were not encouraged, and the opposite vices pressed, by the praise and blame, the favorable and the unfavorable sentiments, of mankind.

Mill belongs to a large class of moral and political philosophers who think that the principles of society fundamentally improve human beings. Most of those principles—certainly in Mill's day, perhaps in our own as well—are religious. Mill maintains that in an important sense religion has therefore been tremendously useful to us as a society.

Mill further maintains, however, that we could be conditioned by society without appealing to religion. The principal tools used by society to shape our involuntary beliefs, according to Mill, are authority and education. But authority and education are not essentially bound to religion. Mill points out that much of what we believe in the domain of science, for example, we believe on the basis of authority. I believe quite strongly, for example, that plants gain nourishment through a process of photosynthesis and that the dark side of the moon is colder than Wisconsin in the winter. But I believe these things not on the basis of personal investigation, but on the shared authority of others. Likewise, Mill emphasizes the tremendous influence of education in shaping our beliefs. I believe that Tallahassee is the capital of Florida, that Abraham Lincoln was the sixteenth president of the United States, and that the North American jet stream flows west to east. I believe these things in part because I was taught them in grade school. Mill means to suggest that through secular education future generations might acquire a deep, involuntary conviction that, say, stealing and murder are wrong even without those prohibitions being associated with religious belief.

Society, according to Mill, also has powerful tools for directly influencing our actions. He suggests that people's actions are deeply influenced—perhaps more than they realize—by forces of public approval and disapproval. We don't generally cheat and lie, Mill suggests, in large part because we know that others will disapprove of our cheating and lying, and we wish to stay in the good graces of our fellow humans. Conversely, people have gone to war, fought duels, and endured terrible hardships because they have sought the approval of others. Indeed, Mill goes so far as to suggest that these social considerations are the primary motivations even in the case of staunch believers. The believer, Mill implies, can't help being more influenced by the immediate and visible approval and disapproval of his fellow humans than the indirect and invisible approval and disapproval of God. Mill's overall point, once again, is that the social goods that might be thought to flow from religious beliefs can be achieved through secular means. Although religion has been useful for the promotion of social virtues, it is by no means essential to them.

21.5. Is Religion Privately Useful?

Mill begins his consideration of the private utility of religion by asking "what it is in human nature which causes it to require a religion; what wants of the human mind religion supplies, and what qualities it develops" (124). He rejects the suggestion that religion is most deeply rooted in fear, arguing that belief in gods is prior to many of the fears they might be called upon to assuage. He instead finds a more noble source in the gap between "the narrow region of our experience" and the "boundless sea" of the world around us that we wish to explore and understand. In the absence of experience, religious imagination, according to Mill, fills the gap—it offers to explain the unexplained by appealing to God. Mill concludes that the value "of religion to the individual, both in the past and the present, as a source of personal satisfaction and of elevated feelings, is not to be disputed" (126).

As in the case of public goods, however, Mill maintains that while religion has indeed been privately useful, the goods that it provides might also be obtained without religion. No doubt drawing on his own personal experience, Mill suggests that poetry has the potential to "supply the same want" traditionally supplied by religion, the want of "ideal conceptions grander and more beautiful than we see realized in the prose of human life" (126). Mill essentially thinks that religion is a need-fulfilling fantasy that inclines toward belief. But, he thinks, we might—as poetry demonstrates—have an alternative need-fulfilling fantasy without belief. We might fill the gap between our limited knowledge and our more expansive needs by nonreligious products of the imagination. Coopting terms, Mill suggests that poetry in this sense might be reckoned a kind of "religion," of which the "outward good works . . . are only a part" and whose "essence" is "the strong and earnest direction of the emotions and desires towards an ideal object, recognized as of the highest excellence, and as rightfully paramount over all selfish objects of desire" (130). Such a religion, Mill suggests, could be called the "Religion of Humanity."

Thus far, Mill has mostly been content to argue that the goods afforded by religion might also be engendered without the aid of religion. Nearer to the end of his essay, however, he moves from defense to offense, arguing that a secular Religion of Humanity would, in fact, represent an improvement over traditional religion in at least three respects. First, he maintains a Religion of Humanity would be disinterested in a way that traditional religion is not. He argues that a Religion of Humanity "carries the thoughts and feelings out of self, and fixes them on an unselfish object, loved and pursued as an end for its own sake," whereas traditional religion tempts the believer "to regard the performance of his duties to others mainly as a means to his own personal salvation" (130). Second, Mill maintains, in effect, that a Religion of Humanity would not demand the intellectual contortions required by traditional religion, especially with respect to the problem of evil. Finally, third, Mill maintains that a Religion of Humanity would not be committed to "the moral difficulties and perversions involved in revelation itself" (132). In not being bound to accepted creeds or historical texts, humanists are free to craft a moral code without allegiance to canonical texts or religious authorities. Because he finds religion useful, Mill—in contrast to some outspoken atheists—does not think that religion should just be abandoned. Rather he thinks it should be replaced by something secular and humanist. In doing so, Mill was an early pioneer of a movement to find a positive replacement for religion, a replacement that might hope to keep what is best about religion while abandoning its nonessential elements.

21.6. What Is Secular Humanism?

Early chapters explored at some length various commitments of the Judaic-Christian-Muslim tradition. Atheists, of course, reject many of those beliefs. Typically, they don't believe that there is an omniscient god, that we have immortal souls, that there is life after death. Those are all things that atheists usually do *not* believe. But what do nonbelievers positively believe? What nonnegative doctrines do they hold? Unfortunately, if not surprisingly, there is no clear, unanimous answer to that question. The nonreligious come in at least as many varieties as the religious. Nonetheless for purposes of comparison, evaluation, and discussion, it might be helpful to have a sense of at least one nonreligious movement often referred to as "secular humanism." Secular humanism is a modern descendant of what Mill referred to as the Religion of Humanity. Indeed, secular humanists often trace their roots back to intellectual figures such as Spinoza, Hume, and Mill.

So what do secular humanists believe? Fortunately for us, secular humanists have attempted to capture their core commitments themselves. In 2003 the American Humanist Association published an updated precis of its beliefs. The results are generally known as the *Humanist Manifesto III* (earlier versions having been published in 1933 and 1973). The document states a commitment to the following beliefs (quoted with omissions and with titles inserted):

> Knowledge
> Knowledge of the world is derived by observation, experimentation, and rational analysis. Humanists find that science is the best method for determining this knowledge as well as for solving problems and developing beneficial technologies.

Naturalism
Humans are an integral part of nature, the result of unguided evolutionary change. Humanists recognize nature as self-existing.

Ethics
Ethical values are derived from human need and interest as tested by experience. Humanists ground values in human welfare shaped by human circumstances, interests, and concerns and extended to the global ecosystem and beyond. We are committed to treating each person as having inherent worth and dignity, and to making informed choices in a context of freedom consonant with responsibility.

Meaning
Life's fulfillment emerges from individual participation in the service of humane ideals. We aim for our fullest possible development and animate our lives with a deep sense of purpose, finding wonder and awe in the joys and beauties of human existence, its challenges and tragedies, and even in the inevitability and finality of death.

Many people who would not identify themselves explicitly as being secular humanists might find much in this set of commitments attractive. It is a broadly naturalist picture of human beings and their place in the world. It suggests that human knowledge is grounded in human capacities rather than, say, revelation or sacred texts. It suggests that humans are of a piece with the natural world, that they do not reign above it or possess supernatural powers such as immortality or libertarian free will. It suggests that ethics and purpose are both rooted in human nature and serve our shared ends. Murder is wrong because it is harmful to human welfare, and our lives are important because we, and our fellow human beings, care about them.

Many today will find the commitments of secular humanism reasonable. Indeed, many are likely to find them to be almost self-evident. But they are not self-evident, and secular humanism, like religious traditions, has its opponents. Although this is not the place for an in-depth exploration of objections to secular humanism, it might nonetheless be helpful to highlight three objections that have been raised against the secular humanist tradition as well as some sense of how secular humanists might respond to those objections.

First, and most obviously, religious believers may object precisely to the secular component of secular humanism. Insofar as secular humanism denies core commitments of religious belief, proponents of those denied beliefs may be expected to object to secular humanism. This difference seems almost definitional and largely inevitable. Sometimes a finer point is put to this charge, however, with the suggestion that secular humanism is antireligious in a stronger sense, that proponents of secular humanism do not just deny religious beliefs but are intolerant of religious beliefs and the religiously minded. No doubt this is true of some secular humanists, just as it is true that some religiously minded people are intolerant of the nonreligious. But as Mill's own example suggests, there seems to be nothing essential about secular humanism that binds it to intolerance. The secular humanist and the religious observer must disagree—per definition—about religion, but neither the humanist nor the believer must hold a prejudicial view of the other.

Second, it is sometimes suggested that secular humanism is committed to a pernicious relativism or immoralism. One can appreciate the source of this concern. To somebody who sees morality as being grounded in the divine, it can understandably seem as though the secular humanist—in rejecting those foundations—must be rejecting morality itself. As we saw earlier (chapter 16, section 3), however, religious belief is not obviously essential to either living a good life nor even to holding objective views on morality. There is simply no denying that many secular humanists are good, law-abiding people. They raise families, participate in civic activities, and care for others. Furthermore, as naturalists, they may embrace any number of objective views on morality. Like other naturalists, they may hold, for example, that morality is grounded in human emotions, or pure reason, or in the agreements we make with one another. While it is easy to see why someone who takes God to be the deepest source of morality might see the denial of God as entailing immorality, the denial of God simply does not obviously entail a pernicious relativism or immoralism.

Third, it is sometimes suggested that secular humanism really doesn't stand for anything substantive. It is just a hodgepodge of independent ideas and traditions awkwardly fitted together as a replacement for religion. Even here I think one can find some sympathy for the objection. Secular humanism does not draw on an age-old tradition that might give its beliefs and practices the feeling of inevitability. Nor does it recognize any canonical texts that have to be accepted or command authority. As revisions to the *Humanist Manifesto* make clear, secular humanists have had to essentially make things up as they have gone along. They have had to decide what beliefs they should accept and what practices make sense for them. When compared with religious traditions that reach back centuries, even millennia, the various commitments and practices of secular humanism might appear to be arbitrary. But it is not clear that this amounts to a real objection to secular humanism. The fact that the beliefs and practices of traditional religions are well-worn does not by itself show that they are superior. Presumably when many of the commitments and practices of traditional religions were first introduced, they may have seemed equally arbitrary and ad hoc. Why should Shabbat begin at sundown? Why should wine be used at Mass? Why should prayers be said five times a day? Furthermore, and finally, the secular humanist might see the seemingly arbitrary and ad hoc nature of their commitments and practices as a virtue rather than a vice. They might see it as an advantage of secular humanism that it can freely develop and evolve with time. They may see it as a virtue, not a vice, that secular humanism is not wedded to the outlines of the *Humanist Manifesto* of 1933 and indeed may look forward to the development of the *Humanist Manifesto IV*. Once again, while it is easy to appreciate the thrust of the objection that secular humanism is in some ways an arbitrary and ad hoc work in progress, it is not clear that that objection should raise a serious concern on the part of the secular humanist.

Further Study

American Humanist Association, https://americanhumanist.org/. A large portal website for "Humanists, Atheists, and Freethinkers."

Greg Epstein, *Good without God: What a Billion Nonreligious People* Do *Believe*. New York: HarperCollins, 2010. An engaging overview of secular humanism.

Philip Kitcher, *Life after Faith: The Case for Secular Humanism*. New Haven, CT: Yale University Press, 2015. An accessible defense of secular humanism from a leading contemporary philosopher.

Stephen Law, *Humanism: A Very Short Introduction*. New York: Oxford University Press, 2011. An excellent, short, accessible introduction to secular humanism.

Christopher Macleod, "John Stuart Mill." *Stanford Encyclopedia of Philosophy* (Summer 2020 edition), ed. Edward N. Zalta, https://plato.stanford.edu/archives/sum2020/entries/mill/. Helpful overview of John Stuart Mill's philosophical thought with an extensive bibliography.

John Stuart Mill, *Autobiography*. London: Penguin Books, [1873] 1989. Widely reprinted and in the public domain.

John Stuart Mill, *Three Essays on Religion*. Ed. Louis J. Matz. Ontario: Broadview Press, 2009.

22

Nietzsche's *On the Genealogy of Morality*

What Do "Good," "Bad," and "Evil" Mean?

22.1. The Setting

Friedrich Nietzsche was born on 18 October 1844 in a small town southwest of Leipzig, Germany. His father—a Lutheran minister, like his father before him—died when Nietzsche was only four years old. Nietzsche's older brother passed away six months later. From that point on, Nietzsche was raised by his mother in the company of his grandmother, aunts, and his younger sister.

At the age of fourteen, Nietzsche was sent to boarding school near Naumburg. There he became acquainted with the work of Richard Wagner. Wagner's music and friendship would come to have a profound influence on Nietzsche's own thinking, work, and life. After graduating from boarding school, Nietzsche enrolled at the University of Bonn in 1864 in theology and philology. In 1865 Nietzsche followed his instructor in philology, Wilhelm Ritschl, to the University of Leipzig and quickly established a scholarly reputation of his own. Around this time Nietzsche was introduced to another major influence when he accidentally discovered Schopenhauer's *The World as Will and Representation* in a local bookstore.

In 1869—at the remarkably young age of twenty-four—Nietzsche accepted a position in classical philology at the University of Basel in Switzerland. In 1870 the Franco-Prussian War broke out, and Nietzsche served as a hospital attendant. His service appears to have had long-term consequences for his always fragile health. During this period, Nietzsche published several books to mixed reviews, including *The Birth of Tragedy* (1872), *Unfashionable Observations* (1873–76), and *Human, All-Too-Human* (1878). In 1879 Nietzsche's poor health forced him to resign from his position in Basel.

For the next ten years or so, Nietzsche led an almost nomadic existence, wandering from country to country, often visiting family, friends,

Saints, Heretics, and Atheists. Jeffrey K. McDonough, Oxford University Press. © Oxford University Press 2022.
DOI: 10.1093/oso/9780197563847.003.0022

and acquaintances, and seeking relief from his physical maladies. Many of Nietzsche's most important works date from this period, including *Daybreak* (1881), *The Gay Science* (1882), *Thus Spoke Zarathustra* (1883–85), *Beyond Good and Evil* (1886), and *On the Genealogy of Morality* (1887). Astoundingly, in what turned out to be his last productive year, Nietzsche added almost a half-dozen new books to this list, including *The Case of Wagner* (May–August 1888), *Twilight of the Idols* (August–September 1888), *The Antichrist* (September 1888), *Ecce Homo* (October–November 1888), and *Nietzsche Contra Wagner* (December 1888).

In 1889, while in Turin, Nietzsche witnessed a horse being whipped in the street, threw his arms around the animal's neck, and experienced a mental breakdown of some sort. Although the cause of the breakdown cannot be known with certainty, it left Nietzsche incapacitated for the remainder of his life. After being briefly committed to a sanatorium in Jena, Nietzsche was taken home by his mother, and later fell under the care of his anti-Semitic sister Elisabeth, whose sympathies led to Nietzsche's coming to be associated with the Nazi movement in Germany. (A concise discussion of the Nazis' appropriation of Nietzsche's writings can be found in the introduction to Nietzsche [1998], vii–xv). Mentally incapacitated from the time of his breakdown, Nietzsche died 25 August 1900.

Nietzsche has always been—and remains—a difficult, controversial philosopher. His writings are often unconventional and can seem more concerned with provoking reflection rather than defending reasoned theses. His *On the Genealogy of Morality* is perhaps his most accessible work in a traditional philosophical sense. Over the course of three essays, it presents a series of theses with potentially profound implications for our understanding of religion. In this and the next two chapters, we look more closely at Nietzsche's views on religion as expressed in those three essays, taking up one essay per chapter. As the discussion shows, Nietzsche's three essays together provide a blistering—often exaggerated—critique of religion and religious morality, but a critique that is in many ways more complex and nuanced than Nietzsche's often overheated rhetoric might at first seem to suggest.

22.2. Three Big Ideas

The first essay of Nietzsche's *On the Genealogy of Morality* introduces three big ideas. It may be helpful to start by getting all three out on the table before working through them more carefully one at a time. The first big idea is simply that of giving a *genealogy* of morality. Nietzsche suggests that the values and morals associated with the Judeo-Christian-Muslim tradition should be investigated not on the assumption that they are God-given but rather on the assumption that they have evolved through human predilections, aims, needs, and circumstances. One goal of Nietzsche's genealogy of morality is to uncover the supposedly lost origins of human morals.

The second big idea is the idea of an *inversion of values*. In the process of carrying out his genealogical investigation, Nietzsche claims to have discovered something shocking. The religious tradition, according to Nietzsche, has succeeded in inverting an older moral scheme, essentially turning human valuations on their heads. What was once called "good" is now called "evil," and what was once called "bad" is now called "good." This is the central idea of Nietzsche's so-called transvaluation of values.

The third big idea is that of *evaluating* moral values themselves. Nietzsche maintains that religion has managed not only to invert an older set of values, but that it has in many ways left us worse off as a result. Although Nietzsche's attitude toward earlier and later moral views is complex, it is nonetheless clear that he thinks it is important that we appreciate what has been left behind, or plowed under, by the rise of religious morality.

22.3. Genealogy of Values

The idea that morality should be investigated historically is not new with Nietzsche. Earlier thinkers had traced ethical obligations back to an original state of nature, to fundamental human inclinations, to the desire to maximize overall utility, and so on. When Nietzsche talks about "English psychologists" he is alluding to philosophers who had made such earlier attempts, including—and in spite of the epithet—the Scottish Hume, the German Paul Rée, and his own earlier self.

Nietzsche opens the first treatise of the *Genealogy* by noting that he finds these psychologists' approach perplexing. By Nietzsche's lights, they are on the right track insofar as they attempt to find a naturalistic account of human morality, that is, insofar as they attempt to trace ethical norms back to human nature. Nonetheless, he finds it odd that they should try to ground what is arguably most profound about human nature—morality—in what is most mundane—that is, human passivity, usefulness, and forgetfulness:

> These English psychologists whom we also have to thank for the only attempts so far to produce a history of the genesis of morality—they themselves are no small riddle for us. . . . What do they actually want? One finds them, whether voluntarily or involuntarily, always at the same task . . . of seeking that which is actually effective, leading, decisive for our development, precisely where the intellectual pride of man would least wish to find it (for example in the *vis inertiae* of habit or in forgetfulness or in a blind and accidental interlacing and mechanism of ideas or in anything purely passive, automatic, reflexive, molecular, and fundamentally mindless)—what is it that always drives these psychologists in precisely *this* direction? Is it a secret, malicious, base instinct to belittle mankind . . . . Or a little subterranean animosity and rancor against Christianity . . . . Or even a lascivious taste for the disconcerting, for the painful-paradoxical . . . . Or finally—a little of everything, a little meanness, a little gloominess, a little anti-Christianity, a little tickle and need for the pepper? (1.1; this chapter follows the translation of the *Genealogy* in Nietzsche [1998])

Whatever their motivations might be, Nietzsche accuses all such earlier genealogists of lacking a true historical spirit, and of thinking, in spite of themselves, in an essentially ahistorical manner. He finds evidence for this in the (alleged) historical implausibility of their accounts of morality. According to Nietzsche, they offer accounts such as the following:

> "Originally"—so they decree—"unegoistic actions were praised and called good from the perspective of those to whom they were rendered, hence for whom they were *useful*; later one *forgot* this origin of the praise and, simply because unegoistic actions were *as a matter of habit* always praised as good, one also felt them to be good—as if they were something good in themselves. (1.2)

But as a historical hypothesis, Nietzsche thinks this defies credulity:

> Now in the first place it is obvious to me that the actual genesis of the concept "good" is sought and fixed in the wrong place by this theory: the judgment "good" does *not* stem from those to whom "goodness" is rendered! Rather it was "the good" themselves, that is the noble, powerful, higher ranking, and high-minded who felt and ranked themselves and their doings

> as good, which is to say, as of the first rank, in contrast to everything base, low-minded, common and vulgar. (1.2)

Nietzsche's idea here is that it is implausible to suppose that the meaning of the word "good" was first fixed by those who were the beneficiaries of altruistic actions. Rather, he contends, the meaning of "good" must have originated as a self-evaluation of the strong, as a self-assessment of those in a position to perform altruistic actions and decide how words would be used. (Nietzsche might like following analogy: it is the parent rather than the child who gets to decide how the terms "good" and "bad" are applied; "good snacks," for example, are snacks that parents think are good, not snacks that children think are good.)

Nietzsche finds further evidence of the error of the "English psychologists" in the psychological implausibility of their accounts.

> In the second place, however: quite apart from the historical untenability of that hypothesis concerning the origins of the value judgment "good," it suffers from an inherent psychological absurdity. The usefulness of the unegoistic action is supposed to be the origin of its praise, and this origin is supposed to have been *forgotten*: —how is this forgetting even *possible*? Did the usefulness of such actions cease at some point? The opposite is the case: this usefulness has been the everyday experience in all ages, something therefore that was continually underscored anew; accordingly, instead of disappearing from consciousness, instead of becoming forgettable, it could not help but impress itself upon consciousness with ever greater clarity. (1.3)

Nietzsche's suggestion here is that it is psychologically implausible that morality should have evolved because it is useful and that we have simply forgotten those origins. If the "English psychologists" were right, he claims, then since the most obvious thing about morality is its usefulness, we could hardly forget that ethical norms evolved precisely because they are so useful. (He thinks broadly utilitarian views are better on this score—they, he maintains, are at least psychologically coherent.)

As a philologist, Nietzsche reports that he was first directed toward a better account of the origin of morality by a linguistic pattern.

> The pointer to the *right* path was given to me by the question: what do the terms coined for "good" in the various languages actually mean from an

> etymological viewpoint? Here I found that they all lead back to the *same conceptual transformation*—that everywhere the basic concept is "noble," "aristocratic" in the sense related to estates, out of which "good" in the sense of "noble of soul," "high-natured of soul," "privileged of soul" necessarily develops: a development that always runs parallel to that other one which makes "common," "vulgar," "base" pass over finally into the concept "bad." (1.4)

Nietzsche's claim here is that in many languages the word "good" has its connotative roots in power, strength, and wealth, while the word "bad" has its connotative roots in weakness, dependence, and poverty. He takes this to be an important clue to the true origin of morality. And he takes the fact that this might be surprising today to imply his central thesis, namely, that the meaning of moral terms has undergone a massive transformation, what he sometimes calls a "transvaluation of values," and which earlier we called an "inversion of values."

22.4. Inversion of Values

Nietzsche's story about how, over the course of history, our moral values became inverted begins in earnest with his discussion of religious authorities, or "the priestly class." Nietzsche maintains that, like other powerful aristocratic classes, members of the priestly class refer to themselves as good and "pure" and others as bad and "impure." But, importantly for Nietzsche, the view of the priestly class is inherently unstable since the priestly class, according to Nietzsche, is necessarily less healthy and robust than other aristocratic classes:

> From the beginning there is something *unhealthy* in such priestly aristocracies and in the habits ruling there, ones turned away from action, partly brooding, partly emotionally explosive, habits that have as a consequence the intestinal disease and neurasthenia that almost unavoidably clings to the priest of all ages. (1.6)

Nietzsche thus holds that the priestly class is something of an intermediary, inherently unstable class. They are in a position of power and thus command the ability to decide what is good and bad. But they are turned away from the actual world, not joyous and healthy, and are thus prone to inventing cures that only further undermine what is best in humans. As Nietzsche puts it, "What they themselves invented as a medicine against this diseasedness of theirs—must we not say that in the end it has proved itself a hundred times more dangerous in its aftereffects than the disease from which it was to redeem them?" (1.6).

Nietzsche suggests that historically the aristocratic priestly class broke off from the nonpriestly aristocratic classes and eventually came to rival them. The Judeo-Christian-Muslim tradition, according to Nietzsche, defines itself in opposition to ancient or "knightly" aristocratic value judgments that have "as their presupposition a powerful physicality, a blossoming, rich, even overflowing health, together with that which is required for its preservation: war, adventure, the hunt, dance, athletic contests, and in general everything which includes strong, free, cheerful-hearted activity" (1.7). Fueled by jealousy and hate, the priestly class is supposed to have turned these values of the "knightly aristocracy" on their head. Instead of strength, weakness is valued; instead of pride, humility; instead of wealth, poverty. Precisely those things which were formerly associated with the "good" are relabeled as "evil" and those things that were formerly called "bad" are called "good." This is Nietzsche's central thesis of the transvaluation of values.

One might wonder at this point *how* the priestly class is supposed to have pulled off this inversion. After all, the proponents of the good-bad morality are presented as being stronger and more powerful, and the proponents of the good-evil morality are presented as being sick and weak. It is crucial here, Nietzsche suggests, that the weakness of the latter requires them to be more careful, more crafty, more "prudent":

> The human being of *ressentiment* is neither sincere, nor naïve, nor honest and frank with himself. His soul *looks obliquely* at things; his spirit loves hiding places, secret passages and backdoors. . . . He knows all about being silent, not forgetting, waiting, belittling oneself for the moment, humbling oneself. A race of such human beings of *ressentiment* in the end necessarily becomes *more prudent.*

Nietzsche thinks none of this is true of the strong, the noble:

> To be unable for any length of time to take his enemies, his accidents, his *misdeeds* themselves seriously—that is the sign of the strong, full natures

> in which there is an excess of formative, reconstructive, healing power that also makes one forget. (1.10)

Nietzsche suggests that—out of necessity, as it were—the weak plot the overthrow of the strong, while the strong are, as it were, having such a good time, and are so full of themselves, that they fail to pay attention to the looming threat. The nonpriestly aristocratic class may be strong, but the priestly class—of necessity—is more clever, and eventually wins the day.

22.5. Evaluation of Values

In the ninth section of the first book of the *Genealogy*, Nietzsche confronts an important objection to his account of morality. Suppose we accept that modern morality has its origins in religious values, even in the values of the weak, in the values of the "mob." So what? How can we say that one value system is better than another without presupposing a value system by which to judge? Nietzsche puts the worry himself as follows:

> That the lambs feel anger toward the great birds of prey does not strike us as odd: but that is no reason for holding it against the great birds of prey that they snatch up little lambs for themselves. And when the lambs say among themselves "these birds of prey are evil; and whoever is as little as possible a bird of prey but rather its opposite, a lamb,—isn't he good? There is nothing to criticize in this setting up of an ideal, even if the birds of prey should look on this a little mockingly and perhaps say to themselves: "*we* do not feel any anger towards them, these good lambs, as a matter of fact, we love them: nothing is more tasty than a tender lamb." To demand of strength that it *not* express itself as strength, that it *not* be a desire to overwhelm, a desire to cast down, a desire to become lord, a thirst for enemies and resistances and triumphs, is just as nonsensical as to demand of weakness that it express itself as strength. (1.13)

Indeed, the worry might be even worse than this: we might wonder, hasn't religious morality—by Nietzsche's own lights—shown its superiority by dint of the fact that it has won out? The challenge therefore stands: what exactly is wrong with good-evil (that is, religious, as opposed to the ancient good-bad) morality?

In trying to articulate what he finds so distasteful about good-evil morality, Nietzsche raises a number of considerations. Perhaps his most central idea is that good-bad morality is primarily inward directed and self-affirming while good-evil morality is essentially grounded in *ressentiment* and consequently is outward directed and other-denying:

> Whereas all noble morality grows out of a triumphant yes-saying to oneself, from the outset slave morality says "no" to an "out-side," to a "different," to a "not-self": and *this* "no" is its creative deed. This reversal of the value-establishing glance—this *necessary* direction toward the outside instead of back onto oneself—belongs to the very nature of *ressentiment*: in order to come into being, slave-morality always needs an opposite and external world; it needs, psychologically speaking, external stimuli in order to be able to act at all,—its action is, from the ground up, reaction. The reverse is the case with the noble manner of valuation: it acts and grows spontaneously, it seeks out its opposite only in order to say "yes" to itself still more gratefully and more jubilantly. (1.10)

Another prominent idea in the first treatise is that good-evil morality is necessarily founded on deception, even self-deception, and a moral and metaphysical lie. Nietzsche makes the point with comical flourish:

> "I understand, I'll open my ears once again (oh! oh! oh! and *close my* nose). Now for the first time I hear what they have said so often: 'We good ones—*we are the just*—what they demand they call not retaliation but rather 'the triumph of *justice*'; what they hate is not the enemy, no! they hate '*injustice*,' 'ungodliness'; what they believe and hope for is not the hope for revenge, the drunkenness of sweet revenge . . . but rather the victory of God, of the *just* God over the ungodly; what is left on earth for them to love are not their brothers in hate but rather their 'brothers in love,' as they say, all the good and just on earth."
>
> —And what do they call that which serves them as comfort against all the sufferings of life—their phantasmagoria of the anticipated future blessedness?
>
> —"What? Did I hear right? They call that 'the last judgment,' the coming of *their* kingdom, of the 'kingdom of God'—*meanwhile*, however, they live 'in faith,' 'in love,' 'in hope.'"
>
> —Enough! Enough! (1.4)

One last idea: Nietzsche also seems to think that the influence of good-evil morality leads to something like a flattening of the human spirit. It makes the world less dangerous, more civilized, more equal, but in this Nietzsche sees a decline rather than an advance. He suggests that modern society founded on good-evil morality is to the more "barbaric" societies of "Roman, Arab, Germanic, Japanese nobility, Homeric heroes, Scandinavian Vikings" as caged animals are to wild beasts. Indeed, he suggests that good-evil morality so flattens the nobility of human nature as to make it boring and uninteresting so that it must ultimately lead to nihilism (a point we return to in chapter 24).

In closing, Nietzsche does not see the development of good-evil morality as a total loss. The *ressentiment* that he finds so repugnant does have an important upshot. In being forced to look inward, the proponents of the good-evil morality are also forced to reflect, to think, to "scheme." In doing so they become, in a sense, deeper, more interesting animals:

> With the priests *everything* simply becomes more dangerous, not only curatives and healing arts, but also arrogance, revenge, acuity, excess, love, lust to rule, virtue, disease;—though with some fairness one could also add that it was on the soil of this *essentially dangerous* form of human existence, the priestly form, that man first became *an interesting animal*, that only here did the human soul acquire *depth* in a higher sense and become *evil*—and these are, after all, the two basic forms of the previous superiority of man over other creatures! (1.6)

Here we get an early hint that Nietzsche's attitude toward the Judeo-Christian-Muslim tradition is more complicated than it might at first appear. That tradition, Nietzsche suggests, has plowed under something healthy and proud and has left us sick and neurotic. But it has also changed us in important, profound ways, ways that may yet open up new possibilities for humankind. In the next two chapters, we see Nietzsche further develop both sides of his ambivalent attitude toward the morality of traditional religion.

22.6. Debunking Religion and Morality?

Nietzsche's *Genealogy of Morality* is a famous example of an argument form that has recently received a great deal of attention from contemporary philosophers. Although there are many variations and details, the basic shape of the argument proceeds in three steps. First, a commonly held view is identified as a target. Second, a genealogy of that view is given, according to which the truth of that view is not relevant. If the genealogy is correct, proponents of the view do not hold their view *because* it is correct but rather for other reasons all together. Third, it is concluded that the view in question has been undermined and should be rejected. Following current parlance, we may call arguments of this broad form "genealogical debunking arguments."

Genealogical debunking arguments in the domain of religion are common. One such argument suggests that religious belief arises out of a kind of wish-fulfillment (see, for example, Freud 1927). It would be great if an all-powerful benefactor were watching out for us. It would be great if someone would someday reward all good deeds and rectify all wrongs. It would be great if we could live forever in eternal bliss, if our deceased loved ones were waiting for us in eternity, and so on. These things are so attractive and so appealing—so the debunking argument goes—that we have come to believe them in spite of the evidence to the contrary. We have come to believe them independently of any evidence that they might be true. The debunker concludes that once we appreciate that the true origins of religious belief are desire rather than evidence, we should abandon religious belief even at the price of decreasing our psychological comfort.

Another line of thought draws on contemporary evolutionary theory (see, for example, Wilson 2002). It is possible that religious belief, or a disposition to religious belief, has been evolutionarily advantageous. Religious belief might promote group cohesion or coordination—or it might be a side effect of some other evolutionary development that is itself advantageous. For example, perhaps natural selection favors clan identities and clan identities lead to religious identities. If some such evolutionary story is correct, then it could be the case that humans have come to hold religious beliefs in a way that does not turn on religious beliefs being true. Again, the debunker concludes that once we accept some such evolutionary story, we should abandon religious belief.

Religious debunking arguments are interesting, and I suspect generally quite powerful for the way people think about religion today. They are, however, controversial among philosophers. One concern that philosophers raise is that genealogical debunking arguments don't usually show precisely that religious beliefs are *false*. It is perfectly possible for some genealogical story to be correct and yet for the belief it is supposed to undermine to be true.

Even if, for example, religious beliefs are widely held because of an evolutionary process that is itself indifferent to their truth, that doesn't necessarily imply that they are false. Even if the genealogical story is correct, the targeted belief might be true. The debunker is, I think, implicitly assuming something like a parsimony constraint. This is not unreasonable. We do the same all the time in science and everyday life. If that's right, the debunker's thought is that having found a particular explanation of some phenomenon—in this case, religious belief—no other explanation is needed, and thus, by a principle of parsimony, allowed. In short: if, for example, religious belief can be explained in evolutionary terms, no other explanation is needed nor permitted. That is not an unreasonable thought, but it does leave a gap between the premises of the argument and the purported conclusion.

Another and perhaps more significant concern that philosophers have raised is that it is often very hard to evaluate debunking stories themselves. Here is a possible story about how religious beliefs came to be: throughout history, people have had genuine, true religious experiences. Those experiences have been passed down and recorded from generation to generation and inform the beliefs of the religiously observant today. Their religious beliefs continue to be nourished even now by divine assistance. That is one possible story about religious belief formation. It is not a debunking story. Here's another possible story: People have never had genuine religious experiences. There is no God and thus no divinity providing continuous assistance to religious belief. In truth, religious belief is ultimately grounded in an evolutionary push that favors religious beliefs that are nonetheless utterly false. Both stories are at least vaguely coherent, and both, I think, could be true. But how are we supposed to decide between them? More generally, there seem to be many possible genealogical stories for any given target, but it is often extremely difficult—perhaps impossible—to determine which genealogical story is true. In many cases, the status of particular debunking genealogies seems to be as controversial as the beliefs they are intended to debunk.

Further Study

Sigmund Freud, *The Future of an Illusion; Civilization, Society and Religion: Group Psychology; Civilizations and Its Discontents, and Other Works*. London: Penguin Books, 1927. A famous collection of essays that offer, among other things, an account of the formation of religion as wish-fulfillment.

Brian Leiter, *Routledge Philosophy Guidebook to Nietzsche on Morality*. New York: Routledge, 2002. An excellent, more advanced guide to Nietzsche's views on morality and his *Genealogy of Morality*.

Kelby Mason, "Debunking Arguments and the Genealogy of Religion and Morality." *Philosophy Compass* 5, no. 9 (September 2010): 770–78. A nicely written, helpful introduction to genealogical debunking arguments.

Friedrich Nietzsche, *On the Genealogy of Morality*. Trans. with notes and introduction by Maudemarie Clark and Alan J. Swensen. Indianapolis, IN: Hackett, 1998. A fluent, modern translation of Nietzsche's *Genealogy* together with a helpful introduction and notes.

Robert Wicks, "Friedrich Nietzsche." *Stanford Encyclopedia of Philosophy* (Spring 2009 edition), ed. Edward N. Zalta, http://plato.stanford.edu/archives/spr2009/entries/nietzsche/. An excellent, brief introduction to Nietzsche's life, works and thought.

D. S. Wilson, *Darwin's Cathedral: Evolution, Religion and the Nature of Society*. Chicago: University of Chicago Press, 2002. Offers an evolutionary account of the formation of religion emphasizing group selection.

23

Nietzsche's *On the Genealogy of Morality*

Whence Conscience, Bad Conscience, and Guilt?

23.1. The Origin of Conscience

The second treatise of Nietzsche's *On the Genealogy of Morality* takes up the topic of conscience—in particular, bad conscience. Not surprisingly, Nietzsche rejects the view that conscience is a kind of divinely implanted moral sense that tells us right from wrong. He likewise rejects the thought that a bad conscience is a morally healthy response to having performed a bad action. In opposing these widespread views, Nietzsche once again offers a naturalistic genealogy of the origins of conscience and of bad conscience. The first main piece of that account is presented primarily in the first three sections of the second treatise and focuses especially on the origin of conscience itself.

Nietzsche begins by noting that from a naturalistic perspective our feelings of moral obligation, of moral duty—of being bound by a promise or commitment—are at least prima facie puzzling. Such feelings might well seem to be unique to human beings. Martha (my dog) all too frequently does things she's not supposed to do, and she is generally submissive when caught, but it is hard to imagine that she would feel badly about getting into the garbage because she thought that it was simply wrong, that she would feel badly because she thought that she owed it to her owners not to do such things. If human beings are reckoned to be sophisticated animals, they might well appear to be the only animals that have a distinctively moral sense of right and wrong. They might appear to be the only animals that have a *conscience*.

In the beginning of the second treatise, Nietzsche suggests two conditions that have helped to make feelings of conscience possible in humans. The first is a regularity of behavior supported by societal constraints:

Saints, Heretics, and Atheists. Jeffrey K. McDonough, Oxford University Press. © Oxford University Press 2022.
DOI: 10.1093/oso/9780197563847.003.0023

> As we have already grasped, the task of breeding an animal that is permitted to promise includes, as condition and preparation, the more specific task of first *making* man to a certain degree necessary, uniform, like among like, regular, and accordingly predictable. The enormous work of what I have called "morality of custom"—the true work of man on himself for the longest part of the duration of the human race, his entire *prehistoric* work, has in this its meaning, its great justification—however much hardness, tyranny, mindlessness, and idiocy may be inherent in it: with the help of the morality of custom and the social straightjacket man was *made* truly calculable. (2.2; this chapter follows the translation of the *Genealogy* in Nietzsche [1998])

This first constraint indeed makes good sense. If my behavior were too erratic or too unpredictable, I would not be in a position to make any promises, nor would anyone be justified in taking my word if I did. If, for all I know, tomorrow I fly off to San Francisco and become a street performer, I can't make a significant promise to return student papers the next day, and students wouldn't be in a position to take me at my word if I did make them such a promise.

According to Nietzsche, the second condition requisite for the emergence of conscience is memory. More specifically, we might say that what Nietzsche really requires is a nonselective memory. If I am going to be a creature capable of making a promise, it is essential that I don't simply forget whatever obligations I have that I don't wish to fulfill. The second treatise thus opens with the following words:

> To breed an animal that *is permitted to promise*—isn't this precisely the paradoxical task nature has set for itself with regard to man? . . . That this problem has been solved to a high degree must appear all the more amazing to one who can fully appreciate the force working in opposition, that of *forgetfulness*. Forgetfulness is no mere inertial force as the superficial believe; rather it is an active and in the strictest sense positive faculty of suppression. . . . Precisely this necessarily forgetful animal in whom forgetting represents a force, a form of *strong* health, has now bred in itself an opposite faculty, a memory, with whose help forgetfulness is disconnected for certain cases,—namely for those cases where a promise is to be made. (2.1)

What Nietzsche finds remarkable about our memories is that we do not just remember things that are in our best interest to remember. I recall a debt, an obligation, a misstep even when doing so is painful and against my own immediate self-interests. This is, of course, crucial to the convention of making promises, agreeing to contracts, and of moral obligations more generally, but how it could have emerged in a naturalistic setting is indeed an intriguing question.

Nietzsche suggests that a dark truth lies behind both of these conditions necessary for moral obligation, namely, that human beings had to be conditioned to regularity and memory by painful constraints imposed by others. Humans only came to have the capacities necessary for making promises because others would mete out painful consequences:

> How does one make a memory for the human animal? How does one impress something onto this partly dull, partly scattered momentary understanding, this forgetfulness in the flesh, so that it remains present? . . . As one can imagine, the answers and means used to solve this age-old problem were not exactly delicate; there is perhaps nothing more terrible and more uncanny in all of man's prehistory than his *mnemo-technique*. "One burns something in so that it remains in one's memory: only what does not cease *to give pain* remains in one's memory"—that is the first principle from the most ancient (unfortunately also longest) psychology on earth. (2.3)

The capacity to be reliably regular and remember obligations, according to Nietzsche, is rooted in the practice of punishment: one came to remember because forgetting was made painful, and pain is, in Nietzsche's words, "the best mnemonic." The original natural tendency toward a healthy spontaneity and forgetfulness was driven out by constraints and punishments imposed by society.

It is worth noting that although Nietzsche thinks that conscience literally has a long and painful history, he nonetheless thinks that it is far from being a tragic waste. That long and painful history, he claims, finds its vindication in the capacities to which it gives rise:

> If . . . we place ourselves at the end of the enormous process, where the tree finally brings to light that *to which* it was only the means: then we will find as the ripest fruit on its tree the *sovereign individual* . . . in short, the human being with his own independent long will, the human being

> who *is permitted to promise*. . . . The proud knowledge of the extraordinary privilege of *responsibility*, the consciousness of this rare freedom, this power over oneself and fate, has sunk into his lowest depth and has become instinct, the dominant instinct: —what will he call it, this dominant instinct . . . ? But there is no doubt: this sovereign human being calls it his *conscience*. (2.2)

Through a long and painful history, Nietzsche maintains, human beings thus emerge with a new, profound capacity: the ability to commit oneself to a future action come what may, to make a promise that serves as a guarantee, to take responsibility for one's actions in a way that is simply impossible for lower animals.

23.2. The Origin of Bad Conscience

Nietzsche takes himself to have given an account—or at least the outlines of an account—of how conscience arose in human beings. The next step in the overarching argument of the second treatise is to ask how specifically *bad* conscience arose. For all that has been said so far, humans could have developed a "long" memory enabling them to make promises, and yet never have developed a *bad* conscience, never have felt *self*-reproach for not having fulfilled an obligation. They might have behaved much in the way that people often behave with respect to the speed limit: they remember that there is a speed limit, they even recognize a certain obligation to go the speed limit, and they generally drive somewhere around the speed limit lest they get a speeding ticket. But while people might regret getting caught speeding, or might feel bad if they were to cause an accident that could have otherwise been avoided, most people don't reproach themselves for speeding per se. (No one lays awake at night reprimanding themselves for driving a bit too fast that day.) So, once again, the next step in Nietzsche's argument is to explain how people come to make *themselves* feel bad for their mistakes and "bad" actions.

An important clue, according to Nietzsche, is to be found in "the very material concept of debt" (2.4). A debtor owes or promises something to a creditor. The creditor expects to either be paid according to the agreement, or to be able to extract an equivalent payment in some other way, usually by causing the debtor to suffer:

> In order to instill trust in his promise of repayment, to provide a guarantee for the seriousness and the sacredness of his promise, to impress repayment of his conscience as a duty, as an obligation, the debtor—by virtue of contract—pledges to the creditor in the case of non-payment something else that he "possesses," over which he still has power, for example his body . . . his freedom or even his life. . . . Above all, however, the creditor could subject the body of the debtor to all manner of ignominy and torture, for example cutting as much from it as appeared commensurate to the magnitude of the debt. (2.5)

The idea here is that a debtor-creditor contract entitles the creditor to extract a payment equivalent to what was loaned. Where that payment cannot be met in accordance with the original agreement, the creditor may take an equivalent degree of suffering from the creditor. (Incidentally, Nietzsche thinks it is obvious that the aim of punishment is not, as some have suggested, reform of the offender; rather, Nietzsche assumes, it is, in its most basic form, literally a payment of satisfaction to the offended.)

Reflection on the nature of punishment thus reveals a "dark truth" according to Nietzsche: the extraction of suffering from the debtor must be a measurable good to the creditor. That is to say, the suffering of the debtor must be equivalent for the creditor to some amount of bread, gold, or property.

> Let us make clear to ourselves the logic of this whole form of compensation: it is foreign enough. The equivalence consists in this: that in place of an advantage that directly makes good for the injury (hence in place of a compensation in money, land, possession of some kind) the creditor is granted a certain *feeling of satisfaction* as repayment and compensation,—the feeling of satisfaction that comes from being permitted to vent his power without a second thought on one who is powerless, the carnal delight "*de faire le mal pour le plaisir de le faire*," the enjoyment of doing violence. . . . The compensation thus consists in a directive and right to cruelty. (2.5)

Nietzsche sees it as a deep and fundamental truth that, like all creatures, humans take enjoyment in the execution, the "outflowing," of their wills. One manifestation of such an "outflowing" is to cause others to suffer. As Nietzsche coldly puts it, "To see somebody suffer is nice, to make somebody suffer even nicer" (2.6). Perhaps it is worth noting that in making this claim Nietzsche does not commit himself to the necessity of making others suffer;

there are other ways in which a will to power might be discharged, for example, composing a symphony, designing a statue, or writing a treatise on the origins of morality.

Nietzsche suggests that in precivilized times, human beings' instinct toward cruelty found a range of natural outlets. One could inflict suffering on those defeated in battle, those who caused offense, those who were simply weaker, and so on. Such natural outlets, however, were severely curtailed when societal constraints were imposed on people, and it is ultimately in this curtailing that Nietzsche proposes to find the origins of bad conscience:

> I take bad conscience to be the deep sickness into which man had to fall under the pressure of that most fundamental of all changes he ever experienced—the change of finding himself enclosed once and for all within the sway of society and peace. Just as water animals must have fared when they were forced either to become land animals or perish, so fared these half animals who were happily adapted to wilderness, war, roaming about, adventure—all at once all of their instincts were devalued and "disconnected." From now on they were to go on foot and "carry themselves" where they had previously been carried by the water: a horrible heaviness lay upon them. They felt awkward doing the simplest tasks, for this new, unfamiliar world they no longer had their old leaders, the regulating drives that unconsciously guided them safely—they were reduced to thinking, inferring, calculating, connecting cause and effect, these unhappy ones, reduced to their "consciousness," to their poorest and most erring organ! I do not believe there has ever been such a feeling of misery on earth, such a leaden discomfort—and yet these old instincts had not all at once ceased to make their demands! (2.16)

With the imposition of societal constraints, Nietzsche maintains, the natural outlets for human instincts to cruelty were sharply curtailed. One could no longer count on being able to release one's hostilities on one's enemies, on those who caused offense, or even on one's weaker fellows. The wild instincts of human beings, Nietzsche suggests, were literally as ill-suited to society as a fish's instincts to dry land.

Nietzsche maintains that the instinct for cruelty, however, did not go away like the gills of the fish that took to land. Instead, he claims, those instincts redirected themselves. Unable to inflict suffering on others, people resorted to inflicting suffering on themselves:

> All instincts that do not discharge themselves outwardly *turn themselves inwards*—this is what I call the *internalizing* of man: thus first grows in man that which he later calls his "soul." . . . Those terrible bulwarks with which the organization of the state protects itself against the old instincts of freedom—punishments belong above all else to these bulwarks—brought it about that all those instincts of the wild free roaming human turned themselves backwards *against man himself.* Hostility, cruelty, pleasure in persecution, in assault, in change, in destruction—all of that turning itself against the possessors of such instincts: *that* is the origin of "bad conscience." (2.16)

Here we finally have Nietzsche's account of how not merely conscience, but *bad* conscience arises. It is the result of frustrated instincts being redirected against their very owners. It is literally a kind of self-cruelty. It is causing oneself to suffer in lieu of causing others to suffer.

Given his analysis of bad conscience, it may be surprising that Nietzsche has a mixed attitude toward it. While he clearly sees self-caused suffering as a dismal abomination in itself, he also suggests that it once again makes possible a previously unimagined range of potentialities:

> Let us immediately add that, on the other hand, with the appearance on earth of an animal soul turned against itself, taking sides against itself, something so new, deep, unheard of, enigmatic, contradictory, *and full of future* had come into being that the appearance of the earth was thereby essentially changed. . . . Since that time man is *included* among the most unexpected and exciting lucky throws in the game played by the "big child" of Heraclitus, whether called Zeus or chance—he awakens for himself an interest, an anticipation, a hope, almost a certainty, as if with him something were announcing itself, something preparing itself as if man were not a goal but only a path, an incident, a bridge, a great promise. (2.16)

Bad conscience, while unhealthy in and of itself, is thus treated by Nietzsche as a stage in the development of a more profound creature capable of much greater feats. It is a source of a deeper, more reflective, more expansive nature, and, for example, of the artist's ability to suffer for the sake of creating something new and beautiful.

23.3. The Origin of Moral Guilt

Up to this point, Nietzsche still has not given us his account of how the distinctively *moral* phenomenon of bad conscience or moral guilt is supposed to arise within his naturalistic framework. We have, in effect, been provided with accounts of two more primitive, more basic phenomena: (i) the phenomenon of conscience understood merely as the capacity for long-term, nonselective memory and will; and (ii) the phenomenon of (amoral) bad conscience understood as the capacity to inflict suffering upon oneself. What remains to be done is for Nietzsche to provide an account of how conscience, or "guilt" understood as a capacity for moral self-reproach, arose out of these more primitive capacities. He sets himself to this task starting at section 19. (So as to make things less confusing, I use the term "moral guilt" for this phenomenon in what follows. Nietzsche himself sees "conscience," "bad conscience," and "guilt" as all denoting the same psychological phenomenon as it evolves through the course of human history, and so switches back and forth between these terms more freely.)

I think the notion of moral guilt that Nietzsche has in mind is probably much less pronounced today than it was in Nietzsche's own time, and contemporary readers might find it difficult to put their fingers on it. It is perhaps most at home in a religious context, and I think that is generally the way that Nietzsche considers it. As an example, reflect on Pascal, who believed that we are born guilty, irredeemably stained, and deserving of damnation. Or think of Martin Luther, who is reported to have felt such guilt at his failure to live up to the demands of his own inner conscience that he would vigorously whip himself in contrition. This kind of moral guilt goes beyond, I think, the self-reproach characteristic of bad conscience in having a sense of failing someone or something else. Pascal and Luther thought that they had failed not just themselves but that they had let God down and needed to atone—insofar as it is possible—to the divine. This extreme sense of guilt is, I think, what Nietzsche means to take up under the heading of moral guilt.

Nietzsche's account of moral guilt has its first step in his application of the debtor-creditor relationship to an individual and the society in which she lives. Just as one may owe something to a particular person, so too, Nietzsche maintains, one can owe something to the society in which one lives:

> The community, too, thus stands to its members in that important basic relationship, that of the creditor to his debtor. One lives in a community, one enjoys the advantages of a community (oh what advantages! we sometimes underestimate this today), one lives protected, shielded, in peace and trust, free from care with regard to certain injuries and hostilities to which the human *outside*, the "outlaw," is exposed . . . since one has pledged and obligated oneself to the community precisely in view of these injuries and hostilities. What happens *in the other case*? The community, the deceived creditor, will exact payment as best it can, one can count on that. . . . The anger of the injured creditor, of the community, gives him back again to the wild and outlawed condition from which he was previously protected: it expels him from itself,—and now every kind of hostility may vent itself on him. (2.16)

According to Nietzsche, one can not only be indebted to other particular persons, but also to a tribe or community. Just as I can owe my neighbor a loaf of bread, I can owe the state taxes or lawful behavior.

Nietzsche next claims, however, that debts can be owed not only to one's current society, but also to the founders of that society, to one's societal ancestors.

> The civil-law relationship of the debtor to his creditor . . . was once again . . . interpreted into a relationship . . . of *those presently living* to their *ancestors*. Within the original clan association . . . the living generation always acknowledges a juridical obligation to the earlier generation, and particularly to the earliest one, which founded the clan. . . . Here the conviction holds sway that it is only through the sacrifices and achievements of the ancestors that the clan *exists* at all,—and that one has to *repay* them through sacrifices and achievements: one thereby acknowledges a *debt* that is continually growing, since these ancestors, in their continued existence as powerful spirits, do not cease to use their strength to bestow on the clan new benefits and advances. (2.19)

The idea here is not, I think, hard to grasp. Just as one can owe a debt to one's current society, so one can owe a debt to the previous ages of one's society that made one's current society possible. Today, this sentiment is perhaps more pronounced in some societies than in others. Some societies appear to place a greater emphasis on acknowledging the contributions of their ancestors, and it is perhaps no coincidence that ancestor worship was a common practice in many of the societies that Nietzsche would have studied as a classical philologist. Nonetheless, founding myths and a sense of debt to earlier generations in some degree seem to be a part of every society. One sees it present in the United States, for example, in respect shown to "the founding fathers" and war veterans, and during commemorative holidays.

Although common, Nietzsche thinks that the notion of generational debt is inherently dangerous, for it suggests that what one owes to is forever increasing. As the society continues to grow and flourish the debt grows too (and if things go wrong, one can always attribute the decay of the society to a failure to properly repay the owed ancestral debt). Over time, Nietzsche claims, the ancestors become elevated to the status of gods, and the debt owed becomes insurmountable. This process by which debt and guilt are ever increased reaches its peak, according to Nietzsche, in Western monotheism:

> If one imagines this brutal kind of logic carried through to its end: finally, through the imagination of growing fear the progenitors of the *most powerful* clans must have grown into enormous proportions and have been pushed back into the darkness of a divine uncanniness and unimaginability:—in the end the progenitor is necessarily transfigured into a *god*. . . . For several millennia the feeling of guilt toward the deity did not stop growing and indeed grew ever onward in the same proportion as the concept of god and the feeling for god grew on earth and was borne up on high. . . . The rise of the Christian god as the maximum god that has been attained thus far therefore also brought a maximum of feelings of guilt into appearance on earth. (2.20)

Nietzsche thus claims that a distinctively moral sense of guilt comes into being through the long process by which people are led to believe that they owe something they can never repay to the gods. In lieu of full payment, they inflict suffering upon themselves in partial restitution. The intensity of this moral guilt increases in direct proportion to the debt owed and the magnitude of the deity worshiped. In this account, the Western tradition's postulation of an infinitely great god gives rise to the greatest possible moral guilt.

Given his account of the origins of moral guilt, we can see why Nietzsche is hopeful that the rise of atheism will loosen its grip:

> Assuming that we have by now entered into the *reverse* movement, one might with no little probability deduce from the unstoppable decline of faith in the Christian god that there would already be a considerable decline in human consciousness of guilt as well; indeed the prospect cannot be dismissed that the perfect and final victory of atheism might free humanity from this entire feeling of having debts to its beginnings, its *causa prima*. Atheism and a kind of *second innocence* belong together. (2.20)

Again, Nietzsche's reasoning here—whether or not one agrees with it—is at least not hard to follow. He has argued that distinctively moral guilt is essentially connected with the postulation of a divine being (or beings) to whom we owe something that we can never fully repay. Our inevitable failure to repay those debts in turn gives rise in us to terrible feelings of guilt—think again of Pascal's feelings of being irredeemably stained and Luther's self-flagellations. From this picture, a release from those terrible feelings of guilt might reasonably be expected to accompany a rise of atheism itself.

Although Nietzsche thus seems to think that atheism is now our best hope for escaping the tyranny of moral guilt, it is worth noticing that he also suggests that there is no necessary link between guilty conscience and theism. Indeed, he holds that for the ancient Greeks, the postulation of gods served exactly the opposite end, helping to limit bad conscience, helping them to hold moral guilt at bay:

> For the longest time these Greeks used their gods precisely to keep "bad conscience" at arm's length, to be able to remain cheerful about their freedom of soul: that is the reverse of the use which Christianity made of its god. . . . Thus the noble Greek wondered for centuries in the face of every incomprehensible atrocity and wanton act with which one of his equals had sullied himself. "A god must have beguiled him," he said to himself finally, shaking his head. (2.23)

Thus, according to Nietzsche, the emergence of feelings of moral guilt—of self-inflicted suffering—is intimately tied to the emergence of the Judeo-Christian-Muslim tradition (although features of Christian doctrine, Nietzsche holds, are particularly effective here). Nietzsche's story as to how this came to pass is explored more fully in the third treatise under the guise of the meaning of ascetic ideas. We turn to that story in the next chapter.

23.4. Should We Obey Our Conscience?

Conscience is usually presented as a kind of inner nagging voice that is supposed to speak up when we violate our own moral principles. That core thought is, I think, consistent with two rather different pictures of the status of those moral principles. In one picture, the moral principles in question are thought of as being innate and absolute. The principles are objective, timeless laws of morality. Conscience is like an infallible inner voice reminding us to stay the moral course and harassing us when we stray from the moral straight and narrow. When people speak of an inner "moral compass," I think they often have this first picture of conscience in mind.

From another perspective, conscience is essentially content neutral. It is still like a nagging voice, but it just echoes whatever moral principles you happen to have, regardless of how you acquired them. If you were brought up with one belief system, you might feel guilt when you do one thing. If you were brought up with another belief system, you might feel guilt when you do just the opposite. In this picture, conscience has no moral authority in its own right. It is not like a moral compass pointing you toward true North. Rather it is like a nagging parent enforcing whatever the house rules happen to be.

In an engaging piece titled "The Conscience of Huckleberry Finn," the contemporary philosopher Jonathan Bennett argues that conscience and sympathy can provide important checks on one another. In developing his thesis, Bennett suggests that sympathy may be understood in very general terms as a sort of fellow feeling. Sympathy occurs when I take on the pleasure and pain of others, when I rejoice in their triumphs and commiserate with their sorrows. Sympathy in this sense is obviously often a good thing. It promotes kindness to others and places an important check on meanness and cruelty.

Interestingly, however, Bennett argues that sympathy is not always a good thing. Parents with infants often discover that they have to sleep train their infants after around six months of age. If they are not sleep trained, the kids may not sleep properly at all, which is bad for the kids as well as for their exhausted parents. In many cases sleep training is an obviously good thing. But it can also be incredibly hard, precisely because the parent's sympathies are incredibly strong. The urge to immediately pick up your child as soon as she starts crying can be so powerful that many parents simply cannot do it. In this case, sympathy seems to stand in the way of our doing what is right, and you can imagine many other cases to the same effect. The surgeon may have to overcome her natural sympathies in performing a necessary surgery.

The soldier may have to overcome his natural sympathies in defending a just cause.

If a blind attachment to sympathy would lead us astray in some cases, Bennett argues that in other cases it may provide an important check on conscience. He suggests one such case can be found in the story of Huckleberry Finn. As Bennett draws the lesson, Huck accepts a bad morality according to which he thinks people can be owned. He thinks that in helping his friend Jim escape from slavery, he—Huck—has done something wrong. Through some nice textual work, Bennett makes a strong case that the character of Huckleberry Finn really is portrayed as feeling guilty—as panged by his conscience—by his decision to help Jim. Fortunately, in this case, Huck's sympathies pull in the other direction and win the day. Bennett offers the story of Huckleberry Finn as an example of how sympathy may act as a check on conscience.

Bennett suggests that one moral that we might draw from reflecting on the relationship between sympathy and conscience is that two imperfect principles are better than one. To his way of thinking, conscience is a guide to morality, but a fallible guide. Sometimes conscience gets things right, but sometimes it gets things wrong. Sometimes it goads us into doing the hard but right thing, but sometimes—as in the case of Huckleberry Finn—it does just the opposite. Sympathy is much the same. Sometimes it leads us to help those in need and sympathize with those in trouble. But sometimes it encourages us to take an easier path away from what most needs to be done. Bennett concludes that we are better off for having both a conscience and sympathy since they can thus serve as a check on one another. We should be wary, he thinks, of principles that grate too strongly against our sympathies and of sympathies that we can't square with our principles.

In the struggle between conscience and sympathy we might—as Nietzsche implies—see something deeply human. To be a well-functioning human is to be capable of feeling a pull between what we are naturally inclined to do and what our inner voice tells us that we should do. Someone who didn't feel the pull of sentiment would be more machine than man, more a computer than a human being. Someone who couldn't feel the pull of conscience, however, would be more a mere animal than a rational human being. He would be buffeted happily or tragically by his impulses without being able to act on principle. A fully developed human is a being who can act both from sympathy and conscience.

Further Study

Jonathan Bennett, "The Conscience of Huckleberry Finn." *Philosophy* 49 (1974): 123–34, https://www.earlymoderntexts.com/assets/jfb/huckfinn.pdf. An elegant investigation into the relationship between conscience, sympathy, and moral principles.

Brian Leiter, *Routledge Philosophy Guidebook to Nietzsche on Morality*. New York: Routledge, 2002. An excellent guide to Nietzsche's views on morality and his *On the Genealogy of Morality*.

Friedrich Nietzsche, *On the Genealogy of Morality*. Trans. with notes and introduction by Maudemarie Clark and Alan J. Swensen. Indianapolis, IN: Hackett, 1998. A fluent, modern translation of Nietzsche's *Genealogy* together with a helpful introduction and notes.

Mathias Risse, "The Second Treatise in *On the Genealogy of Morality*: Nietzsche on the Origin of the Bad Conscience." *European Journal of Philosophy* 9, no. 1 (2001): 55–81. An excellent, advanced overview of the Second Treatise of Nietzsche's *On the Genealogy of Morality*.

Paul Strohm, *Conscience: A Very Short Introduction*. New York: Oxford University Press, 2011. A helpful, engaging overview of the concept of conscience from early to modern times.

24

Nietzsche's *On the Genealogy of Morality*

No Alternative?

24.1. What Do Ascetic Ideals Mean?

Ascetic ideals are, generally speaking, ideals of self-denial. Nietzsche himself offers as paradigmatic examples "poverty, humility, chastity" (3.8; this chapter follows the translation of the *Genealogy* in Nietzsche [1998]). He rightly points out that such ideals are widely held in high esteem and suggests that they have different significance for artists, philosophers, and religious leaders. The beginning sections of the third treatise offer an account of what ascetic ideals mean, according to Nietzsche, for each of these three groups.

With respect to *artists* (see 3.2.–3.5), Nietzsche—using his one-time friend Richard Wagner as an example—concludes that the significance of ascetic ideals is really parasitic upon the significance they hold for others. He thus declares at the beginning of section 5: "What then do ascetic ideals mean? In the case of the artist . . . *absolutely nothing*! . . . Or so many things that it is as good as absolutely nothing! . . . they [i.e., artists] are far from standing independently enough in the world and *against* the world for their valuations and changes in these to deserve interest *in themselves*!" By Nietzsche's lights, artists have simply reflected the ascetic ideals they find in others. They do not themselves offer an independent basis, justification, or drive for ascetic ideals. The self-denying artist is merely mimicking the ideals he finds in others.

With respect to *philosophers* (see 3.6–3.10)—and here Nietzsche uses Schopenhauer as his principal example—the case is somewhat more complicated. On the one hand, Nietzsche suggests that ascetic ideals are conducive to the pursuit of philosophy. Very roughly, they allow the philosopher to focus all her energies on her work, on her defining practice. Thus, according to Nietzsche, for the philosopher, ascetic ideals promise "freedom from

Saints, Heretics, and Atheists. Jeffrey K. McDonough, Oxford University Press. © Oxford University Press 2022.
DOI: 10.1093/oso/9780197563847.003.0024

compulsion, disturbance, noise, from business, duties, cares; clarity in the head; dance, leap, and flight of ideas; good air, thin, clear, free, dry, as the air in high places is" (3.8). On the other hand, Nietzsche also suggests that the embrace of ascetic ideals has provided philosophers with a kind of cover. By playing the part of the ascetic, philosophers can hope to be grouped together with priests and the like; they can hope to be feared in virtue of their willingness to be cruel even to themselves.

Finally, Nietzsche claims that ascetic ideals find their most central role in the case of ascetic priests, among whom he counts not just religious leaders in the Western tradition, but also the "holy men" of ascetic Eastern religions. For this class of people, Nietzsche claims, ascetic ideals serve as the principal conduit for the priest's will to power; they are what sets the priest apart, the source of his authority, and the means by which he bends others to his will:

> Only now that we have gotten the *ascetic priest* in sight do we seriously begin to tackle our problem: what does the ascetic ideal mean? . . . The ascetic priest has not only his faith in that ideal but also his will, his power, his interest. His *right* to existence stands and falls with that ideal. (3.11)

For Nietzsche, the ascetic priest's whole mode of existence is tied to his belief in ascetic ideals. More than simply mimicking those around him, or paving the way for his other pursuits, the priest's way of living, of realizing himself, is tied to his commitment to ascetic ideals. In short, the ascetic priest just is the person for whom the pursuit of ascetic ideals is his primary means of expressing his will to power.

24.2. The Puzzle of Ascetic Ideals

Nietzsche suggests that it is at least prima facie puzzling that ascetic ideals should be so widely embraced. He insists that every human being is driven by a "will to power," by a desire to express herself, by a need to make her influence felt, by a will to realize her capacities. Given such a picture of human psychology, however, it seems paradoxical that the ascetic ideal of apparent self-denial, self-effacement, and self-restraint should be so popular. Indeed, Nietzsche maintains that an ascetic life appears to be a self-contradiction:

> Here the gaze is directed greenly and maliciously against physiological flourishing itself, in particular against its expression, beauty, joy; whereas pleasure is felt and sought in deformation, atrophy, in pain, in accident, in the ugly, in voluntary forfeit, in unselfing, self-flagellation, self-sacrifice. This is all paradoxical in the highest degree: we stand here before a conflict that *wants* itself to be conflicted, that *enjoys* itself in this suffering and even becomes ever more self-assured and triumphant to the extent that its own presupposition, physiological viability, *decreases*. (3.11)

In the face of this paradox, Nietzsche concludes that the apparent rejection of life by life that we seem to find embodied in ascetic ideals must be only *apparent*. Deep down, such ideals must be rooted in a will to power that we have simply lost track of, in a will to power whose strategy is generally misunderstood. Far from being a genuine denial of life, ascetic ideals properly understood must be an obscured strategy for the promotion of life, for the expression of one's will to power. Nietzsche thus insists that the ascetic ideal is "exactly the opposite of what its venerators suppose—in it and through it life is wrestling with death and against death; the ascetic ideal is an artifice for the *preservation* of life" (3.13).

The central project of the third treatise is to set out Nietzsche's account of "the strategy" of ascetic ideals; that is, to explain how the embrace of ascetic ideals is not really a denial of life, but rather a strategy for preserving it. We look at each stage of Nietzsche's account, but before doing so it might be helpful to quickly sketch the big picture. First, Nietzsche suggests that for a variety of reasons human life is generally full of suffering and misery. Second, this suffering, he claims, would in many cases be simply unbearable if it were thought to be to no end—if it were thought to be pointless. Third, the ascetic priest offers a story that gives meaning to human suffering and misery and thus provides a means for making life bearable in spite—or indeed *because*—of the suffering experienced in it. Fourth, the story is widely repeated and accepted because it is the only strategy on offer, "because it was the only ideal so far, because it had no rival" (Nietzsche 1989, 312). With this overarching narrative in mind, let's look more closely at the details of Nietzsche's account.

24.3. The "Vale of Tears"

The idea that the world is a "vale of tears," a realm of endless, unsatisfied longing and suffering was familiar to Nietzsche from the philosophical writings of Arthur Schopenhauer. Schopenhauer held that engagement with the world, and following one's desires, leads only to further suffering and frustration. Given such a view, the ascetic ideal at least makes prima facie sense: the less one engages with the world and pursues one's desires, the less one is likely to suffer. The paradox that Nietzsche confronts thus arises in part because he agrees with Schopenhauer that human existence is generally shot through with misery, and yet he intends to reject Schopenhauer's proposal to simply withdraw from life.

Nietzsche thinks that human suffering has many sources, including our own instincts for cruelty, self-cruelty, and ambition, and from other sophisticated capacities that have arisen in humans. Picking up shortly after the passage quoted above, he writes,

> Whence it stems, this diseasedness? For man is sicker, more unsure, more changing, more undetermined than any other animal, and this there is no doubt—he is *the* sick animal: how does this come about? Certainly he has also dared more, innovated more, defied more, challenged fate more than all the other animals taken together: he, the great experimenter with himself, the unsatisfied, unsatiated one who wrestles with animal, nature, and gods for final dominion—he, the one yet unconquered, the eternally future one who no longer finds any rest from his own pressing energy, so that his future digs inexorably like a spur into the flesh of every present: —how could such a courageous and rich animal not also belong to the most endangered, the most prolongedly and most deeply sick among all sick animals? (3.14)

It is worth noting that two distinguishable issues are intertwined here. One is the widespread suffering of humanity that Nietzsche posits and seems to think is—at this stage at least—largely unavoidable. Another issue is the sickness or weariness to which such suffering is liable to give rise. The former issue Nietzsche thinks is not a deep problem. Suffering is natural to our state. It is one more psychological and physiological spur to activity, and wishing it away tout court would merely lead to a more desperate misery. The latter, Nietzsche suggests, is a more serious problem and one that he thinks is a genuine danger to humankind. If allowed to fester it leads not so much to greater suffering, greater striving, and greater activity, but to nihilism and a kind of extinction. We might say that for Nietzsche the opposite of health is not suffering but rather apathy.

24.4. "Pointless Suffering"

Earlier we saw Nietzsche suggest that humans instinctively look for someone to blame for their suffering. In the first treatise, he argued that the weak come to see the strong as the cause and reason for their own weakness. This *ressentiment* against the strong eventually leads them to associate the characteristics of the strong with "evil" and define their own goodness in opposition to the features of their "oppressors."

Nietzsche further suggests that in blaming someone for their suffering, the miserable do indeed find some temporary relief from their pain. At the very least, the powerful emotions of hatred and vengeance drown out feelings of misery, and thus temporarily mask or "anesthetize" the original suffering:

> Every sufferer instinctively seeks a cause for his suffering; still more precisely, a perpetrator, still more specifically, a *guilty* perpetrator who is receptive to suffering—in short, some living thing on which, in response to some pretext or other, he can discharge his affects in deed or in effigy: for the discharge of affect is the sufferer's greatest attempt at relief, namely at *anesthetization*—his involuntarily craved narcotic against torment of any kind. (3.15)

In the third treatise, the instinct to find someone to blame for one's suffering is subsumed under a more general principle. Nietzsche suggests that it is not really suffering itself that people detest, but rather suffering *for no apparent reason*. Indeed, people will even invite suffering—whether by signing up for an extra course or paying for a gym membership—as long as they believe that it is a means to some end. ("No pain, no gain!") What is difficult for people to stomach, Nietzsche proposes, is not suffering itself, but *pointless* suffering. This need to find meaning in one's suffering, Nietzsche hypothesizes, is what ultimately explains the remarkable success of ascetic ideals.

24.5. "The Ascetic Priest"

Nietzsche attributes the repeated emergence of the ascetic priest throughout history to the priest's ability to address the misery of human suffering. He is a "physician" to the sick in Nietzsche's view, and his honesty is rooted in his being sick himself—in his believing in his own cures (3.15; 3.20). We might distinguish here three strategies available to the priest for alleviating people's suffering.

The first "innocent" means include the inculcation of mindless distracting habits and of small joys in the mundane features of life, in the soothing effects of hard work, and in the comfort of community relations. As Nietzsche somewhat less generously puts it,

> The means employed by the ascetic priest with which we have thus far become acquainted—the general muffling of the feeling of life, mechanical activity, the small joy, above all that of "love of one's neighbor," the herd organization, the awakening of the communal feeling of power, whereby the individual's vexation with himself is drowned out by his pleasure in the prospering of the community—these are... his *innocent* means in the battle with listlessness. (3.19; see especially 3.18)

In addition to these innocent means, the priest also has at his disposal more dangerous means. We have already encountered some of these less innocent strategies, especially in the first treatise. By finding other people to blame—particularly the strong—the priest offers an explanation for suffering, and a target for strong passions of hatred, anger, and mistrust. These feelings temporarily mask the ordinary suffering of people, and in doing so provide a kind of relief from their workaday misery.

Neither of these first two strategies, however, makes essential use of specifically *ascetic* ideals. Anyone can seek relief in routine. Anyone can offer the comforts of blame. The distinctive innovation of the ascetic priest is to suggest that the miserable have themselves to blame for their own misery:

> "I am suffering: for this someone must be to blame"—thus every diseased sheep thinks. But his shepherd, the ascetic priest, says to him: "That's right, my sheep! someone must be to blame for it: but you yourself are this someone, you alone are to blame for it—*you alone are to blame for yourself!*" . . . That is bold enough, false enough: but one thing at least has been achieved by it, in this way, as noted, the direction of the *ressentiment* has been—*changed.* (2.15)

In claiming that the miserable have themselves to blame for their own misery, the ascetic priest simultaneously provides an explanation, a purpose, and an object of *ressentiment* for suffering. He redirects the hostile feelings of the masses inward, toward themselves. The ascetic ideals are an expression of the self-approbation, self-denial, and self-hatred that the priest offers to the suffering in order to explain their suffering, and thus paradoxically to temporarily relieve that suffering.

This last strategy—the truly ascetic strategy—takes advantage of the human capacity for bad conscience and guilt. Nietzsche suggests that the ascetic priest tells a remarkable story that gives meaning to people's suffering: the gods demand adherence to an impossible set of standards, and people fail to meet those standards and thus merit punishment. Their suffering is transformed into this punishment, and their *ressentiment* is directed inward, at their very animal natures—the supposed sources of their sin and thus of their suffering. This strategy does not actually cure the original source of misery; indeed, it engenders new misery as people inflict suffering on themselves. But it does provide a purpose for that suffering, and it is in this that Nietzsche grounds the attraction of ascetic ideals: "*That* the ascetic ideal has meant so much to man, however, is an expression of the basic fact of the human will, its *horror vacui*: *it needs a goal*,—and it would rather will *nothingness* [i.e., the denial of itself, the ascetic ideals] than *not* will" (3.1).

24.6. No Alternative?

Although Nietzsche concedes that the "treatment" offered by the ascetic priest provides a temporary anesthesia for the suffering of people, he does not think that it cures its underlying basis. Most people are, by Nietzsche's lights, like an alcoholic with a terrible problem she tries to drink away. The alcohol temporarily masks the root cause of her misery but doesn't cure it and leaves her with a bad hangover and sickness to boot (see, for example, 3.21). The most basic, fundamental source of pain for humanity, according to Nietzsche—as has already been hinted at—is not suffering itself, but a failure to find meaning in life. The greatest threat to humanity is, in short, *nihilism*. It is the absence of a worthwhile purpose that people cannot bear; the desire to avoid meaninglessness drives them to radical extremes.

The final explanation according to Nietzsche for the widespread acceptance of traditional religion is that it is the *only* solution that has been offered to the threat of nihilism. Religion has been the only "system" that has truly risen to the challenge of giving meaning to human existence. The human need for some such story has thus guaranteed its success. In support of this conclusion,

Nietzsche attempts to show in a relatively systematic fashion that no other "system" has so far offered a genuine alternative to religion. In the *Genealogy*, Nietzsche is particularly intent to argue that science and philosophy do not offer a response to nihilism. Indeed, Nietzsche maintains that, in two important respects, science and philosophy are complicit in furthering ascetic ideals.

First, Nietzsche suggests that like the "innocent" means inculcated by the Abrahamic tradition, the scholarly work of scientists and philosophers serves as a temporary distraction from our failure to find meaning in our lives:

> Oh, what does science not conceal today! how much it is supposed to conceal, at any rate! The industry of our best scholars, their unreflective diligence, heads smoking night and day, their very mastery of their craft—how often does all that mean trying to conceal something from themselves? Science as a means of self-anesthetic: do you know that? (3.23)

It is not hard to see at least some grain of truth here. Scholarly work can be so engrossing that it may drown out other concerns, even concerns that seem to be obviously integral to a complete and meaningful life. Marx famously decried religion as the opiate of the people. One might wonder if he wouldn't today see work as the most widely used narcotic of the masses.

Second, Nietzsche thinks that science and philosophy both share an unquestioned devotion to truth that is part of the ascetic ideal. According to Nietzsche, the scientist optimistically seeks truth without questioning its worth. Truth for the sake of truth! The philosopher, as Nietzsche presents her here, is less sanguine about our ability to reach truth. She takes objections seriously, entertains doubts, never insists on her conclusions. She is more Socratic. But this, Nietzsche maintains, only belies her even more slavish devotion to truth. These last "idealists of knowledge," as Nietzsche calls them, "believe they are all as liberated as possible from the ascetic ideal." But, he writes, "I will tell them what they themselves cannot see. . . . This ideal is quite simply their ideal as well. . . . They themselves are its most intellectualized product, its most advanced front-line troops and scouts, its most insidious, delicate and elusive form of seduction: . . . These are very far from being free spirits: because they still believe in truth" (3.24). Nietzsche's point here is not entirely clear. One possible interpretation, however, is that Nietzsche means to suggest that the search for truth—whether carried out optimistically or pessimistically—is itself an unquestioned ideal entirely consonant with the ideals of the Abrahamic tradition. Scientists and philosophers have let an unquestioned drive for the truth crowd out the more foundational question of what might make our lives meaningful.

It is worth noting that Nietzsche does suggest that an alternative solution to the problem of nihilism is possible. Although we don't really get his positive account in the *Genealogy*, elsewhere he emphasizes a somewhat obscure doctrine of "the eternal recurrence." In *Ecce Homo*, for example, he tells us,

> My formula for greatness in a human being is *amor fati*: that one wants nothing other than it is, not in the future, not in the past, not in all eternity. Not merely to endure that which happens of necessity, still less to dissemble it—all idealism is untruthfulness in the face of necessity—but to *love* it. (Nietzsche 1989, 258)

What to make of this doctrine is still much debated. Some commentators see in it an opening shot for existentialism and the idea that we must learn to embrace the lack of meaning in life, and in doing so overcome nihilism as an obstacle (see, for example, Leiter [2002], 287–288). Alternatively, one might see in Nietzsche's doctrine the suggestion that one may find meaning in the suffering of life by recognizing that it is necessary for the emergence of human nature in all its wonderful, interesting complexity. In short, one might see in Nietzsche's eternal recurrence the suggestion that one must come to see human existence—suffering and all—as capable of intrinsic justification, and thus not as standing in need of an independent source of value.

Further Study

Lanier Anderson, "Nietzsche on Truth, Illusion, and Redemption." *European Journal of Philosophy*, 2005. Advanced, engaging discussion of truth, illusion and redemption in Nietzsche's philosophy.

Scott Jenkins, "Time and Personal Identity in Nietzsche's Theory of Eternal Recurrence." *Philosophy Compass*, 2012. A helpful introduction to the metaphysics of Nietzsche's doctrine of eternal recurrence.

Brian Leiter, *Routledge Philosophy Guidebook to Nietzsche on Morality*. New York: Routledge, 2002. An excellent guide to Nietzsche's views on morality and his *Genealogy of Morality*.

Friedrich Nietzsche, *On the Genealogy of Morality*. Trans. with notes and introduction by Maudemarie Clark and Alan J. Swensen. Indianapolis, IN: Hackett, 1998.

Friedrich Nietzsche, *On the Genealogy of Morals and Ecce Homo*. Trans. with commentary by Walter Kaufmann. New York: Random House, 1989.

25

James's *The Will to Believe*

The Right to Believe?

25.1. The Setting

William James was born in 1842, two years before Nietzsche, in New York City. His father was independently wealthy and a noted Swedenborgian theologian. James was the eldest of five siblings. His brother Henry was a famous novelist, and his sister Alice was a distinguished diarist. The family was intellectually vibrant and strongly supportive of James's intellectual pursuits.

In his youth, James aspired to be a painter and studied under the American portraitist William Morris Hunt. Although clearly talented, James soon concluded that he would never be a first-rate painter and abandoned art as a professional pursuit. After a brief stint as an enlisted soldier in the American Civil War, James attended the recently formed engineering school at Harvard, the Lawrence Scientific School. He soon switched career paths again, however, and enrolled at the Harvard School of Medicine in 1864. He received his MD degree five years later. After briefly teaching physiology, James switched careers yet again. In 1874 he began teaching psychology at Harvard, establishing the first-ever American psychology lab. In 1880 James shifted careers once more, finally becoming an assistant professor of philosophy at Harvard. His parents must have breathed a sigh of relief to find out that their ambitious son wouldn't turn out to be an engineer, doctor, or scientist after all—but rather a philosopher!

Over the course of his long career, James published a number of seminal works. His *Principles of Psychology* was published in 1890 and followed two years later by an abbreviated version. These works would help to establish James as the leading American psychologist of his time. Having drifted from psychology to philosophy, in 1897 James published a collection of essays titled *The Will to Believe and Other Essays in Popular Philosophy*. Around the

Saints, Heretics, and Atheists. Jeffrey K. McDonough, Oxford University Press. © Oxford University Press 2022.
DOI: 10.1093/oso/9780197563847.003.0025

turn of the century, James delivered the Gifford Lectures in Hume's hometown of Edinburgh. The results were published as *The Varieties of Religious Experience*. In these and subsequent works, James developed a system of philosophy that became known as "pragmatism." It is a system of philosophy that emphasizes the practical implications of philosophical belief—a central theme of this chapter's topic.

In spite of his ambitious career, James was sick much of his life and suffered extreme bouts of depression. As a young man, he repeatedly contemplated suicide. Throughout his life he complained of various ailments ranging from back pain to angina. In 1907 he resigned his teaching duties at Harvard in the hopes of completing his philosophical system before his death. In his remaining years, he continued to write and lecture. In 1910 he passed away at his home in New Hampshire. He is buried in Cambridge Cemetery, steps away from Harvard Yard.

25.2. The Ethics of Belief

The Will to Believe is probably James's best-known work (followed by his *Varieties of Religious Experience*). It was written to be given as a lecture to undergraduate philosophy clubs at Yale and Brown. In his opening remarks, James calls the piece "something like a sermon on justification by faith," but that claim is, I think, slightly misleading. *The Will to Believe* is not quite a justification of belief on the basis of faith. It is not an argument for religious belief. Rather, it is a justification of the permissibility of belief on the basis of faith. It is an argument that one *may* believe on the basis of faith. The difference is subtle but important. James would later regret his choice of title and propose that he should have called his essay "The Right to Believe." That, I think, better captures the core thesis of the essay. What James defends in his essay is the idea that, in the absence of conclusive evidence, it is still permissible to hold religious beliefs.

The argument of *The Will to Believe* is, in part, a response to William Clifford's essay "The Ethics of Belief." We encountered Clifford earlier in our discussion of the relationship between faith and reason (chapter 7). In general terms, Clifford defends a view of the relationship between evidence and belief known as *evidentialism*. The evidentialist holds that the only reason to believe something is that it is what is best supported by the evidence. The only reason to believe that Colonel Mustard committed the murder with the rope in the library is that the preponderance of the evidence supports the belief that the colonel did it with the rope in the library. To believe against the evidence would be irresponsible. Doing so would be to violate the most basic normative rule governing belief formation. On this view, it is—as we saw Clifford claim earlier—"wrong always, everywhere, and for anyone, to believe anything upon insufficient evidence."

There is, I think, a certain intuitive pull to evidentialism. But what exactly would be wrong about believing against, or in the absence of, evidence? Clifford gives us two main arguments for accepting evidentialism. The first we might call the argument from unforeseen consequences. Clifford argues that false beliefs can have unexpected consequences and that those consequences can snowball in unpredictable ways. A seemingly innocent little lie can have large repercussions and quickly become a big lie. Ignoring the evidence in what seems to be a trivial matter can have large, unexpected consequences later. That seems right. Probably we have all experienced the ways in which little lies can lead to other lies, and other lies to still other lies. And one can easily imagine how ignoring evidence about a seemingly small thing—"that screw seems not quite right," "that code might have a flaw"—might have disastrous consequences down the line. (Although one might object that Clifford seems to be presenting only one side of the story here. Might not a little lie—"that hat looks nice on you"—have excellent downstream consequences? Might not ignoring many trivial bits of evidence leave time and energy for larger, more important matters?)

Clifford's second argument focuses on intellectual habits. Clifford suggests that believing things without evidence threatens to undermine our general epistemic principles. To his mind, we face an epistemic slippery slope. If we start accepting some beliefs just because they are convenient, might we not be tempted to accept others as well? Over time might we not develop uncritical habits of mind, and such habits of mind might come to have dire consequences? Presumably no one wants their pilot or doctor to habitually believe in the absence of evidence. We might, for example, start off tolerating unproven homeopathic remedies because they seem harmless, but then, with standards lowered, we might allow children not to be vaccinated, with real repercussions. Clifford's reasoning here is hardly conclusive. We might try carefully cordoning off domains of belief. We might demand high standards in some domains and allow more lax standards in others. (Probably we do that already.) Nonetheless, it is not hard to see—and appreciate—the sort of "epistemic habits" worry that Clifford invokes in support of his evidentialism. Bad habits are a real thing, and it seems wise to at least keep an eye on them.

25.3. The Varieties of Belief

James frames his response to Clifford's evidentialism by making some important clarifications and distinctions. He begins by defining a *live hypothesis* as a hypothesis that "appeals as a real possibility to him to whom it is proposed." Notice that whether a hypothesis is live may vary from person to person, from era to era. That the Boston Bruins are likely to win the Stanley Cup may be a live hypothesis to you, but not to your Canadian neighbor. That the sun goes around the earth might have been a live hypothesis in the twelfth century but no longer is today. Whether or not a hypothesis is live is thus relative to particular believers at particular times. It is not an absolute, independent qualification.

James next defines an *option* as "a decision between two hypotheses." We might be more inclined to call an option a "choice." Using James's language, we could say that we face many, many options every day. You faced the option this morning of getting up or staying in bed, of coming or not coming to class. Later today, you'll face further options still: to study or not, to eat dinner or not, and so on.

James says that an option is *forced* if it is necessary to pick one or the other of two hypotheses. Setting aside the possibility of showing up late or leaving early, coming to class or not looks like a forced option. You have to either come to class or not come to class. To take a more pertinent example, Pascal suggests that the belief in God is a forced option. According to Pascal, we have to either believe in God or not believe in God. If one insists that one might abstain from either option—if one insists, for example, that agnosticism avoids both the hypothesis that God exists and the hypothesis that God does not exist—then one is, in effect, denying that the hypothesis of God's existence is forced in James's sense.

James calls an option *momentous* if it matters greatly which hypothesis of an option one takes. Coming to class or not was probably not a momentous option. Which shirt to wear today was almost certainly not a momentous option. James gives us no clear criteria for deciding which options are momentous and which are not. Perhaps choosing a college was a momentous decision. Whether to get married or not, and if so, to whom, is even more likely to be a momentous decision. Your choice of career and whether to have children are also better candidates for momentous decisions than, say, deciding what you'll eat for lunch or what you'll wear to the gym.

With his framework in place, James suggests that religious belief is an option that is forced and momentous. Forced: We either have to believe or not believe. Like Pascal, James counts agnosticism as a form of not believing. Momentous: Whether we believe or not makes a big difference. If we take religion seriously, James suggests, it will affect our whole lives in far-reaching and profound ways.

James furthermore maintains that for many people religion remains a live option. That is just to say that for many the choice of whether or not to believe remains an open question. Two points are worth noting here. First, James isn't interested in proselytizing. Unlike Pascal, he's not interested in converting people to religion. Rather his aim is the more modest one of pushing back against evidentialists like Clifford. If James were alive today, one can easily imagine him also pushing back against modern-day evidentialists like Richard Dawkins, Christopher Hitchens, and Daniel Dennett, who—like Clifford—argue that it is intellectually irresponsible to hold religious beliefs.

Second, there is an interesting connection here to the many-gods objection to Pascal's wager that we encountered in chapter 12. The many-gods objection suggested that Pascal's pragmatic argument for belief in the existence of God falters on the possibility of there being many different possible outcomes. Not only might Pascal's god exist, but so too might, say, Jealous—the god that rewards those who don't believe in Pascal's god and punishes those who do. James's distinction between live and nonlive options might be seen as an attempt to head off exactly this kind of objection. James could say that from a pragmatic view, choice is always a choice between live options. He could insist that when someone like him confronts the choice of whether or not to believe, he confronts the choice of believing or not believing in a fairly narrow range of options. Because live options are relative to potential believers, others may confront different options. So be it. And, James could add, it is precisely because my made-up example of Jealous is not a live option for anyone that it feels merely academic. There may be many different live options for different people, but Jealous is not one of them.

25.4. A First Argument

James offers two main lines of argument in support of the permissibility of religious belief. In connection with the first argument, James suggests that when it comes to belief we have two central goals. First, we want to believe true things. I want to know when class starts, what I'm having for lunch, where I'm supposed to pick up the kids this evening. Second, we want to not believe false things. I want not to be wrong about my home address, about my understanding of today's readings, about when I'm supposed to be at the faculty meeting.

James points out that these two goals—believing true things, not believing false things—can come into tension. If, for example, I simply believe everything I hear, I'm likely to come to believe lots of true things. In being extremely credulous, I'll greatly increase my stock of true beliefs. But, of course, following this strategy will also greatly increase my stock of false beliefs. I'll have promoted my goal of believing true things at the cost of my goal of not believing false things. Going to the other extreme, I might believe nothing I hear. I might adopt a skeptical attitude toward everything. This strategy will surely decrease the number of false things I believe. But, of course, it will also greatly decrease the number of true things I believe. I will have promoted my goal of not believing false things at the expense of my goal of believing true things.

James maintains that it is up to each person to decide how to prioritize the goals of believing true things and not believing false things. I'm permitted to be epistemically pessimistic and prioritize not being duped at the expense of missing out on true beliefs. But I'm also permitted to be epistemically optimistic and prioritize believing true things at the risk of being mistaken. The possibility of believing true things must be weighed against the possibility of believing false things, and there is, James maintains, no right answer as to how that weighing must go.

If that is right, it gives James a first reply to Clifford's evidentialism. Assuming that the evidence with respect to religious belief is not conclusive either way, James can frame Clifford's evidentialism as a kind of pessimism. By James's lights, Clifford is very worried about being duped and so is willing to pass up on many true beliefs. James can be magnanimous here. He can grant that there is nothing inherently wrong with Clifford's pessimistic stance. If Clifford wants to be extremely cautious, he can be. But James insists that it should also be granted that there is nothing wrong about taking a more optimistic stance. There is nothing wrong in accepting the risk of believing more false things in the hopes of believing more true things. And, for James, this is especially true in the case of options that are both forced and momentous. If the option is forced, I have to choose. And if the option is momentous, the benefits of being optimistic are potentially enormous.

25.5. A Second Argument

In *The Will to Believe* there is a second, more radical line of thought as well. James suggests that sometimes "faith in a fact can help create that fact." Believing, for example, that you'll do well on the exam might make it more likely that you'll do well on the exam. Believing that you deserve that promotion might make it more likely that you'll be promoted. More significantly, James suggests that morality might be self-fulfilling in this way. We're mostly honest with one another because we believe—have faith?—that other people are mostly honest with us. The fact that people are mostly honest with one another is true, in part, because we believe that people are mostly honest with one another.

James suggests that it would be perverse to say that you don't have the right to believe in such facts without sufficient evidence. It would be perverse to say that you don't have the right to believe that you will do well on the test or that other people are mostly honest with one another. To prevent people from believing such facts would be to undermine the possibility of those facts becoming true. To prevent people from believing such facts would be to endorse a self-fulfilling prophecy with negative consequences.

How does this second line of thought in *The Will to Believe* connect with religious belief? James suggests that the core of religious belief consists of two parts. The first part holds that there is some kind of deity, perhaps a first mover or designer of the world, perhaps something immaterial and extramundane. The second part holds that believing in such a deity makes life better in the here and now. It gives meaning and purpose to our lives (as we saw even Nietzsche concede). Believing in God may make us better, happier, and more thoughtful.

Does believing in God make it more likely that God exists? It seems like the answer to that question must be "no." In this respect, belief in God is not analogous to doing well on an exam or promoting trust among one's fellow beings. Perhaps there is some fictional sense in which we could say that God exists because people believe in God. God could exist in the same sense that Santa Claus or Sherlock Holmes exists. But that is not the sense of existence that interests Clifford or James. And in the nonfictional, objective sense of *existence*, our believing correctly that God exists depends on God's existence, not the other way around.

Perhaps, however, James never meant to suggest that religious belief might bring about God's existence. Rather, it seems more likely that he has two different points in mind. First, while religious belief or, perhaps more precisely, openness to religious belief might not make it more likely that God exists, it might make it more likely that we will gain evidence for God's existence or that we'll be better positioned to whatever evidence there might be for God's existence. Being open to religious belief might make us search for and find evidence that we wouldn't have searched for if we weren't open to religious belief. Being open to religious belief might make it possible to appreciate the evidence that we do find for God's existence.

Second, James could be thinking that religious belief is not only a matter of epistemic—knowledge-gathering—concern. Most religious believers care about whether their beliefs are true, and most also care about what evidence might be marshalled for or against their beliefs. But that's not all they care about. As James is eager to emphasize, religious belief is also important because it can improve one's life; it can give meaning and purpose to one's existence. And that feature of religious belief might indeed be self-fulfilling. That is to say, the aspect of religious belief that gives a person's life a sense of purpose might presuppose—indeed, might only presuppose—religious belief. If it is true that I want to improve my life, and believing in God will make my life better, it may seem that it would be perverse to deny that I have the right to believe in God. Where I have to choose, and where that choice has far-reaching implications for me, who could possibly deny me the right to choose as I wish? How could my choosing to believe be impermissible?

I think we've followed James into some genuinely profound waters here, and much could be said in investigating them further. Here we might restrict ourselves to one subtle but crucial issue concerning the way James frames his discussion. It is an issue that shows one way in which questions of religious belief are doggedly more complicated and difficult than we might have hoped.

Encouraged by Clifford, James approaches his topic as a question about the *right* to believe. The right to hold one's deepest religious belief is an important right and a right that has not always been respected. History is rife with examples of religious intolerance, from the persecution of Christians in Augustine's day to the anti-semitism of Nietzsche's. And, of course, intolerance persists in our own time as well. One need only glance through a newspaper to find governments, societies, and individuals eager to discriminate on the basis of religious belief.

I assume that most of us will be quite liberal with respect to what we think others should be legally permitted to *believe*. Most of us will allow that others should be free to believe whatever they want, even things that we might deem absurd or hurtful. Most of us will think that if history teaches us anything, it is that systematic attempts to prohibit particular beliefs are generally more harmful than those beliefs themselves. Religious toleration in this sense wasn't always the default view. There was a time, for example, when people were regularly asked to take vows of religious conformity—to swear allegiance to a particular religious view or sect. Those who refused to submit to such vows could lose their jobs, have their property taken away, or much worse. It is hard to imagine, however, such a view finding much traction among, say, college students today, and, indeed, it would have found little to no favor even among James's audiences in the second half of the nineteenth century.

Let us grant, then, that people have the legal right to believe whatever they want. A harder question is whether one has a moral right to believe whatever one wants. Suppose you work in the human resources department of a large company. Suppose you receive a complaint of sexual harassment. Clearly it would be wrong of you not to investigate the claim or not follow all legal protocols. But are you otherwise free to believe what you want? Are you free to believe—perhaps with no reason—that the claim must be fallacious or unfounded? Or, to change cases, suppose that a loved one is accused of a crime. The evidence stacks up strongly against her. Is it morally permitted for you to believe against the evidence? Might it even be morally required of you to believe against the evidence? If we shift from a legal sense of right to a moral sense of right, we might find ourselves less certain whether we have the right to believe anything we want, although I suspect that insofar as it concerns private belief alone, most people today would still incline strongly toward toleration. Insofar as your belief is a purely private matter without implications for others, many would think that you have a wide latitude to believe as you wish or simply as you do.

But, as James himself emphasizes, belief is generally not an entirely personal affair. It is generally connected to action, and we might—not unreasonably—be less tolerant about what we think people may do, especially when what they do affects other people. In 2020, Easter Sunday for many Christians fell on April 13. Easter that year also fell in the middle of a global pandemic that had already infected over a million and half people and killed more than a hundred thousand. Many governments had imposed social distancing measures that forbid citizens from assembling in large groups in the hopes of staving off more illness and death. The vast majority of religious groups agreed with those measures and sought out new ways to serve their members—televising sermons, conducting "drive-through" ceremonies, and so on. Some believers, however, defied social distancing measures, insisting that either God would protect them from the disease, or that, if they did die from the disease, they would go immediately to heaven anyway.

Framed as an issue of a legal or moral right to believe, I suspect that even in this case most readers today would be tolerant with respect to belief itself, that they will grant, for example, that one has the legal right, and perhaps even the moral right, to believe that one cannot contract a highly contagious disease at a large church gathering. But in the most difficult cases, a legal or moral right to believe is not, I think, what is primarily at stake. What is primarily at stake is the right to *act* on one's beliefs. On 13 April 2020, government officials and law enforcement officers in the United States had to decide whether they would allow people to attend large church services, knowing—or at least believing on the basis of evidence—that such services could threaten the lives not only of those attending but of other citizens as well. In this case, one can at least appreciate how difficult tensions can arise between the right to believe, the right to act, and the rights of others.

The overarching suggestion, of course, is that the most difficult questions that arise today about religious belief are not typically questions about what one may be permitted to believe—legally or morally—but rather about what one is permitted to do on the basis of one's beliefs. Can one steer government and health policy on the basis of religious belief? Can one offer preferences or discriminate on the basis of religious belief? For us today, I think, the most controversial issues with respect to religious belief are not generally concerned with legal or even moral rights to believe but rather with rights to act on one's beliefs, especially where those beliefs are offered without, or in opposition to, supporting nonreligious evidence.

25.6. Returning to Plato

At the start of this book, I warned readers that we might well end up where Plato left us at the end of the *Euthyphro*, namely, back where we started, hopefully a little wiser, but no more certain, and perhaps even less certain, than when we began. And so, I suspect, it has come to pass. Have we made any progress? Perhaps not, if progress is measured as an accumulation of problems solved and answers settled once and for all. Philosophy in general doesn't make cumulative progress in that way. In this respect, it is like many of our intellectual endeavors. The historical development of art, literature, and music isn't primarily a story about a set of problems solved or questions answered. Hopefully a survey of those fields would put one in a better position to appreciate art, literature, and music, and to form one's own opinions about them, but it wouldn't—and shouldn't—try to force everyone to agree to a given set of conclusions. The development of philosophy, and the study of it, is no different in this respect.

If philosophy shouldn't be expected to make progress in the way that mathematics and science are often assumed to make progress, that doesn't mean that we haven't made any kind of progress in studying it. So, what kinds of progress might we have made? Some kinds of progress will be idiosyncratic to particular readers. Each of us brings to our studies our own background, interests, and expectations. One person might have brought an antecedent interest in the problem of evil or an unarticulated affinity for Spinoza's deism. Another might have hoped to refine his own thinking about the existence of God or humanism. As unique individuals, we may hope to make progress in our own unique ways. Nonetheless, I think it is possible to also identify at least four broad ways in which every reader might hope to make progress in studying the development of the history of philosophy of religion.

First, our world is shaped by its past. Our laws, customs, and even beliefs are all hugely informed by events that took place a long time ago. Many legal systems, for example, still bear marks of Roman laws written before Augustine was born. Many contemporary constitutions express ideals that were inspired by thinkers of Hume's era. A deep understanding of the world around us requires some understanding of how we got here, some understanding of the origins of our current laws, customs, and beliefs. And that holds equally—or perhaps even more so—in the case of religion. In coming to better understand the thought of influential figures like Anselm, Pascal, and Nietzsche, we gain a better understanding of the intellectual landscape that we now take for granted. An increased understanding of both the past and the present is thus one relatively concrete form of progress we can reasonably hope to make in studying the history of the philosophy of religion.

Second, it is common to assume that while solutions are hard, problems are easy. That is, it is common to assume that it is easy to grasp difficulties even if it is hard to grasp their solutions. Philosophy, however, teaches us over and over again that this common assumption is often false. In many cases, it can be every bit as hard to understand a problem as it is to understand its solution. Take, for example, problems of personal identity and free will. It is easy to see that the concepts of personal identity and free will play important roles in our everyday lives. You'll protest if you are accused of a crime that was committed by someone else. You'll feel that you are not entitled to praise for an act that you did against your will. These are common, important concepts. And yet, as we've seen, when we think through them, they raise deep and puzzling questions. What is it that makes you the same person you were as a child? Is it a continuity of body? Of soul? Of memory? What is required for you to will freely? Must you have options? Must you have contra-causal powers? Must you be able to sin? Even where philosophy doesn't yield definitive solutions, it can make progress by helping us to appreciate the shape and depth of a problem—by helping us to appreciate what tensions must be faced, what questions must be asked. When we study the history of philosophy of religion, we can therefore reasonably hope to make progress by gaining a better understanding of the puzzles, difficulties, questions, and mysteries that are raised by religious and nonreligious beliefs alike.

Third, philosophers care about arguments, about the reasons people have for what they believe. Some of those reasons are particular to a given era, background, or person. As we saw, Augustine's understanding of sin, evil, and free will were all heavily conditioned by the Neoplatonic philosophy that he embraced after his rejection of Manicheanism. Aquinas's arguments for the existence of God were similarly influenced by the Aristotelianism of his era. And Hume's skepticism was likewise conditioned by intellectual trends of his time and his own experiences with Scottish Presbyterianism. Some reasons, however, are more general. Almost anyone can see the problem of evil as a—perhaps defeasible—reason to doubt the existence of an omnipotent, omniscient, omnibenevolent God. Almost anyone can see the promise of justice and eternal happiness as a—perhaps defeasible—reason to hope for the existence of the same. Even though philosophy does not, and should not, promise to convince everyone to adopt the same conclusions, we can nonetheless make progress in coming to understand the reasons—both idiosyncratic and general—that people have for holding the beliefs that they do hold. In studying the history of philosophy of religion, we can hope to make progress by understanding the views of others, even the views—or perhaps especially the views—of those with whom we do not necessarily agree.

Fourth, philosophy of religion wrestles with some of the most important issues that we can possibly face. It raises fundamental questions about our deepest nature, about the nature of the world, about what we should hope for and what we should do. These questions could not be of greater importance for us either as individuals or as a society. How we answer them shapes our interactions at familial, state, national, and international levels. How we answer them shapes our everyday attitudes and personal convictions. In studying the philosophy of religion, we give ourselves a chance to form our own beliefs about such essential issues. By engaging with other thinkers past and present, we give ourselves an opportunity to form considered beliefs shaped by our own careful reflection on relevant alternatives and reasons. In studying the history of philosophy of religion, we can hope to make progress by thinking about the reasons we have for our own beliefs, by coming to understand our deepest convictions, and by recognizing our most important commitments.

Even if, at the end of the day, we are left no more certain than when we began, it is hard to imagine an undertaking that holds out the promise of more important kinds of progress.

Further Study

Melvyn Bragg, "William James's 'The Varieties of Religious Experience.'" BBC Radio 4, May 13, 2010, https://www.bbc.co.uk/programmes/b00s9ftw. A roundtable discussion of William James and his masterpiece, *The Varieties of Religious Experience*.

Russell Goodman, "William James." *Stanford Encyclopedia of Philosophy* (Fall 2016 edition), ed. Edward N. Zalta, https://plato.stanford.edu/archives/fall2016/entries/james/. A helpful overview of James's life and thought with an extensive bibliography.

William James, *The Will to Believe, Human Immortality, and Other Essays in Popular Philosophy*. New York: Dover Publications, 1956. An excellent collection of William James's popular philosophical writings, including *The Will to Believe*.

Wayne Pomerleau, "William James." *Internet Encyclopedia of Philosophy*, ed. James Fieser and Bradley Dowden, https://iep.utm.edu/james-o/. A helpful overview of James's life and works.

Index

For the benefit of digital users, indexed terms that span two pages (e.g., 52–53) may, on occasion, appear on only one of those pages.